NO-REGRETS REMODELING

2nd EDITION

How to Create a Comfortable, Healthy Home That Saves Energy

by the Editors of *Home Energy* Magazine

PUBLISHED BY ENERGY AUDITOR & RETROFITTER, INC.

BERKELEY, CALIFORNIA

ICON KEY

1: BEGINNING

2: GOALS

3: FINANCE

4: ENERGY

5: ROOMS

6: FLOOR PLANS

7: WINDOWS

8: AIR SEALING

9: INSULATION

10: SPACES

11: LIGHTING

12: VENTILATION

13: HEATING

14: COOLING

15: WATER

16: CONSTRUCTION

17: MANAGING

HOME ENERGY
SAVER

DANGER ZONE

Text and illustrations © 1997, 2013 by *Home Energy* magazine. All rights reserved.
Requests to reprint all or part of *No-Regrets Remodeling* should be addressed to *Home Energy*
magazine at the address below.

Editor: Jim Gunshinan
Project Manager/Developmental Editor: Carol Venolia
Book Production: Phyllis M. Faber
Book and Cover Designer: Beth Hansen-Winter
Cover Photo: Courtesy of Matt Grocoff
Art Director: Kate Henke
Illustrator: Devin Kinney
Copy Editor: Irene Elmer
Art Production Assistants: Toni White, Mark Barroll
Indexer: Theresa Duran
Proofreader: Karen Stough

Printed in the United States of America on recycled paper.
Second edition. First printing May 2013.
10 9 8 7 6 5 4 3 2 1   12 13 14 15 16

Paperback ISBN: 978-0-9639444-3-6

For information on ordering single, bulk, or corporate copies directly from the publisher, please
call 510-524-5405 or order online at homeenergy.org. Distributed to the trade by Chelsea Green
Publishing Company, 85 North Main St., Suite 120, White River Junction, VT 05001.
802-295-6300; chelseagreen.com.

Library of Congress Control Number: 2013911281

Published by *Home Energy*, The Home Performance Magazine, a program of Energy Auditor &
Retrofitter, Inc., a California not-for-profit corporation dedicated to the dissemination of objective
and practical information on residential energy conservation and efficiency. Please send comments
to Home Energy, 1250 Addison Street, Suite 211B, Berkeley, CA 94702. 510-524-5405;
contact@homeenergy.org; HomeEnergy.org.

TABLE OF CONTENTS

WELCOME

Are you ready to improve your home? Whether you call your project a repair, an upgrade, a renovation, or a remodel, you probably have a lot of questions:

- How do I get started?
- Where can I find help?
- Who handles all the details?
- What will this cost?
- How can I avoid doing things I'll regret later?

You're about to embark on a journey that can be complicated and sometimes exhausting—but it can also be exciting and deeply rewarding. You're going to be making a significant investment in your home, and you want to be sure you're putting that time and money in the right places.

You've come to the right place. *No-Regrets Remodeling* can steer you through this mysterious and potentially overwhelming process. We'll help you understand how your house works, how to get the most bang for your buck, and how to avoid regrets down the road.

We'll provide you with useful information and guide you through thoughtful planning. our goal? For you to complete your remodeling project feeling proud of yourself, pleased at how well everything works, delighted with your lowered energy bills, and enjoying greater comfort at home.

IT'S ALL ABOUT MAKING GOOD DECISIONS

Most remodeling projects fall into one of three categories. Your starting point might be an emergency:

- A broken water heater or furnace
- Storm damage
- A collapsing bathroom floor
- A leaking roof
- A flooded basement or crawl space

or maybe you have the luxury of time to plan:

- A kitchen or bathroom renovation
- Adding space for a growing family
- What to do with your big empty nest
- Upgrading old, worn-out materials and appliances
- Eliminating the drafts and making your whole house more comfortable
- Making related improvements while doing a seismic upgrade

or perhaps you're improving your home to bring it up to date for resale:

- Increasing *insulation* levels
- Upgrading to highly efficient equipment and appliances
- Improving window performance
- Revamping your kitchen or bathroom

Whatever your starting point, this book will be your experienced companion and guide, helping you make decisions you'll feel good about for years to come.

WHAT IS NO-REGRETS REMODELING?

No-regrets remodeling means ending up with an attractive home that meets your needs while being more energy efficient, comfortable, and durable; less costly to operate and maintain; and healthier for you and your family. It also means avoiding expensive, hazardous mistakes or needing to do the job over.

No-regrets remodeling feels good. Ask a family who just installed insulation and high-performance windows; they'll tell you how cozy and quiet the house is now, and how much less energy they're using. Someone who just remodeled the bathroom will be delighted that the new low-flow showerhead means there's enough hot water for everyone—and fewer family fights! And that new *ventilation* system? For the first time, there's no mildew on the walls.

But if you're not well informed, you can end up with regrets—serious regrets. For example:

- You could spend a lot of money and not notice any improvement in your comfort or your utility bills.
- Electrical, plumbing, or carpentry projects can disturb your home's insulation and introduce new air leaks. You might end up feeling too hot or cold, paying more for your monthly utilities, or breathing air laden with toxics, carbon monoxide (Co), mold, lead, or asbestos.
- The wrong choice of window glass can cause unpleasant glare or make your home feel cold in winter and hot in summer—with high heating and cooling bills, to boot.
- Maybe you felt too cold in winter, so you had a bigger furnace installed without sealing air leaks or improving insulation. You might feel a little warmer, but your heating bill could go through the roof.
- Remodeling a kitchen or bathroom without understanding how those alterations cause changes elsewhere in the house can introduce new hot or cold spots. It can even introduce moisture where you don't want it, leading to mold growth and perhaps to respiratory problems.
- If you fix everything else but leave your duct system unsealed, you could be sucking unhealthy air into your home while wasting heating and cooling energy.

All these situations become worse when you confront the expense and hassle of tearing out the work and doing it all over. That's what we call regret-filled remodeling.

WE'RE HERE TO HELP

If you're like most American homeowners, your home is the center of your life and your biggest investment. It's where you renew yourself at the end of the day, spend time with family and friends, and make your little piece of the world a reflection of who you are. You want it to work for you, not against you.

We'll guide you in getting good professional help at every stage, from home analysis through design and construction. If you're a do-it-yourselfer, you'll find additional help in the Resources section.

We'll also help you plan ahead for emergencies, like a broken water heater or air conditioner (A/C), so you'll be prepared to get the best replacement system when you need it. When it's 100°F outside, you will have more control over your destiny if you know what you need, and aren't at the mercy of the first person who shows up to fix your A/C.

PLAN WELL, REAP THE BENEFITS

Time spent planning will pay you back handsomely. Consider your options, make all your decisions before you start (yes, you can do it!), and enjoy a well-executed project.

No-Regrets Remodeling is all about helping you do that planning. Whether you read it from front to back, or dive right into the chapter that addresses your project, we'll give you a solid grounding in the basic information you need to make good decisions.

HOW TO USE THIS BOOK

You'll get the most out of this book if you read all the chapters in order, but we know you may be busy, and you may have a particular project in mind. So we've devised a system of icons that will let you start anywhere in the book, then guide you to other chapters you'll need to read in order to understand how your project relates to other parts of your house.

Throughout the book, you'll find the Home Energy Saver™ (HES) logo in the margin whenever the text describes a step that would benefit from using this valuable online energy auditing tool (HomeEnergySaver.lbl.gov). Developed at the U.S. Department of Energy's Lawrence Berkeley National Laboratory, HES is the first and most widely used online tool for calculating residential energy use; it can provide you with a list of energy-saving upgrades tailored to your home, climate, and local energy prices.

At the end of each chapter, you'll find a Resources section to lead you to more information. You'll also find a General Resources section at the back of the book. Glossary words are *italicized* the first time they occur; you'll find definitions in the Glossary at the back of the book.

Here are some paths you might take through *No-Regrets Remodeling*:

Got an urgent situation?

- Water heater broke: Go straight to Chapter 15.
- Furnace quit: Go to Chapter 13—but you'll be even better off if you start with Chapter 4 (and get the home performance assessment recommended there), and then read Chapters 8 and 9. If you follow the advice found there, you might need a much smaller furnace.
- A/C died: Go to Chapter 14—but once again, start with Chapters 4, 8, and 9 to save money and increase your comfort.
- Storm damage to windows: Check out Chapter 7.
- Tree branch through your roof: Go to Chapters 8, 9, and 10 to take advantage of this opportunity to increase your comfort, lower your utility bills, and make your home last years longer.

Want to be prepared for future surprises?

- Read the chapters on windows and doors (Chapter 7), heating (Chapter 13), cooling (Chapter 14), and water heating (Chapter 15).
- Decide in advance what kind of equipment you want to get when the need arises, and whom you'll call to install it.
- Read Chapter 17 and create a Homeowner's Manual to organize your decisions and plans.

Have a single project in mind?

- Put in a new skylight: Read Chapter 11 to understand how best to use that natural light, and Chapter 7 for information about skylights themselves. But also read Chapters 4, 8, 9, and 10 to take advantage of this opportunity to make related improvements.
- Improve your home's insulation: Read Chapter 9 for sure, but also Chapters 4, 8, and 10 to avoid a regret-filled remodeling.
- Upgrade your windows: Chapter 7 and—you guessed it—Chapters 4, 8, 9, and 10, so you won't miss related opportunities. And Chapters 11, 13, and 14 will help you understand how those windows relate to your lighting, heating, and cooling schemes.

Planning a major remodel?

- Start with Part I (Chapters 1–4) to get the big picture about what to do—how to proceed, how to plan, how to finance your project and take advantage of rebates and incentives, and how to figure out which energy improvements will do you the most good.
- If you want to alter specific rooms or change your floor plan, look at Part II:

  ◆ If you're considering remodeling your kitchen, bathroom, home office, media room, or laundry, lean on Chapter 5 to help you focus on the things you need especially in those rooms.
  ◆ If you're thinking of adding on or changing your floor plan, Chapter 6 will help you rethink the layout of your whole house.

- No matter what you're doing to your house, read Part III! Chapters 7–10 are about the core of no-regrets remodeling. They'll help you understand how the parts of your home work together, expose some common myths to help you avoid trouble, and make you savvy about the basics of windows, doors, air sealing, and insulation.
- Part IV covers aspects of the home that you rely on daily: lighting, ventilation, heating, cooling, and water. You might wonder why we didn't start right off with these topics. It's because you'll do a much better job upgrading these aspects of your home after you understand the material in the preceding parts—especially Part III.
- Part V will help you where the rubber hits the road:

  ◆ Chapter 16 will help you with getting your building permit, getting bids from contractors, and living through the actual installation or construction.
  ◆ Chapter 17 is about living well in your remodeled home after the work is done. Don't overlook this chapter; it will help you manage your energy usage and keep your home in good condition for years to come.

Whatever your project, read Chapter 17 before you begin the physical work on your house. The section on creating a Homeowner's Manual will guide you in documenting the work and storing equipment manuals for future use. It's especially valuable to photograph any work that will be covered up, such as plumbing or electrical work in the walls, so that you know what's in there if you need to make repairs or upgrades later.

CRUCIAL GOALS

No matter how small or large your home-improvement project will be, keep these important goals in mind:

- *Energy efficiency*—Reducing the amount of energy used to operate your home
- **Safety and health**—During construction, for you and your workers; afterward, for your whole family
- **Comfort**—Feeling warm in winter, cool in summer, free of nasty drafts, and easily able to see whatever you're doing
- **Water efficiency**—Enjoying water without wasting it, indoors and out
- **Durability**—Building so that all the parts of your house last as long as possible
- **Value**—Targeting your expenditures to maintain or increase the value of your home, both in the marketplace and in your day-to-day experience
- **Whole-house systems thinking**—Knowing how each part of your house interacts with the others, for your own peace of mind

READY TO GET STARTED?

It's time to begin your remodeling journey. If you pay attention to the details and follow our suggestions, you stand an excellent chance of ending up very satisfied with your remodeling project.

Chapter 1

? WHERE TO BEGIN? HOW TO PROCEED?

Good planning can help you

- use less energy;
- save time and money;
- minimize mistakes and avoid backtracking;
- get reliable help; and
- not be fooled by common myths.

Whether you're buying a new water heater or remodeling your entire house, tackling home improvement may seem overwhelming. But information and good planning can put you back in charge. Take the time to read this book, dig into the resources, get professional advice, and plan your projects carefully before you jump in. You'll reap the benefits for many years.

WHAT'S YOUR STARTING POINT?

As we mentioned in the introduction, there are three common starting points for home-improvement and remodeling projects:

1. Something is broken and you need to fix it fast.
2. You want your house to look and function better, and you have time to plan ahead.
3. You're upgrading your house for sale.

In any of these situations, there is a right way and a wrong way to proceed. Let's start with some important tips.

Emergency Repairs

Maybe you'll turn on the shower and get no hot water, wake up shivering to find the heat off, or come home on a hot day to learn that the A/C isn't working. Sometimes it's a major failure requiring professional help, but often it's a minor problem that anyone with the right information can solve in a few minutes. Avoid making hasty decisions; they can be expensive. Can you find a temporary way to stay cool, warm, or clean while you consider your options?

Maybe the pilot light is off on your water heater or furnace. If you don't have a pilot light and you still don't have heat, make sure the power is on to the equipment. If the access panel on your furnace came loose, a safety switch may have turned off the blower motor. Or perhaps a circuit breaker has tripped and needs to be reset. If your A/C is moving air but the air isn't cold, check the circuit breaker for the condenser and check the outside disconnect.

CREATE A HOMEOWNER'S MANUAL TODAY FOR SMOOTH SAILING TOMORROW

Before you even have mechanical problems, we suggest that you create a Homeowner's Manual for your house (Chapter 17). This pulls together all your equipment and appliance manuals, maintenance checklists, and plans for future home projects to help you manage your home.

A Homeowner's Manual can save you time, money, and headaches by providing you with the information you need to keep your home running smoothly, use energy wisely, and handle minor crises quickly and easily when they come along.

Study the manual for the malfunctioning equipment. Follow the trouble-shooting instructions. If that doesn't correct the problem, call in a professional.

If you need to replace a piece of equipment, this is an opportunity to upgrade. Learn about energy-efficient, comfortable options in Chapters 4 and 5.

Natural (and Other) Disasters

Sometimes you're looking at a disaster. Hail breaks windows; trees fall on the roof; storm water enters the house; a pipe breaks, flooding the basement. But a disaster can be an opportunity to make much-needed improvements. If storm damage takes out your furnace, you can replace it with a better model. Broken windows can be replaced with high-performance units.

Take Your Time

Going with the quickest repair may not be cost-effective or in your long-term interest. It's usually worth spending a little time and money to have a trained *home energy professional* inspect your home (Chapter 4). Then you'll have the information you need to choose the best heating system, or decide what type of windows to install. You'll also have a list of improvements that you might make along with your repairs.

Your insurance may not cover everything the home energy pro suggests doing, but the extra cost of most upgrades will be low, and will pay off for many years in energy savings and a more-comfortable, healthy home. Don't fall prey to a sales-driven service that wants to put in a new furnace or other equipment without considering your whole home and any other improvements that might be appropriate for your situation.

Remodeling When You Have Time to Plan

Planning a remodeling project means doing more than just redesigning your floor plan and picking out finish materials. This is the time to evaluate and correct structural defects, identify moisture problems, and deal with any hazardous materials that may be disturbed during renovations. Keep in mind that your home is made up of many interrelated systems. Any changes you make will probably affect how your entire house works.

For example, if you install a powerful new kitchen range hood, it may create enough *negative pressure* to cause *backdrafting*. This means that the *flue* gases from your furnace, water heater, and fireplace are sucked back into the house, rather than rising up and out through their vents. The result? You're breathing combustion by-products, including *carbon monoxide (CO)*. This can make you very sick or even kill you. You can avoid this by making changes to your furnace, water heater, or fireplace—if you plan ahead.

When you replace windows and doors, consider how to keep rain out of the walls. This may require removing siding around the new windows in order to *flash* and seal them properly to the existing wall. If you don't do this, water may get into the wall. The result? Rotten siding and mold in the house.

MYTH: SAVING ENERGY REQUIRES SACRIFICE.

TRUTH: High-quality renovated homes use less energy and are more comfortable than the average house. They have fewer drafts, fewer hot and cold spots, cleaner air, and lower energy bills.

MYTH: HIGH-EFFICIENCY HEATING AND COOLING EQUIPMENT WILL GUARANTEE ENERGY SAVINGS.

TRUTH: While equipment performance is important, overall home performance and the delivery of heated or cooled air or water are more important than the efficiency of the equipment itself. Poor delivery (caused by uninsulated ducts and pipes) can waste more energy than efficient equipment will save. Because a very efficient house doesn't use much energy, don't spend money on super-high-efficiency equipment until you have air-sealed and insulated your house (Chapters 8 and 9) . . . *if* it still makes sense.

If you are planning a major interior renovation or an addition, this is an excellent opportunity to make your whole house more energy efficient, healthy, and sustainable—at little, if any, extra cost.

Upgrading for Sale

Savvy buyers are looking for energy-efficient home features. As we explain in Chapter 3, these features may improve your home's value. Consult with a home performance assessor, architect, or building contractor to find out which improvements will get the most bang for your buck.

WHEN TO BRING IN THE PROS

Skilled professionals have experience that you may not have, and they know what pitfalls to avoid. But they are not infallible; they're subject to prejudices, particularly if they aren't well versed in energy efficiency technologies and practices. Find professionals who are knowledgeable and cooperative, and assemble a team that will work together to bring your project to fruition.

> **MYTH: RECYCLED AND NATURAL MATERIALS WILL MAKE MY HOME "GREEN."**
>
> TRUTH: Don't spend extra money on green building materials without making the efficiency improvements your home needs to operate without wasting resources.

Should I Get a Home Performance Assessment?

Yes. A comprehensive *home performance assessment* will help you make informed decisions for both planned renovations and emergency repairs. Make sure you get a thorough assessment (Chapter 4)—one that includes water use, energy use, *indoor air quality* (IAQ), combustion safety, structural integrity, and moisture management.

Your home performance assessment will also help you plan future projects, many of which may be surprisingly inexpensive. A thorough assessment will reveal the hidden defects in your house and provide a baseline against which you can measure your proposed and completed improvements. Best of all, being informed in advance means you won't be at the mercy of the first person who shows up to fix your A/C when it's 100°F outside.

Do I Need an Architect?

If you're considering structural or floor plan changes, it's a good idea to bring in an architect or residential designer early on.

If you are making changes to your home's floor plan or structure, consider hiring an architect or residential designer. These professionals understand the big picture and how the parts work together. Their expertise can save you headaches—and possibly enough money to cover their fee. Look for an architect whose experience, design style, and communication skills fit well with yours. Interview candidates until you find the right one.

Don't confuse a drafter with an architect. An architect provides the technical knowledge and creativity to turn your dreams and needs into workable, satisfying, three-dimensional concepts, then translate those concepts into forms and materials. The drafter records all that on paper. (In other words, architects may provide drafting services, but not every drafter is an architect.)

Should I Hire a Contractor?

You may be able to do some of the work yourself, either acting as the *contractor* (managing subcontractors, timing, and materials flow) or doing the actual labor. But construction has become very specialized; without the right skills, you may not do the work in the most efficient and effective way.

Major renovations usually require hiring a licensed contractor. In most locations, plumbing, *HVAC* (heating, ventilation, and air conditioning), and electrical work must be done by licensed contractors.

Design-build companies offer both design and construction services, eliminating the finger pointing that often occurs in the traditional architect-contractor-homeowner triangle. Designer-builders tend to develop more practical solutions because of their construction experience, and they seldom exceed their cost estimates. Make sure you like both the design and the construction reputation of a design-build firm before you sign on.

Choosing an appropriate building contractor is key to your project's success.

PLANNING MAKES EVERYTHING GO BETTER

Poor planning leads to forgetting things, which leads to do-overs, which run up the cost and delay the job. Planning ahead lets you consider your options and determine the sequence of tasks. It also means working out the details, so that construction professionals can give you their best price and finish their work quickly. All this saves money and time, and keeps everyone happier.

Would you rather start without proper planning, take eight months to finish, and go over budget? Or would you like to take a few months to plan, start later, finish in three months, and come in under budget? We thought so.

Plans Are an Important Part of Planning

When making design or structural changes to your house, you should have professional *construction documents (CDs)*. A rough sketch is not enough when investing this much time and money. Often needed for permits, useful for working out construction and finish details, and helpful for managing the work, complete CDs help ensure that everyone is working with the same information.

CDs can also be part of a contract to help you get what you expect (they are also called *contract documents*). When you've settled on your final design, you will have detailed drawings for budgeting, negotiating contracts, permitting, and managing the project to a successful completion.

Begin with *as-builts* drawings of your house as it is now. If you have the original from which your house was constructed, those should do—but make sure you add any changes made to your house since it was built. If you don't have original drawings, you can hire a drafter, residential designer, or architect to produce a set for you. A typical set of as-builts will include floor plans, *elevations* (side views), and perhaps *sections* (cutaway views). Use these as-builts as a base for considering changes you want to make. If you're redesigning parts of your home, your architect, designer, or drafter may add

> MYTH: SOLAR PANELS ARE THE BEST WAY TO LOWER ENERGY BILLS.
>
> TRUTH: Solar panels cost a lot. You may be able to save more energy than they will ever produce by making simpler, less-expensive improvements to your home. Get professional advice on the best options for your situation.

Floor plans give you a bird's-eye view of your home's layout.

ELEVATION EAST

ELEVATION WEST

An elevation is a view of your house from one side.

MYTH: REPLACING WINDOWS WILL SAVE LOTS OF ENERGY.

TRUTH: In most climates, windows are the last thing to consider replacing. Insulation, air sealing, heating and cooling improvements—even adding storm windows or insulated shades—may save more energy.

Opening a window is a no-cost way to cool your house when the weather is good.

roof plans, structural drawings, electrical and mechanical diagrams, a site plan with landscaping and drainage, and *details* (close-up drawings of crucial elements, such as footings, roof eaves, and window flashing).

HOME IMPROVEMENT NEEDN'T BE EXPENSIVE

It's common to assume that home improvement is expensive. But many projects cost little, if anything, and make your house function better.

No-Budget Energy-Saving Improvements

Much of the energy we waste in our homes can be saved by changes in behavior, like dressing for the weather—lightly in summer, more heavily in winter.

When the weather is nice, open windows and doors instead of running your A/C. In some hot climates, you can keep the house open mornings and evenings, then close it up as the temperature rises. Use ceiling fans to keep you cool. (Note: Fans only cool when they're blowing on you, so don't waste energy running them when you're not there.) Keep curtains or blinds closed when sun is shining in, particularly on west-facing windows.

To stay warm in mildly cool climates, you might keep the house closed during the morning and evening, and open it up in the middle of the day to let in warm air. Open blinds to let in the sun's heat and keep the house warmer.

Turn off lights when you aren't in the room. Turn electrical equipment and appliances off when you're not using them. TVs use about half their lifetime energy when they are off, just so we can use a remote control to turn them on. You can use a power strip (manual or smart) to turn off any electronics that use a remote control or have a digital display that's always on.

Don't keep an extra freezer or refrigerator unless you really need it. If you do, keep it full—these appliances use more energy when they are empty because it's harder to cool air than to cool a solid. (If the refrigerator is only partly full, fill the rest of it with jugs of water to reduce energy use.) If you replace an old freezer, don't keep the old, inefficient model running just because you have it. Turn it off when it's not needed or buy a smaller, more-efficient model.

How About a No-Budget "Addition"?

Homeowners often feel that their home is too small, and that they need to add space. This is sometimes true, but often there is underused space that can be repurposed or reorganized. You can rearrange furniture to use a room more efficiently. There may be doors you don't use but keep open, cutting down on useful floor area; keep them closed and see if your rooms feel bigger.

If you have a formal living or dining room that you rarely use, turn it into a TV room, office, or bedroom. An armoire can do the trick.

Finally, look at the stuff you own. What can you get rid of to free up space? You may have a whole room's worth of things you can sell or give away to gain floor space. For more ways to better use space, see Chapter 6.

Low-Budget Improvements

Here are some inexpensive ways to save energy and money:

- Replace incandescent bulbs with *compact fluorescent lights (CFLs)* or *light-emitting diodes (LEDs)* (Chapter 11).
- Install timers or occupancy sensors on fans and lights (Chapter 11).
- Plug electronics into *smart power strips* (Chapter 4).
- *Caulk* and weather-strip doors and windows (Chapter 8).

Moderate-Budget Projects

If you have a modest budget, here are some more possibilities:

- Paint dark rooms a lighter color to use less electric light (Chapter 11).
- Replace older appliances and electronics with ENERGY STAR-rated models (Chapter 4).
- Install a high-quality furnace filter (make sure your furnace can handle the extra pressure, or the new filter may restrict the airflow, reducing the efficiency and effectiveness of the system) (Chapter 13).
- Install storm windows (Chapter 7).
- Seal heating and cooling ducts (Chapter 8).
- Replace plumbing fixtures with high-efficiency models (toilets, showerheads, faucets); rebates may be available (Chapters 5 and 15).
- Insulate hot-water pipes (Chapter 15).
- Install a demand hot-water pump if you have to wait a long time for hot water (Chapter 15).

PLANNING PROJECTS YOU CAN DO TODAY:

- Make an appointment with a home performance assessor (Chapter 4).
- Start a Homeowner's Manual for your home (Chapter 17).
- Try no-budget changes that use space and energy better.

PLANNING PROJECTS THAT WILL TAKE MORE TIME:

- Carefully consider your goals for this project (Chapter 2).
- Interview architects and contractors.
- Have someone draw as-builts of your house (or find the ones you have).
- Get professional advice about the appropriate scope of your project, to make sure related items aren't overlooked.

RESOURCES

"Choosing a Good Contractor" (Home Energy Saver): hes.lbl.gov/consumer/happen-choosing

"How to Choose a Green Architect/Contractor" (Natural Choice Directory): naturalchoice.net/articles/architect.htm

"You and Your Architect" (American Institute of Architects): aia.org/value/yaya/index.htm

Chapter 2

CLARIFY YOUR GOALS NOW FOR BEST RESULTS LATER

Why set goals before diving into your project? To help you

- get satisfying results, both short-term and long-term;
- get better value for your investment; and
- minimize missed opportunities.

When remodeling beckons, the urge to *do* something is almost irresistible. Some homeowners grab their tool belts and start swinging the hammer without a thought about their goals. But the wiser course of action often begins with inaction—or, more accurately, with planning (Chapter 1).

The first step is to scrutinize your needs and wants. Whether you envision a comprehensive overhaul, a one-room addition, or a quick fix, take time for introspection. You'll create a sound footing that will guide your work in the near and long term. Your goal setting can be quick and dirty or meticulously detailed; either way, it's a crucial step in your no-regrets remodeling.

FROM DREAMS TO GOALS

Planning often starts with discontent, which breeds desires, which give rise to dreams and visions. You probably have plenty of those! The trick is translating those dreams and visions into goals, plans, and physical realities.

Remodeling affects everyone in the household. Who lives there now, and for how long? Find out what they like and don't like about the house. Ask them about their visions and goals for the house and how their needs may change over time. It may not be realistic to let your six-year-old design your kitchen, but find out what she wants for her bedroom, the family room, the backyard.

A Step-by-Step Process

The following process will keep you on track as you explore your wants. If you live with others, work through these steps together:

1. Start by articulating your dreams and visions. Jot down some simple bullet points, or talk it through with your family or a friend.
2. Then set your dreams and visions aside for the moment. Once you start exploring your needs, wants, opportunities, and constraints, your thoughts are likely to change. It's common for a family to approach an architect saying, "We'd like to add a family room behind the garage," and then end up building something quite different.
3. Now consider your long-term plans. Will you stay in the house indefinitely? Sell in ten years? Give it to your kids? Rent it out?
4. Consider your goals for the remodel. Think in terms of performance

---

TAKE COMFORT INTO ACCOUNT

Now consider what *does* work well about your home. What rooms or other spaces do you enjoy spending time in?

List all the rooms and functional outdoor spaces in and around your house. Note the positive features and shortcomings of each. Now think of each room or space in terms of *comfort*. What about that room makes you comfortable or uncomfortable, and in what way? Is it pleasantly or unpleasantly

- warm or cool?
- drafty or breezy?
- light or dark?
- musty or odiferous?
- cramped or cozy?
- sterile or cluttered?
- large or small?
- high or low ceilinged?

Are the answers different at different times of day or in different seasons?

rather than physical solutions. What do you want to *accomplish*? What doesn't work well and should be *fixed*? Recall what made you want to remodel in the first place. For example, you might want

- lower utility bills and a smaller *carbon footprint*;
- more space (make a list of exactly what you need space for);
- kids' rooms closer to (or farther from) yours (will this change when the kids get older or leave home?);
- space for overnight guests without compromising privacy (saying this is more helpful than saying, "I want a guest room"; the first is about performance, the second leaps to a solution);
- to have 15 people over for Thanksgiving dinner (again, this is more useful than saying, "I need a larger dining room").

5. Now compare your long-term plans with your remodeling goals. Do you notice any conflicts or inconsistencies?
6. Prioritize your remodeling goals. You might simply number each goal on your list #1 (top priority), #2 (secondary), or #3 (relatively low priority). Or devise a spreadsheet showing different priorities for different household members. It can be helpful to indicate which part of the house will be affected by each goal; some natural groupings or affinities may appear. These questions may help you prioritize:

- Which of your goals are most important to you?
- Which are you most willing to spend money on?
- Which will provide an immediate benefit *and* a long-term benefit?
- Which will benefit you more in the short term but less in the long term, and vice versa?
- Would you be willing to defer or reconsider some of these goals if your needs change over time? If so, which ones?

After you assign a number to each goal, look at your #1 priorities and rank them from most to least important.

CONSIDER YOUR LIFESTYLE

Once you've identified and prioritized your family's goals, consider them in the context of how you all spend your time:

- How much of each person's time is spent at home?
- Indoors? Outdoors?
- In what rooms or spaces?
- Doing what (include hobbies and recreation)?
- At what times of day?

Make a list, or consider creating an activity timetable. This might help you realize that it makes sense to have one room rather than several to accommodate movie watching, Wii, exercise, and computer use (assuming these activities don't occur at the same time). This kind of planning can really save money.

Also think about what may change as time passes. Consider your likely activities one, three, five, and ten years hence.

CONSIDER A PHASED MASTER PLAN

If your budget won't let you do everything at once, a master plan for future improvements can be invaluable. Having a phased master plan allows you to do what you can in the short term while looking forward to making more improvements later. It also allows you to defer improvements you're less certain about, or for which you think your objectives may change over time.

Be sure to tell your architect or designer about your future wishes as well as your current plans. Your team can help you formulate a master plan to be implemented over time, planning the current improvements in ways that make future improvements easier.

Here's an example of how master planning can save you money and headaches. In 2007, the Martins completely remodeled their kitchen. In 2009, they hired an architect to design a family room addition to the house. Once they explored their vision, it turned out that they'd put the stove in the perfect place for a doorway into the family room. They weren't willing to remodel the kitchen a *second* time to accommodate that doorway, so their new plans were compromised. If the Martins had created a phased master plan before remodeling their kitchen, the house would have been much more functional and pleasant.

Get clear about what qualities and factors are most important to you, then compare notes with other household members.

RANK YOUR QUALITATIVE PREFERENCES

Before proceeding to the design phase, it's important for you to be clear about what matters most. Each decision maker should rank the following factors from most (1) to least (10) important (it's okay to disagree):

- Aesthetics
- Comfort
- Function
- Durability
- Energy efficiency
- Maintenance
- Budget
- Schedule
- Utility bills
- Environmental impact

Share your rankings with your design and construction team. This information will help you make the inevitable trade-offs that come up in the course of design.

WHAT'S NEXT?

Keep in mind that remodeling can have a life of its own; what actually happens may well deviate from your initial expectations. If you remain open-minded, you'll be able to face the unexpected opportunities and challenges with a level head.

For satisfaction all around, involve everyone in your household in setting goals and planning your project.

GOAL-SETTING PROJECTS YOU CAN DO TODAY:

- Make notes on what everyone likes and dislikes in your home.
- Start a file of ideas you like clipped from magazines.
- Bookmark web sites that show appealing projects.
- Discuss your hopes and expectations with your family.

GOAL-SETTING PROJECTS THAT WILL TAKE MORE TIME:

- Organize all your visions, goals, and priorities into a file to share with your architect or designer and your building team.
- Create your own priority table.

RESOURCES

Energy Free: Homes for a Small Planet. Ann Edminster, Green Building Press, 2009

The Home Design Handbook: The Essential Planning Guide for Building, Buying, or Remodeling a Home. June Cotner Myrvang and Steve Myrvang, Holt Paperbacks, 1992

Natural Remodeling for the Not-So-Green House: Bringing Your Home into Harmony with Nature. Carol Venolia and Kelly Lerner, Lark Books, 2006

The Northwest Green Home Primer. Kathleen O'Brien and Kathleen Smith, Timber Press, 2008

Chapter 3

Chapter 3
HOW TO FINANCE YOUR REMODELING PROJECTS

How can understanding your financial options help you plan? It can

- familiarize you with available financing programs;
- allow you to take advantage of government incentives and *tax credits*;
- help you decide whether to pay cash or finance your project;
- determine how much money you can borrow; and
- show you how to get a loan to upgrade a distressed home.

Carefully weighing your options for funding your remodeling projects can help you make decisions about scope and timing.

You've got the desire, you're ready to start planning your home-improvement project—but how will you pay for it? These days, is it smarter to pay cash or borrow? And how can you evaluate the array of lending and rebate programs?

Many government and utility programs are available to reward you with tax credits, rebates, and *loans* for energy efficiency upgrades. If you're shopping for a home, you can take advantage of loan programs that help you purchase and upgrade a home that needs work.

SHOULD YOU SELF-FINANCE?

Should you spend your savings on this project or finance all or part of it? To answer this question, consider the scope of your project.

If you plan to make simple upgrades—replace a water heater or insulate the attic, for example—you may be able to pay cash and eliminate *interest* payments.

Phasing may also allow you to work with available cash. If you have several upgrades in mind, you can decide when to do each one based on how much money you have on hand. You may want to bring in an architect and a general contractor to help you determine how to break the project into phases, how best to sequence those phases, and what each phase will cost.

But if you're going to do a more-extensive remodel, you'll want to think about the total cost, how long the remodeling will take, how much it will disrupt your lives, and whether you'll want to move out during construction. If you don't have enough cash on hand to cover the whole project, you may want to borrow money to get the job done as soon as possible.

There can be a downside to paying cash. Let's say you're considering cashing in a mutual fund to pay for your remodel. The problem is that you'd be taking a liquid asset (money that's available when you want it) and sinking it into a fixed asset (money that is not readily accessible). You might lose earnings from that liquid asset (interest, dividends, capital gains). Also think about whether you'll have sufficient liquid reserves in case of an emergency.

TAILORED FINANCING IN PHASES

Kelly Lerner remodeled her California home in three phases. First, she improved a bedroom and turned the garage into a family room. Then she turned the basement into a master suite. Finally, she added a dining room and remodeled the kitchen. She paid cash for the first two phases and borrowed for the final push.

"Remodeling room by room gave me time to get to know the site and house and create a much better design," says Kelly. "Completing projects one at a time and paying as I went saved thousands on interest payments and kept me from overspending." When she needed to borrow for her final phase, she was well positioned with a low loan-to-value ratio.

TABLE 03.01: OPTIONS AND MONTHLY PAYMENTS FOR A $10,000 LOAN

Fixed Interest Rate	Loan Term	Monthly Payment	Source	Type
4.5%	5 years	$186.43	Credit union	Unsecured 2nd mortgage
13.99%	10 years	$155.00	Remodeling contractor	Unsecured 2nd mortgage
7.99%*	10 years	$125.00	Remodeling contractor	Unsecured 2nd mortgage
8.75%	15 years	$ 99.94	Remodeling contractor	
5.00%	30 years	$ 54.00	Mortgage lender	Cash-out refinance

*Some unsecured loans allow the contractor to buy the interest rate down, hence the lower rate for this loan compared with the one directly above it.

DANGER ZONE: BEWARE THOSE SIX-MONTH NO-INTEREST LOANS

If you are absolutely sure you can pay off a loan in six months, a short-term no-interest loan can be a good deal. However, many people fall into the trap of not paying off the loan by the sixth month, and then find themselves paying interest at 18–23%. Consider what you are stepping into before you start sinking.

A mortgage professional can help you explore financing options.

SHOULD YOU BORROW?

The advantage of borrowing is that you keep your cash liquid and use someone else's money to improve your home. You may also be eligible to deduct the interest on your 1040 Schedule A (check with a tax professional). Let's look at some options for funding a remodel.

Table 03.01 shows several options for a $10,000 loan. Figures are based on *interest rates* as of this writing. While interest rates will change, this example provides a good idea of what the monthly payments might be at various interest rates and loan terms. Determine the size of the loan you need and multiply for an estimate of your monthly payment. The lender may be a credit union, bank, remodeling contractor, or mortgage lender.

Notice that the loan with the lowest interest rate has the highest monthly payment. That's because it also has the shortest loan term. So look carefully at those great-sounding deals with low rates and short terms. Make sure you can handle the monthly payments before you leap.

Cash-Out Refinance

In Table 03.01, the 5% 30-year loan option looks pretty good. But this is a *cash-out refinance* loan. This means that you would have to refinance your first mortgage in order to get that $54 monthly payment. The rule of thumb is that if your current mortgage interest rate is 1% higher than the new interest rate (or more), a cash-out refinance can be a good deal.

In order to evaluate whether a cash-out refinance is worthwhile for you, work with a mortgage professional to get an estimate of the financing costs (such as origination fees, *underwriting,* and *title insurance*) and learn what costs will be included in the new mortgage and what your new payments would be. Typically, the financing costs can be included in the new mortgage.

Secured and Unsecured Loans

There are two types of loan: secured and unsecured. A *secured loan* is recorded as a *lien* against your property. An *unsecured loan* is not secured by any property, so there's nothing to collect against in case of default. As a result, an unsecured loan is easier to get but more costly than a secured loan. In both cases, the borrower must make monthly payments, but a secured loan will be paid in full when the property is sold.

Secured loans are provided by banks, credit unions, and licensed mortgage professionals. Unsecured loans are provided by a lender who has qualified a remodeling contractor to offer you a loan. These contractors are bonded to ensure that they will complete the job.

Energy-Efficient Mortgages

The *energy-efficient mortgage (EEM)* is a *Federal Housing Administration (FHA)* program that you can use to purchase or refinance a house and make specific energy improvements, adding the cost of those improvements to your mortgage. Participation requires a home performance assessment by a *Home Energy Rating System (HERS)* professional. An EEM pays only the home performance assessment and energy improvements. The amount of the loan is limited to 5% of the property's appraised value.

How to Apply for a Loan

Find out what your *FICO credit score* is before you apply for a loan. Several Internet sources offer a free credit report, but check out the promotions they're hooking you into before you push the button. TriMerge offers the best credit report, because it includes all three bureaus: Equifax, Transunion, and Experian. If credit reports confuse you, you can go through a mortgage lender or a credit bureau; for $20–40, they will obtain a TriMerge report, explain it, and advise you on how to improve your score.

If you're applying for a secured loan with a longer payback term, you'll be required to document your assets (checking and savings accounts, investments) and your income and obtain an appraisal of your home's value.

Loan-to-Value Ratio

When you apply for a secured loan, the *loan-to-value (LTV) ratio* is a key element; the lower your LTV, the better your available interest rate. The LTV is the ratio of your property value to the amount you will owe. Your property's value is determined relative to homes sold within the past 90 days.

The easiest way to estimate your home's value is to plug in your address on Zillow.com; it will show you the value of neighboring homes that sold recently. This isn't as accurate as an appraisal, but it will give you an estimate.

Now add the balance you owe on any current mortgages to the amount you hope to borrow. Divide the result by your home's current value. The result is the LTV (see sidebar on next page).

HELP FOR MAKING A DISTRESSED PROPERTY MORE ENERGY EFFICIENT

Are you hunting for a bargain fixer-upper? As this book goes to press, there are many distressed homes on the market. These properties have two things in common: They usually need repairs and the prices are very low. As a result, many people are able to purchase a home who couldn't do so before. FHA can help out with a 203K mortgage, which

- offers 3.5% down (gift funds are acceptable);
- offers 30-year financing;
- accepts a nonresident co-borrower (such as your parents' income);
- is *assumable* on resale (at today's low rates); and
- includes $35,000 of renovation in a first mortgage.

If you're interested, work with a mortgage professional who is experienced with both the 203K and the energy-efficient mortgage. These can be combined to produce an effective renovation solution.

Tax credits and rebates can significantly offset the initial costs of energy-efficient upgrades.

TAX CREDITS AND OTHER INCENTIVES

The federal government, states, and many municipalities encourage thoughtful use of energy resources, often providing tax credits for energy efficiency upgrades.

Tax deductions are nice, but a tax credit is subtracted from your final tax bill—cash in your pocket after you file! Available tax credits come and go; check the Resources section and research currently available options.

The federal government currently offers the Residential Energy Efficiency Tax Credit and the Renewable Energy Tax Credit for specific improvements to your property. Check with your remodeling contractor and the ENERGY STAR web site for requirements, then file the paperwork with your taxes.

There are also utility *rebates*, water company rebates, manufacturer rebates, and sales. Search for these on the Internet or in the newspaper.

WILL THIS UPGRADE INCREASE THE VALUE OF MY HOME?

The full cost of a remodeling project is rarely reflected immediately in the value of a home, especially when home prices are down. Furthermore, most homeowners who make whole-house energy upgrades stay in their homes to reap the benefits. Consequently, we have little historical data on how these upgrades affect resale value.

If you are considering selling your home soon, only cosmetic improvements (painting, visible repairs) will increase your home's value. If you plan to stay in your home, consider how the upgrade will increase the home's value to you; greater comfort and lower energy costs are immediate tangible returns on your investment. Your home's value will increase over time.

If you sell your home in the future, the key to ensuring a high return on your investment is to tell the Realtor and appraiser about any improvements you've made. Keep copies of your home performance assessments, product labels, and energy bills, before and after remodeling. Show your appraiser the R-29 insulation in the roof and the invoice for the new high-performance furnace, along with the performance assessment and the lower utility bills. A knowledgeable

---

LOAN-TO-VALUE CALCULATION EXAMPLE

Estimated home value
$500,000

Amount owed on first mortgage $350,000

New remodel loan (second mortgage) $ 50,000

Total mortgage balance
$400,000

Total mortgage balance/ Home value = LTV (%)

$400,000 Total mortgage balance/$500,000 Home value = 80% LTV

TABLE 03.02: COST VS. VALUE, NATIONAL AVERAGE

Type of Remodel	Cost	Resale Value	Cost Recouped
Deck addition	$10,350	$7,259	70.1%
Window replacement (wood)	$12,229	$8,258	67.5%
Bathroom remodel	$16,552	$10,293	62.2%
Roofing replacement	$21,204	$12,257	57.8%

Source: *Remodeling* magazine, "Cost vs. Value Report 2009–10" (remodeling.hw.net/2011/costvsvalue/national.aspx).

TABLE 03.03: YOUR CREDIT SCORE AND LOAN OPTIONS IN A RESTRICTIVE CREDIT MARKET

Credit Score	Loan Options
Less than 640	Very difficult and expensive
640 to 679	A few good options
680 to 719	Good options
720 plus	The best options

appraiser will check the energy efficiency box on your appraisal form and indicate increased value.

Another way to establish the increased value of your remodeled home is to have it certified through a green-building program (Chapter 4). A study by Earth Advantage Institute found that green-certified homes in Portland, Oregon, sold for an average of 30% more than non-green-certified homes, based on sales of existing homes between May 1, 2010, and April 30, 2011.

FINANCING STEPS YOU CAN TAKE TODAY:

- Review your savings and cash flow to determine whether you can self-finance, or if not, what monthly loan payments you can afford.
- Review your credit score and learn how to qualify for a loan.
- Investigate available tax credits and incentives.
- Consult with a lending professional.

FINANCING STEPS THAT WILL TAKE MORE TIME:

- Improve your credit score, if necessary.
- Determine the cost and timing of your home-improvement project.
- Apply for financing, rebates, and credits.

RESOURCES

Credit Reports:
- annualcreditreport.com
- freecreditreport.com

Energy-Efficient Mortgages:
- eemeasy.com
- eemtraining.com/energy-efficient-mortgages
- resnet.us

"Federal Tax Credits for Consumer Energy Efficiency" (ENERGY STAR): energystar.gov/index.cfm?c=tax_credits.tx_index

Green Earth Equities: Bringing Wow & Green to Foreclosed Homes: greenearthequities.com

Green MLS Toolkit: greenthemls.org

Remodel Estimates: remodelestimates.com

Residential Energy Services Network (RESNET): resnet.us/directory/raters

Includes the Home Energy Rating System (HERS) tool, a directory of certified professionals, and more.

203K Rehab Program: fhainfo.com/fha203k3.htm

U.S. Department of Energy:
- "Tax Credits, Rebates, & Savings": energy.gov/savings
- The Tax Incentives Assistance Project: energytaxincentives.org
- Database of State Incentives for Renewables and Efficiency: dsireusa.org

A 203K mortgage makes it easier to finance and improve a distressed property.

Chapter 4

IT'S SMART TO MAKE ENERGY IMPROVEMENTS

What can a more-energy-efficient home do for you? It can

- give you more control over your energy consumption and expenses;
- make your home more comfortable;
- help your equipment and appliances last longer; and
- improve your home's IAQ.

No matter what level of remodel or improvement you're planning, it's smart to include energy improvements. Here's why:

- Remodeling gives you a once-in-several-decades opportunity to make energy improvements in spaces that are usually inaccessible.
- As fuel costs rise, energy improvements may pay for themselves.
- Energy production and consumption cause pollution, habitat destruction, and climate change; lowered energy use lessens all three.
- Making your home more energy efficient makes it more comfortable, durable, and healthful.

The bad news: many homes waste a lot of energy. The good news: you can probably reduce that waste significantly without making a huge sacrifice.

HOW DO WE USE ENERGY IN OUR HOMES?

If you want to save energy, it helps to know how you're using it now. The Average U.S. Household Energy Use pie chart can help you understand where home energy dollars tend to go. As you can see, heating and cooling together account for over half (54%) of the energy used in the average U.S. home, with heating dominating. The next-biggest chunk (22%) goes to appliances, then water heating at 18%.

If you want to save energy, you might want to improve the efficiency of your heating-and-cooling system first (Chapters 13 and 14), and then work on your water-heating efficiency (Chapter 15). Lighting and appliances together account for nearly one-third of the energy use in the average home. In fact, energy use for these items has nearly doubled since 1978, when most of us had fewer TVs and no personal computers or entertainment centers.

How Much Energy Is Your Home Using Now?

What you need to know next is how *your* home uses energy. You can find this out using an online tool (see "A Yardstick for Home Energy Use"), or by hiring a home energy professional to do a home performance assessment.

U.S. Household Energy Uses. Courtesy of the U.S. Department of Energy Buildings Energy Data Book, 2012.

Use Home Energy Saver (hes.lbl.gov) to find out how much energy your home consumes for each end use, and to investigate the role of behavioral and operational factors.

TABLE 04.01: WAYS TO ASSESS YOUR HOME'S ENERGY USE

Type of Assessment	How It Works
Online survey	Input information about your home and energy bills, and learn how your energy use compares to that of others.
On-site walk-through	Home energy pro does visual inspection and makes recommendations.
Diagnostic testing inspection	Home energy pro adds diagnostic testing for infiltration and duct leakage to visual inspection.
Comprehensive home performance assessment	Home energy pro adds further testing and analysis, including combustion safety, thermal imaging, and HVAC testing where necessary.
Home energy modeling	Home energy pro does inspection, testing, and data gathering and creates a model of the home's energy performance. This helps you determine how best to spend your energy retrofit dollars.

A blower door is used by home energy pros to measure air leakage.

A home energy professional will interview you about your needs and then suggest the appropriate level of assessment. This assessment could include

- inspecting the insulation and the air barrier;
- inspecting the house for moisture problems;
- pressure testing for air leakage and duct leakage;
- thermal imaging to pinpoint air leakage, insulation, or moisture problems;
- inspecting and testing for hazards, such as CO or gas leaks;
- computerized energy modeling; and
- providing a prioritized list of cost-effective improvements.

No matter what level of remodeling you're doing, a home performance assessment with energy modeling will probably be worth the price. You want to use less energy, but where should you start? Would adding more attic insulation be better than replacing the windows? Should you insulate the walls, or do they already have insulation?

An *energy-modeling* analysis of your home, using specialized software, can help you answer questions like these. Based on the energy pro's inspections, measurements, and testing, the modeling software analyzes your home's heat flows, equipment efficiencies, and other factors. Then it prints out a chart showing how much energy your home uses, and for what.

Let's look at two pie charts, produced by energy-modeling software, for a poorly insulated, leaky bungalow in Atlanta, Georgia. The first chart shows that this homeowner needs to heat his house more efficiently. The second one zeroes in on the culprits: the house is too leaky, the ducts are too leaky, and the walls need insulation.

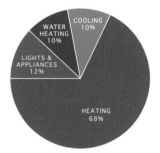

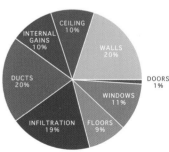

TOP: Energy consumption for an old, leaky, poorly insulated house in Atlanta, GA. BOTTOM: Looking more closely at the heating energy consumption in the Atlanta house, we see how heat is being lost. ("Infiltration" refers to the air leaking in or out of the house, and "internal gains" means heat added by such factors as cooking, appliances, and body heat.)

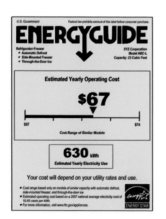

The EnergyGuide label helps consumers compare the energy efficiency of appliances: 1. Estimated energy consumption on a scale showing a range for similar models. 2. Estimated yearly operating cost based on the national average cost of electricity.

HOW MUCH ENERGY AND MONEY CAN YOU SAVE?

Depending on your climate and how energy efficient your home is, you may be able to save 20% to 100% on your utility bills. Some home performance contracting companies offer guaranteed energy savings.

Reduce Your Energy Use before You Invest in Technology

Your home continually loses heat in winter and gains heat in summer. The rate of heat loss or gain is affected by your home's *building envelope*—the insulation and air barrier that separate your indoor *conditioned* (heated or cooled) *spaces* from *unconditioned spaces*. The poorer your building envelope, the harder your heating and cooling systems have to work.

So it's always a good idea to improve the building envelope first, and then upgrade the heating and cooling equipment. If your house loses a lot of heat in winter, installing a more-efficient furnace won't reduce your energy bills as much as installing a more-efficient furnace in a well-insulated, air-sealed house. And some of the money you put into improving the building envelope may come back to you, if it enables you to buy a smaller, less-expensive heating-and-cooling system.

Choosing and Using Appliances

Your appliances can have a big impact on your energy bills. Look for two colorful items when you're shopping:

- The yellow EnergyGuide label shows how much energy a particular appliance uses in a year and how it compares to other appliances in the same category. (Having an EnergyGuide label doesn't necessarily mean that an appliance is energy efficient.)
- The blue ENERGY STAR logo indicates that the appliance has met the ENERGY STAR requirements for products in its category.

These days, many products use energy even when they're turned off, creating what's called a *vampire, phantom,* or *standby load.* Some of those vampire loads are valuable and some aren't. An internal clock in your computer may be a useful vampire load, while a "power off" light on your TV is unnecessary. According to Lawrence Berkeley National Laboratory, vampire loads are responsible for 5–10% of a home's electricity use.

Devices that don't need to be on 24 hours a day can simply be unplugged when not in use, though in some cases you may have to wait for them to warm up when you restart them. Better still, plug them into a *power strip* that you can turn off. For a little more money, you can get a smart power strip that turns itself off.

Energy-efficient appliances may actually cut your energy bill twice. Efficient appliances use less energy, and this generates less waste heat that must be removed by your A/C in the summer.

SHOULD YOU USE RENEWABLE-ENERGY SOURCES?

Renewable energy comes from sources that will last indefinitely—basically solar, wind, and *hydropower* (generating electricity via moving water).

Solar Energy

If the sun shines on your house or yard, you may be able to use solar energy to heat your house (Chapter 13) or your water (Chapter 15).

You may also want to consider installing a *photovoltaic (PV)* system to generate electricity. A PV professional can analyze your site's solar potential and recommend the best way to capture that solar energy. Mount solar modules on the roof? On a pole? Tracking or fixed mount? Ask an expert.

Here's a four-stage plan for adding solar energy to your home:

1. *Energy efficiency.* Before you install any solar energy system, make some basic energy efficiency upgrades to your home. Spray foam, cellulose insulation, and CFLs are much less expensive than solar modules.
2. *More energy efficiency.* If you install PV now, you're probably paying for wasted energy. Find more ways to make your home energy efficient. These upgrades may be more expensive than the improvements you made in step 1, but they're still less expensive than PV.
3. *Solar electric.* Once you've completed the first two steps, installing new PV panels will be worth the expense. The price of PV has fallen in recent years, so this step has moved ahead of solar thermal in many cases.
4. *Solar thermal.* It used to be cheaper to turn solar energy directly into usable heat than to turn it into electricity. In many cases, that's no longer true. Coupling PV panels with a *heat pump* water heater or even an electric-resistance water heater is often more cost-effective than using a solar water heater (Chapter 15). But if your home is off the utility grid; you live in a warm, sunny climate; or you can get a good deal on a solar water heater, solar thermal may still be your best option. Have a professional evaluate your situation and compare the cost-effectiveness of the two options.

In some areas, tax incentives and rebates can help cover the cost of installing solar thermal and PV systems. Such programs can make it cost-effective to go solar right away (Chapter 3).

Wind Power

Small-scale *wind power* may be an option if you have sufficient space and plenty of wind. To capture this resource, you'll need a tower to get the turbine away from the turbulence near the ground. If your home fills the bill, you could easily generate a lot of excess power to sell back to the utility company.

If your home's roof isn't optimal for a PV array, you can build a south-facing "solar shed" in a sunnier part of your property. Credit Tindall Homes.

GET YOUR HOME WEATHERIZED WITH A "BARN RAISING"

The Home Energy Efficiency Team (HEET), in Cambridge, Massachusetts, builds community spirit while making homes more energy efficient. At HEET's weatherization parties, home energy pros train volunteers to help homeowners reduce energy use.

Once a month, the team leaders pick a house to weatherize. They do a full home performance assessment, then put out the word for volunteers, assemble a materials list, and give the homeowners a price. (Low-income homeowners get everything free; others get free labor and pay for materials.) They also line up musicians and food. On the day of the "barn raising," everyone shows up to work, learn, have fun, and make a difference. (See Resources to start your own HEET.)

A YARDSTICK FOR HOME ENERGY USE

You can get a simple assessment of your home energy consumption by going to the ENERGY STAR Home Energy Yardstick web site (see Resources). Enter your zip code, number of occupants, house size, fuel types, and year's worth of utility bills. You'll receive a score that

- tells you how your home's energy use compares to that of similar homes in your climate region; and
- establishes a baseline against which you can monitor your progress.

Then look at ENERGY STAR's Home Energy Advisor for ways to improve your home's energy efficiency.

These online tools are not as detailed or customized as an on-site home energy assessment, but they provide useful information—and they're free.

Hydropower

Hydropower can be one of the most environmentally friendly and least-expensive sources of electricity for your home, but you've got to have a water source, and it's got to have a significant flow and some vertical drop. Got a creek? If so, have a *micro-hydropower* pro take a look at your site's feasibility.

HOW FAR WILL YOU GO?

Are you ready for maximum energy savings? Several programs and standards will give you a target to aim for.

If your renovation is going to be a complete *gut rehab*—stripping all the building envelope walls down to the studs—you can aim for certification through a new-home program like ENERGY STAR. To qualify, your home must be inspected, tested, and confirmed through energy modeling to meet rigorous criteria for reduced energy use.

Find out if there's a *green building* program in your area that sets standards for home remodeling. Examples of such programs include GreenPoint Rated in California, Minnesota GreenStar, and EarthCraft House in the southeastern United States. Such program guidelines usually call for testing and inspecting the home before and after the work and documenting the improvements made. These programs can help you qualify for rebates and tax incentives that can put thousands of dollars back in your pocket.

If you want to seriously reduce your energy use, consider a *deep energy retrofit*, which targets reducing energy use by 50-90%. This is accomplished primarily by beefing up the building envelope: sealing air leaks, adding wall and roof insulation, and installing high-performance windows. These measures greatly reduce summer heat gain and winter heat loss, so your heating and cooling equipment needn't work as hard to keep your house comfortable. The "1000 Home Challenge," an initiative of Affordable Comfort, Inc. (ACI), aims to support deep energy reductions in 1,000 homes around the country; their web site provides information and support for the process.

Want to go even farther? Consider shooting for *net zero energy (NZE)* or *zero peak* levels of energy performance. A net zero home produces as much energy on-site as it uses over the course of a year. Although in theory this could be achieved by an energy hog of a home with lots of PV, it's generally best to make the home as efficient as possible before installing PV, as previously explained. A zero peak home is designed to draw no electricity from the power grid during peak hours. This lowers the utility company's need for expensive fuel sources and power plants to meet peak demand.

Finally, *Passive House*—a standard developed in Germany and now gaining popularity in the United States—emphasizes improving the building envelope more rigorously than any other standard. Many homes built or remodeled to the Passive House standard can be kept warm in winter with only a small heater; the insulation, air sealing, and ventilation are so effective that body heat and household activities (such as cooking and showering) provide most of the heat. However, this is a challenging standard to meet in new construction, and even more challenging in a remodel.

YOUR HOME IS A COMPLEX SYSTEM

It doesn't pay to improve your home's energy efficiency without considering other aspects of its performance. In the 1970s, for example, there was a big push to insulate and seal up houses. But reducing airflow without adding controlled ventilation reduced IAQ. These supertight homes sealed in pollutants and created combustion safety hazards—problems that had not been common when air flowed more freely through houses. Similarly, adding insulation without controlling the flow of moisture into the attic, wall cavities, and living spaces led to *condensation,* encouraging mold growth.

The field of *building science* addresses such problems by focusing on how houses work as whole systems. Always include building science principles in your home energy efficiency planning, or you're likely to solve one problem while creating three others. Understanding the three fundamental rules of building science can save you lots of money and misery.

Rule 1: Understand Your House as a System

This could be called the "hip-bone's-connected-to-the-thigh-bone" rule, and it's one that a lot of people who work on houses don't grasp. A house is a system with lots of interacting components—framing, electrical, plumbing, heating, cooling, insulation, weather resistance, and so on—each with its associated *trade contractor.* Unless they are specially trained, trade contractors in these various fields may not recognize how their actions affect other parts of the house. This is another good reason to hire a home energy professional; they are trained to take the house-as-system approach.

How well your house works depends on the proper functioning of

- the weather shell;
- the building envelope; and
- the mechanical systems.

The *weather shell* consists of the roofing and siding; it keeps the elements out. The building envelope consists of a continuous air barrier and adjacent insulation; its job is to separate conditioned spaces from unconditioned spaces, such as the attic, garage, and crawl space. The *air barrier* is a layer of materials that block air movement, for example *drywall,* plywood, house wrap, polyethylene, sealants, and some types of insulation. Many homes lack a good air barrier, and a poor remodeling job can create even more air leaks. Collectively, those holes can be like having a window open year-round (Chapter 8).

Mechanical systems—heating, cooling, and ventilation equipment—also have a huge impact on a home's performance. Improperly designed or installed, they can create big differences in moisture content and air pressure between indoors and outdoors. These can affect the comfort, durability, healthfulness, and efficiency (see Rule 3). For best performance, you want mechanical systems that are properly sized, with *distribution systems* (ducts or pipes) that are designed and installed for optimal efficiency (Chapters 13 and 14).

GOING SOLAR TO CUT GREENHOUSE GAS EMISSIONS

Rob and Debbie have been improving the energy efficiency of their California home for years. First they replaced single-pane windows with high-performance windows, increased roof insulation, and swapped out their old furnace for an energy-efficient model with a programmable thermostat. When they added solar water heating, they saw their monthly utility bill drop.

Four years ago, they decided it was time to add PV to their south-facing roof. The *5.4-kilowatt (kW)* array cost $40,000, offset by an $8,000 state rebate and a $2,000 federal tax credit. Their utility costs plunged from $1,300 to $300 a year.

Better still, since installing PV, they've saved 16.72 tons of greenhouse gases, 23,879 kWh of electricity, and $6,450 in utility bills, according to their utility's online monitoring system.

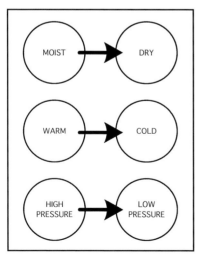

Managing the migration of moisture, heat, and air is crucial to home energy efficiency, comfort, and longevity.

Rule 2: Build for Your Climate

Ever pick up a home improvement magazine or watch a TV show about renovating your home? Remember the sheet of plastic that they attached to the studs before they installed the drywall? That was the *vapor barrier*; it keeps water vapor from migrating through the wall. Did they tell you which climate regions call for a vapor barrier and where to install it? Probably not. But you can't build to the same specifications in all climates without creating trouble. It matters a lot whether your climate is wet or dry; hot, cold, or mixed.

That vapor barrier, for example, may be a good idea in Minneapolis or Miami, but forget it in Memphis. In Minneapolis, the humid air is mostly inside the house, so the vapor barrier goes on the inside face of the studs. In Miami, the humidity is mostly outside, so the vapor barrier goes on the outer stud face. In Memphis, whichever side you install a vapor barrier on is going to be wrong half the year—and the trapped moisture will encourage mold growth. Make sure your designer and contractor know the right way to build for your climate (Chapter 8).

Rule 3: Control the Flow of Moisture, Heat, and Air

Moisture, heat, and air all flow naturally from areas of "more" to areas of "less." Moisture moves from wet to dry areas; heat moves from hot to cold areas; air moves from high-pressure to low-pressure areas.

Pondering these three basic flows will help you understand

- how moisture finds its way into your walls, floor, and ceiling, where it can wreak havoc;
- why that heat you're paying for in winter will constantly flow to the colder outdoors (and why it's important to slow it down with insulation); and
- what makes air move around, into, and out of your house—and how to prevent combustion appliances from backdrafting.

If you don't take these flows into account, you could waste money and energy, feel uncomfortable, and even damage your home. For a no-regrets remodel, the design and construction of your home's envelope must slow or stop all three flows; two out of three is usually not good enough.

There's much more to building science than these three rules. Chapters 8 (air sealing), 9 (insulation), 10 (attics, basements, and more), 12 (ventilation), 13 (heating), and 14 (cooling) will deepen your understanding of building science and show you how to incorporate sound practices into your remodeling project.

HOME ENERGY IMPROVEMENTS YOU CAN MAKE TODAY:

- Replace old incandescent bulbs with CFLs or LEDs and save 75% on lighting costs (Chapter 11).
- Unplug electronics when they're not in use, or put them on a smart power strip.
- Set your thermostat a bit lower in winter and higher in summer.
- Reduce your water heater temperature to 120°F (don't set it lower, or bacteria could grow in the water). You can run hot water into a glass and use a medical, candy, or meat thermometer to check its temperature.

- Keep cool with fans, which cost less to operate than air conditioning (Chapter 14).
- Wash clothes in cold water. The hot water you use for a load of laundry consumes more energy than the washing machine itself.
- Load up your dishwasher. Running a partially full dishwasher means more loads, which means using more energy.
- Maintain your clothes dryer. If your dryer vent doesn't allow the hot, moist air to move easily to the outside, it's wasting energy and creating a fire hazard. Clean the lint trap after each load; clean the main duct yearly.

HOME ENERGY IMPROVEMENTS THAT WILL TAKE MORE TIME:

- Get a home performance assessment to learn how much energy your home uses now and where to make the easiest improvements.
- Replace energy hog appliances with efficient models.
- Improve your heating and cooling distribution systems by sealing ducts, adding insulation, and installing *zoned* controls.
- Improve your home's envelope to cut your heating and cooling needs.
- Explore whether renewable-energy systems make sense for you.

RESOURCES

General

American Council for an Energy-Efficient Economy: aceee.org/consumer
- Consumer Guide to Home Energy Savings Online: aceee.org/consumer
- Residential Sector: Homes & Appliances: aceee.org/portal/residential

BuildingScience.com: buildingscience.com/index_html
Objective, high-quality information about commercial and residential buildings.

Energy Circle: energycircle.com

ENERGY STAR: energystar.gov

Energy Vanguard: blog.energyvanguard.com

Green Building Advisor: greenbuildingadvisor.com

Home Energy magazine: homeenergy.org

Home Energy Saver: hes.lbl.gov/consumer
Analyze your home's energy use, and see how you can save.

PASSIVE SURVIVABILITY

How well would you fare in your home if the power went out for days—or weeks? Can your home handle extended periods of unusually hot or cold weather? What about natural disasters? Alex Wilson of *Environmental Building News* and the Resilient Design Institute calls this "passive survivability" and argues that it should be included in building codes.

The efforts you make to improve your home's insulation, airtightness, passive-solar heating, and natural cooling will all go a long way toward giving you passive survivability in case of disaster.

WHAT'S YOUR CARBON FOOTPRINT?

Does lessening your impact on the environment motivate you to action? Does the increasingly wacky weather (more snow in winter, bunches of tornadoes in spring, long heat waves in summer) make you think maybe there's something to this talk about climate change? If so, you'll probably be interested in determining your *carbon footprint*—the amount of carbon emissions released into the atmosphere as a result of your activities.

Whenever we burn *fossil fuels* (oil, gas, coal), carbon dioxide (CO_2) is released into the atmosphere. If you heat your home with natural gas, fuel oil, or propane, you're responsible for some carbon emissions. The amount depends on how efficient your home is. When you use electricity, your home's carbon emissions are a function of how that electricity was generated. Coal-fired power plants generate a lot more carbon emissions than hydropower or nuclear plants.

To figure out your home's approximate carbon footprint, you can use an online *carbon calculator* (see Resources). Your home energy pro may also be able to do carbon emission calculations for you and tell you how much your planned energy improvements will lessen your contribution to climate change.

Residential Energy Services Network: resnet.us

Resilient Design Institute: resilientdesign.org

1000 Home Challenge: thousandhomechallenge.com

U.S. Department of Energy:
- Building America program: www1.eere.energy.gov/buildings/building_america
- *Energy Savers:* energysavers.gov
- *High-Performance Home Technologies: Solar Thermal & Photovoltaic Systems* (Best Practices Series, vol. 6, 2007)
- Home Energy Score: www1.eere.energy.gov/buildings/homeenergyscore
- Home Performance with Energy Star: energystar.gov/index.cfm?fuseaction=hpwes_profiles.showSplash

Home Energy Assessment

Building Performance Institute: bpi.org/homeowners.aspx
Home energy basics and a database of BPI-certified building analysts and contractors.

ENERGY STAR Home Energy Yardstick: energystar.gov/index.cfm?fuseaction=HOME_ENERGY_YARDSTICK.showGetStarted

Home Energy Assessments (DOE): energysavers.gov/your_home/energy_audits/index.cfm/mytopic=11160

Home Energy Efficiency Team (HEET): heetma.com

Home Energy Saver Pro: hespro.lbl.gov/pro

Residential Energy Services Network (RESNET): resnet.us/directory/raters
Includes the Home Energy Rating System (HERS) tool, a directory of certified professionals, and more.

Appliances

ENERGY STAR Most Efficient: energystar.gov/index.cfm?c=most_efficient.me_index

TopTen USA: toptenusa.org

Carbon Footprint Calculators

EPA's Household Carbon Footprint Calculator: epa.gov/climatechange/emissions/ind_calculator.html

The Nature Conservancy's Carbon Footprint Calculator: nature.org/greenliving/carboncalculator/index.htm

UC Berkeley's CoolClimate Carbon Footprint Calculator: coolclimate.berkeley.edu/carboncalculator

Green Building Programs

Build It Green's Greenpoint: builditgreen.org/greenpoint-rated-existing-home

EarthCraft House: earthcrafthouse.com

LEED for Homes: usgbc.org/DisplayPage.aspx?CMSPageID=147

Minnesota GreenStar: mngreenstar.org

National Green Building Standard: nahbgreen.org/NGBS/default.aspx

Passive House: passivehouse.us

Chapter 5

RETHINKING YOUR KITCHEN, BATH, LAUNDRY, HOME OFFICE, OR MEDIA CENTER

What can upgrading special rooms do for you? It can

- make the room more functional by improving its layout;
- save energy and money with more-efficient appliances;
- save water with efficient plumbing fixtures;
- make the room safer with better lighting and finish materials;
- make the room more accessible for a disabled family member; and
- improve IAQ with good ventilation and moisture control.

4' TO 6'

TOTAL < 22'

4' TO 7'

4' TO 9'

AVOID OVERLAPPING THE WORK TRIANGLE WITH AN ISLAND OR TABLE

PLACE THE MICROWAVE NEXT TO THE FRIDGE OR RANGE FOR EASE OF USE

The work triangle is considered the basis of a good kitchen layout.

The kitchen, bathroom, and laundry room are often the most poorly functioning parts of an older home, so they offer great opportunities for functional upgrades and energy efficiency improvements. Or maybe you want to create a home office or media center. This chapter is your home base.

KITCHEN

You're probably in the kitchen several times a day, so you want your kitchen to look good, function well, and perhaps welcome friends and family to gather. With all the appliances and cooking, your kitchen is also a good place to save energy.

Under-cabinet lighting puts light right where you need it, on the work surface, without annoying shadows.

Prep and Work Areas

For safe, practical food prep and work areas, you'll want to focus on three crucial features: electric lighting, natural light, and work surfaces.

Electric Lighting

Kitchens that only have ceiling lighting may have inadequate light and shadows on the work surface. Consider adding high-quality under-cabinet lights (Chapter 11).

Don't over-light with recessed-can lights. Consult a lighting designer, kitchen designer, or interior designer, or do your homework to determine how much and what type of lighting you need. Don't confuse quantity with quality.

Natural Light

Where possible, configure your workspaces to take advantage of windows and skylights. Avoid putting these light sources behind you to minimize shadows on your work surfaces. Also avoid glare, which can occur if the sun shines directly into your eyes or bounces off a shiny surface.

A sunny kitchen can be a joy to work in, as long as the work surfaces are located to avoid glare.

Use Home Energy Saver (hes.lbl.gov) to calculate how much energy your appliances consume.

If nobody is in the kitchen in daytime, natural light may not be a priority. If your kitchen has no windows, you may want to install a *light tube* or paint the walls a lighter color (Chapter 11).

Work Surfaces

Countertops should be durable and pleasing to look at—and stay that way throughout their service life. Do you like to cut food on the countertop, or use cutting boards? Your answer will dictate the best type of work surfaces. Countertops are a long-term investment, so be sure that what you pick will serve you for many years; choose a material that won't look outdated any time soon.

You might want to avoid tile. The grout discolors and erodes, and it should be resealed periodically; many sealants pose health or environmental hazards. Top marks go to unfinished wood, stainless steel, and light-colored, relatively nonporous stone, such as granite or sealed marble. Dark-colored stone may contrast poorly with food, which will increase lighting needs. If you use a stone sealant, make sure it is safe for food contact.

Cooking Appliances

Choosing the right appliances saves energy and makes cooking a pleasure. Kitchens generally have either a range (a cooktop and an oven) or a separate cooktop and one or more ovens. Which is better? Personal preference or budget may drive this decision. A range takes up less floor area and is often the most economical; the more appliances, the higher the price.

Fuel type is another consideration. If you prefer an electric oven but a gas cooktop, you'll probably want separate appliances. And if you have specific wants or needs—say a *steam oven*, a *convection oven*, or a built-in cooktop wok—those needs may dictate your selections.

What Type of Oven?

Convection ovens, which use a fan to circulate air and keep temperatures relatively steady, offer shorter cook times and use 20% less energy than standard ovens. In general, self-cleaning ovens are more energy efficient than ovens that are not self-cleaning. Microwaves have the advantage of cooking the food without heating the cookware or the kitchen, and so use roughly one-third as much energy as conventional ovens to do the same job. There are also hybrid ovens (microwave plus convection, for instance) that have the same energy benefits as microwaves with better cooking results.

Ventilate Right!

Be sure to provide both natural ventilation from windows and mechanical ventilation from a range hood. If your kitchen has no range hood, you should install one, particularly if you have a gas stove. Cooking with gas produces unhealthy combustion by-products which can accumulate without sufficient ventilation. Cooking also produces moisture, which should be exhausted in order to avoid mold and material damage.

Some kitchens have extremely high-capacity fans which require *makeup air* in order to avoid backdrafting. (When a fan pulls large volumes of air out of the house, the vacuum created can draw contaminated air from other sources, such as the basement or garage.) Be sure to have a qualified professional analyze your ventilation needs and specify appropriate equipment (Chapter 12).

Washing Dishes: By Machine or by Hand?

A new, energy-efficient dishwasher saves significant amounts of water and energy compared to hand dishwashing. If your dishwasher is more than seven to ten years old, you may want to buy a new one; some are also very quiet. Dishwasher performance varies, so do your homework.

At the kitchen sink, a low-flow faucet—or one that lets you easily vary the flow rate—can reduce your water consumption without sacrificing function. Also consider installing a foot pedal to activate the faucet; this reduces water waste that occurs when you turn the water on and off.

Refrigeration

Old refrigerators are much less energy efficient than new ones. They are also often the largest single *plug load* in the house. So if your refrigerator is old (average life expectancy is 15 years) or deteriorating, you may want to replace it—it's costing you a lot to run. Recycle your old refrigerator; don't stick it in the garage (relocating the problem) or toss it in the landfill. Some utilities will pay you to recycle them; check with your power company and your waste hauler.

Here's some advice from the American Council for an Energy-Efficient Economy:

> *Size, configuration, and features have a big impact on overall unit energy consumption.* ENERGY STAR *ratings are available for refrigerators [but] different fridge/freezer configurations are treated differently by the* ENERGY STAR *standards, so that it is possible to have an* ENERGY STAR *side-by-side model that uses more energy than a similar size non-* ENERGY STAR *top-freezer model.*

Freezers and Other Cold Storage

If you want a stand-alone freezer, get an ENERGY STAR model, ideally one listed by TopTen USA. If you need a lot of cold storage space, consider storing some foods in the cellar, where it's often cooler than in the main house.

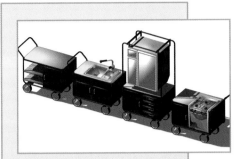

Design by Pliny Fisk.

A KITCHEN WHEREVER YOU NEED IT

At the Center for Maximum Potential Building Systems, in Austin, Texas, codirectors Pliny Fisk and Gail Vittori created a mobile kitchen. It can be wheeled outside, under a shady canopy, to avoid adding cooking heat to the indoors. "Probably the coolest thing about this kitchen," says Pliny, "is its adaptability—inside for winter, outside for summer party buffet."

TABLE 05.01: AVERAGE ENERGY EFFICIENCY OF COOKING APPLIANCES

Cooking Appliance	Energy Efficiency
Induction cooktop (electric)	84%
Conventional electric range	74%
Gas range w/ electronic ignition	40%
Gas range w/ pilot light	20%

Note that while electric appliances are more efficient in terms of the energy they use *in your home*, they are not necessarily more efficient when considered from a broader perspective. Nationwide, the average efficiency of converting fuel to electricity in a power plant is around 30%, while the average efficiency of delivering gas is around 90%. This means that the *effective* energy efficiency of cooking is around 22% (0.3 x 0.74) on a conventional electric range, or 25% on an induction cooktop (0.3 x 0.84), vs. 36% on a gas cooktop with electronic ignition (0.9 x 0.4).

UNIVERSAL DESIGN

At some point, someone in your household may have special access needs, especially in the kitchen. Designing now for universal access later is much less expensive than making changes when the need arises. Be sure to allow enough space, and design critical kitchen features appropriately, to accommodate a range of abilities.

In moderate climates you might even want to install a "cooler cabinet"—once common but now almost forgotten. They are used to store foods, such as grains and some fruits and vegetables, that don't need refrigeration but will keep better at cooler-than-room temperatures. They are built against an exterior wall (preferably one that faces north). The exterior wall is louvered and screened, and the shelves are slatted to allow outdoor air to circulate through the cabinet. To avoid compromising your house's thermal barrier, the cabinet must be well insulated, sealed, and weather-stripped.

BATHROOM

Bath design is not as complex as kitchen design, but many of the same principles apply. Consider these two things in particular:

- Your family's needs will change over time—babies now, teenagers later, and eventually an aging self. Should you incorporate universal-design features now, or at least plan for them? For instance, should you include *blocking* in the walls so that grab bars can easily be added later?
- Whether and how much to renovate a bathroom depends on such questions as: How functional (or dysfunctional) is the room? How dated and worn are the finishes and fixtures? How much do you hate it?

If you're creating a new bathroom, can you compensate for the shortcomings of your other bathrooms, avoiding the need to remodel them? For example, the master bath might be your first choice for a soaking tub, but if you're remodeling the hall bath, could the tub go there instead? Can your new or remodeled bathroom be multifunctional—how about a combination bath-laundry? Or a bath-linen-broom closet? Can you make the bath serve two different rooms or zones in the house by locating it between them?

Ventilation

A window was once considered sufficient to ventilate a bathroom. These days, however, experts advise including mechanical ventilation to avoid moisture buildup, so plan to include an exhaust fan (Chapter 12). For a typical small bathroom or powder room (5 feet x 8 feet or smaller), a fan rated at 50 *cubic feet per minute (CFM)* should be adequate, particularly if it is a good-quality fan. (The better the fan, the quieter it generally is.) Price is a fair—though not perfect—indicator of fan quality. $20? Probably not so good. $200? Probably decent.

The fan's main job is to remove humidity, so it should run for about half an hour after anyone takes a bath or shower. Since most people won't remember to come back to turn the fan off, it's best to install an automatic control to avoid wasting energy. Several options are available, including

- a manual-on/vacancy-off sensor, set to remain on for 30 minutes after it senses no occupant;
- a *humidistat* that senses moisture levels; and
- a timer that you can set before leaving the room.

Another good option is a fan that operates continuously at a low level; its on switch boosts it temporarily to a higher level.

Toilets and Urinals

Many of the latest toilets—whether single or *dual flush*—are very water efficient, ranging from slightly more than 1 gallon per flush (gpf) to around 1.3 gpf, compared with 1.6 gpf for relatively recent models and up to 5 gpf for older ones (Chapter 15).

Urinals may be unconventional in a home, but they can also save water, especially in a male-dominated household. If you choose a *waterless urinal* for even greater water savings, be sure to research maintenance beforehand.

Composting toilets use no water, but it's difficult to get approval for them in many parts of the United States. Many people reject composting toilets because they don't want to deal with human waste, even composted. However, composting toilets have been safely used for many years. Some manufacturers (Clivus Multrum and Sun-Mar, for example) have long track records, and proponents claim that a well-functioning composting toilet is odor free and requires only infrequent maintenance and compost removal.

Bathing

Conventional wisdom dictates having at least one tub in a home. But showers generally use much less water, assuming low-flow showerheads and showers of reasonable duration. A standard 5-foot tub holds 50 gallons. A low-flow showerhead puts out between 1.75 and 2 gallons per minute (gpm), so even a ten-minute shower will use less than half as much water as a tub bath. Showers take up less space than tubs, too, and may fit where a tub won't.

About Showerheads

Low-flow showerheads can cause even the staunchest conservationists to shake their heads; few people will tolerate a trickling shower. But there's more to the shower experience than flow rate; the hydraulic design of the showerhead also plays a major role. Read reviews, pick one that sounds good, and try it out. If you are not satisfied, return it and try another model.

If you have old showerheads, it's easy to swap them out for new ones. Just about anyone with a wrench, Teflon tape, and some elbow grease can manage it. Best of all, many water districts give new showerheads away free. (To test the flow rate on your existing showerhead, turn the faucet on all the way and record the time it takes to fill a 5-gallon bucket. Divide 5 gallons by the number of minutes to find the flow rate in gpm.)

Bathroom Faucets

Bathroom sink faucets present another opportunity to save water (and energy) with minimal expense and effort. Older faucets virtually gush water, yet it takes relatively little water to wash your hands or brush your teeth. If

When remodeling a bathroom, focus on ventilation, water use, and good use of space.

DANGER ZONE: BEWARE!

If you encounter mold or mildew (or even mushrooms) when remodeling a bathroom, take appropriate health precautions (Chapter 12).

SHOWERHEADS CAN BE AN INDIVIDUAL THING

Pete and Chris tried out a lot of new technologies in their Vermont home. Showerheads were no exception, so when some new water-saving models became available, they bought a couple and experimented. Pete really liked one and hated the other . . . but Chris loved the one Pete hated, and couldn't stand the one he liked! The moral of this story is that one size does *not* fit all. You'll need to decide for yourself.

CHOOSING MATERIALS FOR WET ROOMS

Select materials and finishes for kitchens, baths, laundries, and other "wet" rooms to stand up to moisture and the test of time:

- Ask yourself, "Will I love this in five, ten, or fifteen years?"
- Simple, neutral-colored finish choices may seem boring, but they can be jazzed up with colorful towels, curtains, or paint. Hot-pink toilets and turquoise sinks, however, may go out of style.
- The wallboard should not be faced with paper (one of mold's favorite foods). Use products like Fiberock or DensArmor Plus, which are not paper faced.
- Hardwood can be a good choice for kitchens, entries, and even bathrooms if it has a bulletproof finish, as many engineered-wood floorings do, or if it is intentionally rustic looking and will continue to provide the aesthetic you like when it's been exposed to lots of foot traffic, drips, and splashes over the years.
- What type of hardware is best for a wet room? Nothing beats chrome for durability. Stainless steel is another good choice. Most other metallic finishes don't hold up to wear over the years.

you have a faucet you like, but want to save water, just install an aerator. Aim for a flow rate of 0.5–2 gpm for a faucet or aerator. To test flow rate, use the 5-gallon-bucket test described above for showerheads.

If hot water arrives slowly after you turn on the faucet, you may want to upgrade your distribution system (Chapter 15).

One Handle or Two?

Bathroom sink faucets come in two basic types: two handle or one handle (mixer faucets). If you use cold water for hand washing, two handles may save a bit more energy than a mixer faucet, which the person before you may have left at a mixed setting. On the other hand, a mixer faucet may protect you against scalding, depending on your water heater setting and your distribution system. (If it takes a while for hot water to arrive, scalding probably isn't a problem. But if the water is *really* hot, turn down the water heater setting.) Foot pedals may be a good option; see the kitchen section.

LAUNDRY

When space is at a premium, or to make your budget stretch farther, you might combine a laundry with a bathroom, mud room, pantry, family room, or hall closet. Share plumbing, floor space, and doorways with another compatible function whenever possible.

In this era, most laundry rooms have a clothes washer and a clothes dryer. Some storage is essential, and many folks consider a sink obligatory. However, a bath-laundry might have a lavatory sink instead of the more-traditional deep laundry sink. Decide based on your needs, not on convention.

Other desirable amenities include

- folding space—a table or countertop at least 3 feet wide;
- hanging space—clothes pole, hanging rack, clothesline;
- tall storage space, for large boxes and bottles of detergent; and
- access to the outdoors, with a clothesline nearby.

Washers and Dryers

Should you buy new laundry equipment, or keep what you've got? Old clothes washers, like old refrigerators and dishwashers, are far behind their contemporary cousins in efficiency. New models provide dramatic water and energy savings, so if yours is nearing the end of its life expectancy, a replacement is in order. New washers remove more water from clothes than the old models, cutting down dramatically on drying time and dryer energy.

As of this writing, new dryers are more energy efficient than old dryers—but not a lot more. Dryer technology is rapidly evolving, however, so look for new developments in dryer energy efficiency. Make sure your dryer is vented to the exterior (to keep moisture from building up indoors and causing mold growth), and that there are no kinks in the vent duct. Periodically check the duct for lint buildup, which is a fire hazard.

If you're building a new laundry room, or if you have trouble finding a way to exhaust the clothes dryer, consider a *condensing clothes dryer*. This is more energy efficient than a conventional dryer and eliminates the need for an exhaust duct. Consider installing a floor drain or *drain pan* under a condensing dryer (required by code in many areas), just as you should consider installing a drain below any clothes washer or water heater that is in or over living space. An overflow or a burst hose could flood your laundry room.

The best clothes dryer is the sun; be sure to find a good spot for a clothesline. An indoor line is fine, too, if you don't have a place to hang a line outdoors.

Lighting

You need good lighting so you can treat stains before laundering. Make sure the light is strong enough, that it shines directly on the work surface, and that you use energy-efficient bulbs. An inexpensive gooseneck lamp may do the job, making hardwired improvements unnecessary.

HOME OFFICES AND MEDIA CENTERS

The most important things to consider in creating a home office or media center are lighting, electronics, and power managemen.

Lighting

Be sure to avoid glare and reflections on computer and television screens. For paperwork or reading, make sure you have adequate *task lighting*, and less-intense *ambient lighting* (Chapter 11).

Electronics

Your home may contain dozens of electronic items—everything from TVs and sound systems to home office equipment. The more energy efficient you make your home, the larger these electronics loom in your overall energy consumption (Chapter 4).

Most of these electronics have not just two operating modes (on and off) but also a third: standby or low-power mode, signaled by an indicator light that remains on when the device appears to be turned off. Electronics more than two or three years old can draw considerable power, even in standby mode. Their newer counterparts tend to use relatively little power in standby.

Keep or Replace?

Each year, new models are more functional and compact, cost less, and (for a comparable size) use less energy than last year's models. But enormous amounts of energy and raw materials go into the production and distribution of electronics—and disposal adds to already burdened landfills. So before you buy the latest model each year, weigh the hidden costs.

Combining a laundry room with a bathroom, pantry, or other area can save space and money.

When planning a laundry area, include ample folding space, hanging space, and storage.

A "solar clothes dryer" not only gets your clothes dry without consuming electricity or gas but also leaves your clothes smelling great.

A home office concentrates a lot of electricity-consuming equipment in one place; good purchasing and energy management can maximize your comfort and minimize expense.

Your best bet is to identify the big energy hogs and replace them as budget permits. Some of the biggest hogs are

- plasma TVs (liquid-crystal displays use a lot less energy);
- desktop computers (new models use much less energy than older ones; laptops use even less);
- cathode ray tube (CRT) monitors (LCDs are far more efficient);
- multifunction devices (printer-copier-faxes, for example); and
- digital video recorders (DVRs), digital cable, and other set-top boxes.

Phones and other items with *transformers* or chargers also deserve scrutiny. If the transformer or charger is large (roughly the size of a stick of butter), it's probably old and inefficient; if it's much smaller, it's newer and more efficient.

Power Management

Most offices and media centers are inadequately served by plugs; there aren't enough, and they are poorly placed. Include plenty of power outlets in these areas, and locate them so that you can reach them easily.

Many of your electronics are probably *energy vampires*, sucking energy for indicator lights and instant-on features you don't actually need. Switched outlets may help control energy vampires, but in most homes the easiest and most flexible solution is to use smart power strips in key locations. There are several types of smart strip; the most common one consists of a master outlet that controls several dependent outlets, and several more outlets that operate independently of the master. When a device that is plugged into the master outlet is switched on or off, the devices that are plugged into the dependent outlets switch on or off automatically, saving energy. Some smart strips include timers. Research the options or consult your home performance assessor for advice on what would best serve your needs.

OTHER OPPORTUNITIES

Throughout your project, keep an eye open for remodeling possibilities. For example, if you're tearing out wallboard as part of a bath or kitchen remodel, take advantage of that open *wall cavity* to air seal and insulate the wall (Chapters 8 and 9). Your update to one room may facilitate related improvements to other rooms—at a lower cost than if they were done separately.

PROJECTS YOU CAN DO TODAY:

- Replace your old refrigerator or clothes washer.
- Repaint a dark room lighter to reduce your reliance on electric lighting.
- Replace incandescent lighting with CFLs or LEDs.
- Check fan flows. Can your kitchen range hood hold up a sheet of two-ply toilet paper? Can the bath fans hold up a one-ply sheet?

- Check the flow rate on showerheads and faucets to see if replacements or aerators are in order (ask your water district for freebies).
- Get a retractable clothesline or a folding drying rack for the laundry.
- Put computers and entertainment centers on smart power strips.

PROJECTS THAT WILL TAKE MORE TIME:

- Redo your kitchen. Improve the layout, replace outdated appliances, and incorporate universal-design features.
- Add light tubes to windowless baths, closets, and powder rooms.
- Replace moldy wallboard with new, paperless wallboard.
- Phase out your desktop computers and monitors as they age and replace them with TopTen-listed laptops.

RESOURCES

Print

AARP Guide to Revitalizing Your Home: Beautiful Living for the Second Half of Life. Rosemary Bakker, Lark Crafts, 2010

The Composting Toilet System Book. Dave del Porto and Carol Steinfeld, Ecowaters Books, 2000

Energy Free: Homes for a Small Planet. Ann Edminster, Green Building Press, 2009

Good Green Kitchens. Jennifer Roberts, Gibbs Smith, 2006

Universal Design for the Home: Great Looking, Great Living Design for All Ages, Abilities, and Circumstances. Wendy Adler Jordan, Quarry Books, 2008

Your Green Home: A Guide to Planning a Healthy, Environmentally Friendly New Home. Alex Wilson, Mother Earth News Wiser Living Series, 2006

Online

American Council for an Energy-Efficient Economy:
- Home Page: aceee.org/consumer
- Homes and Appliances: aceee.org/portal/residential
- New Refrigerator Standards: aceee.org/press/2011/08/new-refrigerator-standards-coolest-y

"Appliances and Electronics" (DOE/EERE): energysavers.gov/your_home/appliances/index.cfm/mytopic=10020

EfficientProducts.org: efficientproducts.org
Lists efficient computers, monitors, TVs, set-top boxes, battery chargers, and smart power strips.

ENERGY STAR-Rated Products: energystar.gov/index.cfm?c=products.pr_find_es_products

GreenBuildingAdvisor.com: greenbuildingadvisor.com
A resource for building, designing, and remodeling green homes.

TopTen USA: toptenusa.org
Lists the ten most efficient U.S. products in a variety of categories, including dishwashers, refrigerators, freezers, clothes washers, TVs, computers, and monitors.

Chapter 6
CHANGING YOUR FLOOR PLAN

What can improving your floor plan do for you? It can

- make your home better meet your needs and wishes;
- help you respond to changes in household size and needs;
- make your home feel larger without the expense and energy consumption of adding on;
- let you take advantage of natural heating, cooling, and lighting;
- create an income-producing second unit; and
- help you design an addition that will make your whole house more livable and more energy efficient.

The layout of your house—the size and shape of the rooms and how those spaces relate to each other and to the outdoors—has a big impact on how you and your family feel about being at home. It also plays a role in your home's consumption of energy and other resources.

Whether you're planning a major or minor remodel, if your home's layout doesn't meet your needs, it pays to look at your current floor plan with a designer's eye. Maybe your home was fine for a while, but now your circumstances are changing—a growing family, an empty nest, a home-based business, a new hobby, a parent moving in, or just wanting more or different space. Or maybe you want your home to feel lighter and airier, more spacious, cozier—a better place to spend family time. You might want more space for entertaining, or more connection with the outdoors.

Whatever your motivations, the time you spend rethinking your floor plan will pay off in satisfaction, and in value for the money you spend. This is a good time to bring in an architect or residential designer to help you see possibilities you haven't imagined.

JUST ADD ON—OR REDESIGN?

If your family wants spaces your home doesn't provide, it's tempting to just add on. Sometimes that's the best solution, but often a close look at the current floor plan will reveal less expensive ways to meet your needs. Additions cost you twice—once when you pay for the construction, then endlessly as you pay to heat, cool, light, and maintain that new space. And any time you add indoor space, you're losing outdoor space. So before you spend a lot of money and time, take time to consider your options. Wouldn't it be interesting if you could meet your needs without adding on?

When people want more space, often it's because their home's design doesn't meet their current needs. Do you have a living room that is rarely used? Perhaps with minor modifications it could become your new home office. Is

Start with a floor plan of your existing house, then play with different arrangements of furniture, walls, and openings. See if you can get the house you want without the expense of adding on!

the house chopped up into a warren of tiny rooms? Opening some of them up could create a more spacious feeling. Would your formal dining room get more use if you removed the wall dividing it from the kitchen? Or maybe some rooms are in the wrong place—like a sunny, south-facing bedroom that you're never in during the day. Changing how you use your rooms is like no-cost remodeling.

Use Home Energy Saver (hes.lbl.gov) to calculate how enlarging your home could increase your energy use.

How to Approach Redesign

In Chapter 2, you explored what you want your remodeling project to do for you. Now look at your home in relation to your goals. How well does each space meet your needs? What has to change? Think carefully about each space; pay attention to the following things:

- **Function.** How is the space typically used? Do those activities change with the seasons? With holidays or other special occasions? Could a single-use space accommodate different activities at different times?
- **Floor area.** How many people are in the room for normal activities? For special occasions? The type and placement of furniture, and the way people move within the space, help determine how big an area you actually need.
- **Adjacencies.** What needs to be nearby? Do you need to serve a meal, communicate with your family, or keep an eye on the kids from this room? Should some areas be separated, such as the media room and bedrooms?
- **People flow.** How do guests and family members enter your home? The way people walk from one room to another has both practical and aesthetic aspects. Consider the experience you want a friend or a business visitor to have while moving through your home.
- **Orientation to the outside.** Are the views, sunlight, and fresh air appropriate for the way you will use this space? Do you have access to the outdoors?

It's Easy to Try Changes on Paper

Design is fun. Get the whole family involved. Respect everyone's input, and make room for flashes of creative insight. Here's an easy way to do it.

First, document how you currently use your home:

1. Start with the floor plan of your house as it is. If you have a set of plans, get them out and have usable copies made. If you don't have floor plans, measure your house and draw your floor plan on graph paper to scale. A scale of 1/4 inch to 1 foot is common, but a scale of 1/2 inch to 1 foot might be easier to play with if it fits on the paper. Make a few copies. Draw the footprint of each piece of your furniture to scale on another sheet of graph paper and cut it out as you would a paper doll.
2. Now, as a point of reference, position your cutout furniture on the floor plan in its current arrangement (use double-sided removable tape or poster putty). This will serve as a point of reference. Pay attention to how much space there is between the pieces of furniture. Is there room to walk between them?

IS A BIGGER HOME BETTER?

The size of the average American home has gradually increased from about 1,000 square feet in 1950 to 2,300 square feet in 2000. Family size has decreased during that time, so the average floor area per person has ballooned from 290 to 850 square feet. Is all that space really useful?

Bigger homes gobble up more resources. While home size more than doubled between 1950 and 2000, the U.S. Energy Information Administration found that residential natural gas use rose 200% and residential electricity use increased 500%. Have our satisfaction and comfort kept pace with the monetary and environmental cost?

We're starting to figure out that large, poorly designed homes don't bring satisfaction. The quality and functionality of space matter more than the quantity; a carefully designed floor plan and beautifully crafted materials are the key. You want a home that feels good, looks good, and works well for your needs; size is only vaguely related to success in those arenas.

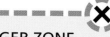

DANGER ZONE

If your new ideas involve opening or moving walls, get advice from an architect, builder, or engineer; those walls may be holding up the floor above or the roof. If you want to raise a flat ceiling to create a *cathedral ceiling*, you'll also want professional advice; that flat ceiling may be holding your walls in place.

IT'S A CABINET! IT'S A BED! IT'S A TABLE!

Every square foot of floor space is precious in Natasha Granoff's three-bedroom, 980 ft² home. So she made her small guest room double as a study by building in a bed that can fold up into a wall cabinet, with a table that can fold down when the bed is tucked away.

Cleverly designed built-ins can make one room do double duty—or triple! Designed and built by Sonoma Woodcraft, J. Jake Pettengill.

3. Copy the plan (you can trace or photocopy it) with the furniture in place so you'll have it to refer to.

Now comes the fun part—trying out different arrangements. Look back at your goals and your analysis of room function, area, adjacencies, flow, and outdoor orientation as you play with new possibilities.

1. Explore changing the uses of rooms by moving the cutout furniture to other rooms that have a better orientation or location for a given activity.
2. Consider how changing doorways, adding openings, or even moving walls might help improve the design. Or how about popping out a window seat or adding a nook?
3. Look at several arrangements, even if your first idea seems perfect; you may come up with something even better.

The goal is to find out how little you'd need to change in order to make the best use of the space you already have in your home. The fewer changes you make, the more you will save in money and energy.

Space-Optimizing Design

Not every activity needs a room to itself; whenever you can make one space or one item serve more than one function, you save yourself room and money. A window seat can be a cozy reading nook or conversation alcove while remaining part of a larger family room; it can also be a guest bed, with the space underneath used for storage. Desk spaces for sorting mail, paying bills, and computer use can be built into a cabinet or closet, allowing you to change a room's use by simply opening a door. Look for ways to turn "wasted space" into a special place: a reading corner, a home office, built-in storage.

If you want to divide a room, you may not need to build a wall. A freestanding bookshelf or tall cabinet can do the job if acoustic separation isn't required; just be sure to bolt it to an adjacent wall in earthquake country. Strategically placed openings can provide selective views into the adjacent space, making both spaces appear larger.

Space-saving furniture can add flexibility with little or no construction. Consider pull-out surfaces, much like the traditional pull-out cutting board in kitchens. These can be used to extend a coffee table for game-playing space, or to extend the work surface in a home office. Dining tables with leaves that pull out or fold up are another classic example. A fold-down ironing board can disappear into the wall.

Sometimes a "micro-addition" is all a room needs. You can save money and natural resources by cantilevering a small area beyond an existing exterior wall to add a window seat or closet, without adding a new foundation.

Family Room or Great Room

Family and great rooms are used in many ways as families grow and change. Over time, a family may use the space as a toddler's playroom, a place to watch movies together, the teenagers' hangout, a corner for paying bills or doing homework, and a place to hold adult parties or community meetings.

Finding creative ways to accommodate many uses may let you avoid building an addition.

You may want a different feel for different activities. Let's say you like your family room to be a comfortable, casual space—but when you invite business colleagues over, you want it to feel a bit more formal. You can save space and even change the mood of the room on an as-needed basis by

- hiding the TV in a cabinet;
- tossing toys into an ottoman that doubles as storage space; or
- making your messy bill-paying desk disappear behind a closet door.

Bedrooms

It is currently fashionable to have a master bedroom suite with a study and large walk-in closets. These features can be accommodated in less space with such creative solutions as

- a window seat or reading nook;
- an alcove for a computer; or
- storage for out-of-season clothes outside the heated area.

Even small kids' bedrooms can comfortably accommodate many uses:

- Kids love using the three-dimensional space of a room. Bunk beds are an old standby solution for a shared bedroom. A new variation for a solo room is to build in a homework desk or closet under a raised bed.
- For a shared bedroom, curtained sleeping alcoves give each child a private space, leaving the middle of the room for playing together. Storage cabinets above and below each bed save even more space.

Bathroom

Bathrooms can feel luxurious without taking up a lot of room. Good natural lighting and plenty of storage space will make even a small bathroom feel accommodating. If you crave a soaking tub, look for a smaller version to save space and water. There are also smaller toilets and sinks; they're just as useful as standard-size ones, but they take up less room.

Need another bathroom and don't know where to put it? One family slipped a small half-bath into the space under the stairway; it works because they used a combination lavatory and toilet. The lavatory sits on top of the toilet tank, and the hand-washing water is reused for flushing.

Storage

Storage areas are essential, but they're often lacking or used poorly. Good storage can make a home function smoothly. It can also keep you from building more house than you really need.

First, look at what you're storing. Are you holding on to stuff that would be better off finding a new home? Are you keeping things inside the house that could just as easily be stored in the garage or a shed?

Don't forget to make the best use of the vertical space in a room. With beds tucked up high, the floor is freed up for seating, books, and play.

BEFORE   AFTER

You may not need an extra bathroom if you remodel a current one to allow multiple users without loss of privacy.

This sink atop a toilet tank not only saves floor space in a bathroom but also saves water; the hand rinse water flows into the tank for use on the next flush.

Next, consider some creative storage ideas. Kitchen storage tricks can be applied in other rooms. You can make your linen or bedroom closet as efficient as a pantry, with shelves on the doors and slide-out shelves. Look for any hollow space that could be turned into storage. Build bookshelves between studs of interior walls; use chest beds that have drawers underneath; install full-depth drawers in the space under the low end of a stairway.

Look outside the heated area of your home for low-cost storage opportunities to free up house space. Maybe there is room on your back porch to add a storage closet for durable items. You might want to build a storage shed in the yard or install floor-to-ceiling storage cabinets in the garage. If your garage has a high ceiling, you might be able to add a storage mezzanine.

NEED LESS SPACE?

What if your problem isn't too little space, but too much? Maybe your children have left home, and you're heating and cooling more house than you use. If moving to a smaller home isn't an option, there are several things you can do.

Cocooning

In the seasons with the highest heating and cooling costs, you could choose to *cocoon* in a few essential rooms and close off the rest, shutting off or greatly reducing the supply of *conditioned* air to the uninhabited rooms. There will probably be some air leakage between the conditioned and unconditioned parts of the house, but you'll probably use much less energy than you'd use to condition your whole house. Or maybe you just want to inhabit one room for a few months, spending most of your time there during the day. The living room or family room might be a good choice. Particularly in winter, it's less important to heat your bedroom or kitchen than it is to heat the spaces where you spend your daytime hours.

You might even choose to air seal your cocoon and beef up the insulation there (Chapters 8 and 9), especially if you don't have the budget to seal and insulate the whole house. Then not only will you be heating or cooling a smaller area, but you'll be able to hold on to that conditioned air longer, saving money on your utility bills twice.

Subdividing Your Home

If you're pretty sure you'll never need all of your house again, and you don't want to move, you may get a double benefit from dividing your house into two or more living units. Not only will you have less house to heat and cool, but you can collect rent on the new apartment. This could even be a good strategy if adult children or aging parents may live with you in the future, providing them with their own adjacent dwelling.

Check into the zoning and other codes in your area before you fall in love with this idea. And get a design professional's input about the best way to divide the space and possibly reconfigure the HVAC system.

DANGER ZONE

When cocooning, you must pay attention to ventilation and humidity levels in the closed-off spaces to avoid mold growth. You can monitor the indoor humidity by using an inexpensive weather station in the closed-off space. A small, efficient bathroom exhaust fan, controlled by a humidity-detecting switch, can provide automatic ventilation (Chapter 12).

OUTDOOR ROOMS

Outdoor rooms are a great way to expand your living space without spending a lot of money. Better still, they're heated by the sun and cooled by the shade and breezes, so they don't consume energy. Well-designed outdoor rooms allow you to enjoy cooking, eating, working, playing, and entertaining outside while providing some protection from the weather. Before the advent of air conditioning, households all over the country had screened porches, summer kitchens, and sleeping porches. Now we can save energy and enjoy the outdoors by reviving these traditions, updated for today's lifestyles.

Porches can be wonderful places to sit, swing, share a meal, do paperwork, or play during mild weather. A roofed, screened porch provides shade and protection from mosquitoes while letting you enjoy sunlight, shade, breezes, and birds. Adding a porch on the south or west side of a house can shade the house from the hot afternoon sun, reducing cooling costs.

Patios or decks are great for entertaining in good weather; their usefulness can be extended with some minor additions. Trellises over the outdoor space can support a shade-producing vine in warm weather while letting in winter sunshine. An operable awning can provide shade or protection from rain. A windbreak can give you privacy while taming the breeze.

Sunrooms allow you to bask in the sun, even when it's cool or breezy outside. You can create a dedicated sunroom, or you can make one by adding storm windows to a screened porch. A sunroom can even provide winter solar heat gain to adjacent rooms via connecting doors or windows (Chapter 13).

A screened porch lets you enjoy the outdoors without being pestered by flying insects. Its roof also provides cooling shade for the house.

ADDITIONS: WHEN YOU REALLY DO NEED MORE SPACE

Have you done your best to use your home more efficiently, but you still need more space? Congratulate yourself; now that you've explored better ways to use your existing space, you may not need as big an addition as you'd thought. Whether or not you'll be adding on, it's always best to look at redesigning your existing floor plan first. This gives you the opportunity to improve the way the whole house functions and feels.

Let's say you need another bedroom. When you reevaluate your current floor plan, you might realize that your existing family room is in the best place for the new bedroom. Then you might notice that adding a new family room to the south side of the kitchen gives you a passive-solar-heated family room closer to the kitchen—and solves the problem of kitchen overheating.

As much as possible, locate your addition so that it will get appropriate sunshine and breezes (Chapters 4, 13, and 14)—and shape your yard to create enjoyable outdoor spaces. Also think about how your addition will change the patterns of sun, shade, and wind in your yard and on the rest of the house. Avoid blocking sun and breezes from existing rooms that need them.

A small sunroom addition is a great place to enjoy the sunshine, even on a cold day, and collect solar heat for the rest of the house.

GOING UP?

Some people think adding a second floor to a one-story house saves money, but this is rarely the case. Unless your foundation is unusually beefy, it will need to be strengthened. Furthermore, the existing framing, wiring, plumbing, finishes, and heating and cooling systems will all be disrupted. Get advice from an engineer and a building contractor before you assume that going up is the easiest thing to do.

Don't overlook the possibility of increasing your conditioned living space without building an addition at all. Converting an attic, basement, garage, or porch into living space gets you more room without increasing your home's size or shape (Chapter 10).

New Construction Brings New Opportunities

Building an addition means building part of your home from the ground up, which allows you to select from a wide range of healthy, resource-efficient options. If your addition will be wood framed, consider specifying *optimum-value engineered (OVE)* framing, which uses considerably less wood than standard framing techniques. Or maybe you'll find that *structural insulated panels (SIPs)* work well with your existing house—and give you a tight, well-insulated structure using very little lumber. There are many other options to choose among. Explore the Resources section and get advice from design and construction professionals who are familiar with green building.

It will also be relatively straightforward to insulate and air seal your addition to higher levels than in the existing house. You might even consider designing your addition as a cocoon that can be heated or cooled during seasonal peaks without paying to condition the whole house.

Design your addition to make the most of every square foot of space. Consider how you might use each room in more than one way. If you're adding a bathroom, you can compartmentalize it for use by several people without loss of privacy—for example, by having a toilet room, a separate bathing room, and a central sink area. This might eliminate the need for another bathroom.

A new stairway can have more than one use; you can make the landing a bit bigger to include a window seat or bookshelf.

An enlarged stair landing can become a small library with a "Zen" view. Deepak Chopra residence; architect and photo, George Beeler.

REDESIGN PROJECTS YOU CAN DO TODAY:

- Move your furniture to better utilize the spaces you have.
- Try out floor plan changes on paper.
- Use bookcases to divide up a room that's too large.
- Acquire space-saving furniture.
- Get rid of unneeded possessions that take up space.
- Close off part of your house and cocoon if you're heating or cooling more house than you need.
- Spend time in your yard, sensing the best locations for outdoor rooms.

REDESIGN PROJECTS THAT WILL TAKE MORE TIME:

- Add new built-ins for increased flexibility and storage.
- Remove or relocate walls, doors, or windows.
- Add window seats or bay windows.
- Build an addition, if you decide you need one.

RESOURCES

Print

Green from the Ground Up: A Builder's Guide to Sustainable, Healthy, and Energy-Efficient Construction. David Johnston and Scott Gibson, Taunton, 2008

Home Enlightenment: Practical, Earth-Friendly Advice for Creating a Nurturing, Healthy, and Toxic-Free Home and Lifestyle. Annie B. Bond, Rodale Press, 2005

Less Is More: A Practical Guide to Maximizing the Space in Your Home. Elaine Lewis, Studio, 1995

Little House on a Small Planet. Shay Salomon, Lyons Press, 2009

Not So Big Remodeling: Tailoring Your Home for the Way You Really Live. Sarah Susanka and Marc Vassallo, Taunton Press, 2009

Not So Big Solutions for Your Home. Sarah Susanka, Taunton Press, 2002

Prescriptions for a Healthy House, 3rd ed. Paula Baker-Laporte, Erica Elliott, and John Banta, New Society Publishers, 2008

Structural Insulated Panels for All Climates. Joseph Lstiburek, Building Science Press, 2008

Your Green Home: A Guide to Planning a Healthy, Environmentally Friendly New Home. Alex Wilson, New Society Publishers, 2006

Online

CalRecycle: calrecycle.ca.gov/greenbuilding/materials

> Lists definitions of green building materials, including product-selection criteria.

Carpet & Rug Institute's Green Label for Carpets and Adhesives: carpet-rug.org/residential-customers/selecting-the-right-carpet-or-rug/green-label.cfm

"Changing Trends: A Brief History of the U.S. Household Consumption of Energy, Water, Food, Beverages and Tobacco," by Diamond, R.C., and M. Moezzi. In *Proceedings of the 2004 ACEEE Summer Study*, 10. Pacific Grove, California. American Council for an Energy-Efficient Economy, Washington, DC, 2004. Report Number LBNL-55011: *epb.lbl.gov/homepages/rick_diamond/LBNL55011-trends.pdf*

Environmental Building News: buildinggreen.com

Green Seal–Certified Products: greenseal.org/FindGreenSealProductsandServices/Products.aspx

Healthy Building Network News: healthybuilding.net

Scientific Certification Systems IAQ and Product Certification: scscertified.com/gbc/indoor_air_quality.php

"Small Is Beautiful: House Size, Resource Use, and the Environment." *Environmental Building News:* buildinggreen.com/auth/article.cfm/1999/1/1/Small-is-Beautiful-House-Size-Resource-Use-and-the-Environment/?&printable=yes

LEFT TO RIGHT: The Beeler house at the time of purchase in 1998. • South side of the house after Phase II: new PV system, solar air heater, and wind-driven turbine ventilator. • Southeast corner of the house after Phase III.

BEELER CASE STUDY

OWNERS: *George and Ellen Beeler*
LOCATION: *Petaluma, California*
CLIMATE ZONE: *Marine*

In 1997, George and Ellen Beeler "decided to get serious about living a green lifestyle." This included living in town to reduce automobile fuel use and improving an existing house. George is an architect with a long-standing commitment to ecological design, so this remodel became a living laboratory.

The house they chose was built in 1940. It had single-pane aluminum windows, the original gas furnace, and no insulation or roof overhangs. There were no available data on the prior owner's energy use.

Phase I (1998)

Upgraded the building envelope:

- added R-30 blown-in cellulose attic insulation;
- added R-13 dense-pack cellulose wall insulation between the 2 x 4 studs at the main living level;
- added R-20 dense-pack cellulose wall insulation between the 2 x 6 studs at the ground floor;
- added R-7 EPS insulation board to the outside of the concrete basement walls;
- closed off basement louvers that had been vented to the outside; and
- replaced the existing single-glazed aluminum windows

with low-e2 glass in fiberglass frames with argon fill. (Replacing the single-glazed arched window in the living room would have been too expensive, so they kept it and added an R-4 triple-honeycomb shade.)

Improved the comfort systems:

- replaced the existing 60% efficient furnace with a 96% efficient sealed-combustion condensing natural-gas furnace with a high-efficiency air filter, and a very efficient variable-speed blower, allowing use of manual dampers to shut off heat to unused rooms;
- added a multisetback thermostat;
- replaced the conventional water heater with a tankless model;
- chose the most efficient ENERGY STAR appliances (when the PV system was installed in Phase II, having paid $100 more for the refrigerator saved $1,000 in PV panels);
- changed almost all the incandescent lights to fluorescents or CFLs; and
- added a whole-house fan for night cooling.

Reduced water use:

- installed water-efficient fixtures and appliances;
- installed a Taco on-demand hot-water circulation pump;
- installed high-efficiency drip irrigation (using nonpotable shallow-well water); and
- installed a 1.5-gallons-per-flush toilet.

Phase I Results

Energy use for space and water heating was reduced by 70%, and electricity use was reduced by 80%.

Phase II (2005)

Added renewable-energy systems:

- installed a 2.5kW PV system;
- installed Solar Wall solar air heating;
- added a roof overhang over south-facing windows for summer shading;
- captured passive-solar heat gain by opening window coverings during the day and closing them at night; and

EXISTING WINDOW PRE-1998   NEW WINDOW 1998

Wood trim needs painting & sealing almost every year

Single glazed aluminum windows are R-1, replaced except for nonconditioned garage

New Low E² fiberglass windows = R-4

Recycled HDPE trim looks new 12 years later. It covers aluminum clad adhesive flashing over window flanges

GOOD WORKMANSHIP!
No voids in the insulation from settling!

Dense pack cellulose insulation was blown into all exterior walls and interior wall of the garage in 1998.

This wall was opened up in 2010 for additional earthquake strengthening

Cellulose also fills voids around wiring & pipes

Phase III Results

Blower door tests before and after air sealing showed a 35% reduction in infiltration. Natural-gas use for space heating and water heating was reduced from 185 to 154 therms per year. Water use dropped to 48 gallons per day, a 43% reduction since 2003 (before which there had been dramatic water use reduction, but those data aren't available).

- installed a wind-driven turbine ventilator for natural ventilation and whole-house night cooling.

Further reduced water use:

- installed steel roofing to harvest rain-water in the future;
- captured storm water to recharge the groundwater; and
- installed a graywater system for irrigation.

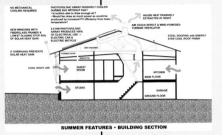

Phase II Results

Summer comfort was greatly improved. In the first year, the PV system brought electricity consumption from the utility down to zero and produced over 1,465 kWh, reducing the household CO_2 production by 4,301 lb. Solar air heating reduced annual natural-gas use from 309 therms in 2001 to 167 therms in 2006. (However, higher thermostat settings to accommodate Ellen's fibromyalgia brought natural-gas use up to 185 therms by 2009.)

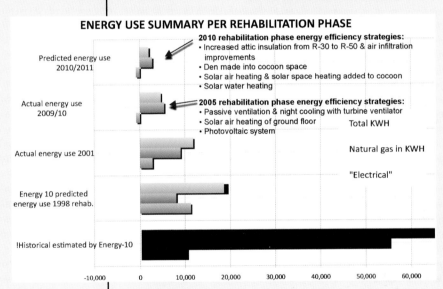

Phase III (2011–12)

Aiming to meet the 1000 Home Challenge, the Beelers improved the energy efficiency of their house before adding more renewable energy to achieve net zero energy:

- turned the den into a cocoon for Ellen, whose fibromyalgia requires warmth;
- added a solar air-heating duct to the den cocoon;
- improved air sealing to reduce air infiltration;
- increased attic insulation from R-30 to R-50;
- insulated the hot-water pipes;
- reinforced the house structure against earthquake and severe wind;
- improved water efficiency by replacing the toilet with a 0.8-gallon-per-flush Niagara Stealth model;
- installed new kitchen and bath faucets with separate hot- and cold-water valves (to minimize hot-water use); and
- installed more-efficient exhaust fans in the kitchen range hood and the bathroom.

Lessons Learned

George says they would have done a few things differently if they'd known in 1998 what they know now:

- prepare a phased rehabilitation master plan (the phasing shown above wasn't planned);
- improve the building envelope enough in Phase I to eliminate the need for a conventional heating system;
- invest in a very-high-efficiency water heater for space heating and *domestic hot water*;
- perform quality assurance testing as work progressed;
- obtain additional financing to add a sloped roof in Phase I, to make possible major air sealing in the attic and an increase in roof insulation to R-50;
- replace the stucco siding, to make possible major air sealing in the walls and the installation of 2-inch rigid insulation board to raise total wall R-value to 26; and
- reduce the size of west- and north-facing windows since the existing windows are much larger than they need.

Chapter 7

CHOOSING WINDOWS AND DOORS

What can better windows and doors do for you? They can

- increase indoor comfort summer and winter;
- lessen noise from outside; and
- lower your heating and cooling bills.

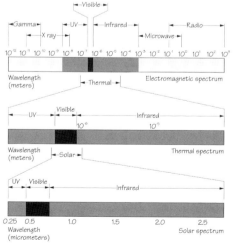

Windows let in light, air, heat, and views of the outdoors. High-performance windows let you optimize these factors for comfort and energy efficiency.

Use Home Energy Saver (hes.lbl.gov) to calculate how much energy and money you can save with window upgrades.

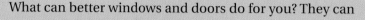
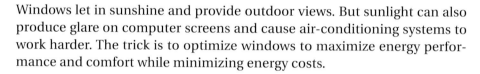

The electromagnetic spectrum. (Note the wavelength scale changes between the three charts.) Reprinted from *Residential Windows*, 3rd ed., by John Carmody et al.

Making good choices about your windows and doors can greatly improve your home's operating costs, comfort, and appeal. But extracting the truth from web sites, advertising literature, and sales claims can be frustrating. Take time to understand how windows and doors function, and you'll have the tools you need be a savvy shopper in a complicated marketplace.

KNOW YOUR WINDOWS

Windows let in sunshine and provide outdoor views. But sunlight can also produce glare on computer screens and cause air-conditioning systems to work harder. The trick is to optimize windows to maximize energy performance and comfort while minimizing energy costs.

Many improvements have been made in window technology in recent decades, with more to come. New *high-performance windows* resist heat gain and loss much better than older single-pane windows. But don't assume you have to buy new windows. Older windows can be improved by adding storm windows, shades, blinds, and shutters, inside and out.

How Windows Work

Windows and glass doors play an important role in the energy performance of your home. A single pane of clear glass is a poor insulator, and most older windows let air in around their edges. Today, many technologies have improved window energy performance. But to admit light and keep your views clear, windows are usually much less insulating than walls and ceilings. The greatest difference between windows and the rest of your outer wall is that windows allow greater heat transfer and passage of light.

Window glass is often referred to as *glazing*. Thus, a window with a single pane of glass may be called single glazed, and a window with two layers of glass, or a double-pane window, may be called double glazed.

Windows have three characteristics that you need to understand:

- visible transmittance;
- solar heat gain coefficient; and
- insulation value (R- or U-value).

50

Visible transmittance (VT) indicates how much of the light that falls on a window passes through it. A single-glazed clear window has a VT of about 0.6. A heavily *tinted*, multiglazed window may have a VT of 0.15 or less.

Windows also transmit radiation we can't see: shorter wavelengths in the *ultraviolet (UV)* part of the spectrum, and longer wavelengths in the *infrared (IR)* part. The sun's visible and infrared radiation bring solar heat into your home. Ultraviolet radiation causes damage and fading, so you may want to control it as well.

The *solar heat gain coefficient (SHGC)* tells you the fraction of *solar radiation* that comes through a window as heat gain, compared to how much solar radiation strikes that window from outside. An imagined window that transmits all the available solar radiation has a SHGC of 1; one that transmits none has a SHGC of 0. Real windows fall somewhere between. For example, a single-glazed clear window with a relatively small frame may have a SHGC of 0.84, whereas a multiglazed window with special coatings and an inert gas between the panes may have a SHGC of 0.25 or less.

It's crucial that you understand the implications of different VT and SHGC ratings if you want to select the best window for a given facade of your home.

Well-Insulated Windows

During cold weather, windows with high insulation values are much warmer on their inside surface than are windows with low insulation values. This provides several benefits:

- Occupants are more comfortable.
- Condensation on glass is reduced or eliminated.
- Thermostat set points can be lowered without sacrificing comfort.
- Energy consumption and cost are reduced.

On hot summer days, well-insulated windows make your house more comfortable and reduce the need for air conditioning. This is particularly true of windows exposed to direct solar radiation that have a low SHGC. With well-insulated windows, you can feel comfortable at a higher thermostat setting—and if you're in the market, you may be able to meet your reduced cooling needs with a smaller, less expensive cooling system.

The insulation value of walls and ceilings is often expressed as an *R-value*. (R stands for resistance to heat flow.) Modern homes in much of North America have R-20 walls and R-40 attics. By contrast, older single-glazed windows have an R-value of about 1. Double-glazed windows with special coatings may have an R-value of 3. Nowadays, multiglazed superwindows with special coatings and inert-gas-filled cavities may have an R-value of 10 or more.

Window systems, however, are generally rated not by their resistance to heat flow but by the inverse: their thermal transmittance, or *U-factor*. A material with an R-value of 10

HOW HEAT MOVES

Energy is transferred from warmer to cooler areas in three ways:

- *conduction* (transfer directly from one object to another, as from your hand to a cold metal railing);
- *convection* (transfer via movement of a liquid or gas, such as air, to heat or cool objects); and
- *radiation* (transfer through space, as when shorter-wavelength IR solar radiation strikes earth, or longer-wavelength IR heat radiates from a hot woodstove).

All three modes of heat transfer play a role in how windows function; understanding them will help you make good choices.

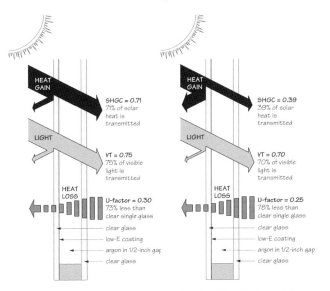

LEFT: Center-of-glass properties for double glazing with a high-solar-gain low-e coating. RIGHT: Center-of-glass properties for double glazing with a low-solar-gain low-e coating. Reprinted from *Residential Windows*, 3rd ed., by John Carmody et al.

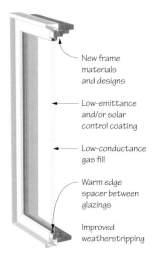

New frame
materials
and designs

Low-emittance
and/or solar
control coating

Low-conductance
gas fill

Warm edge
spacer between
glazings

Improved
weatherstripping

Technological advances have significantly improved window energy performance in recent years. Reprinted
from *Residential Windows*, 3rd ed., by
John Carmody et al.

has a thermal transmittance of 1/10, or 0.1. The lower the U-factor, the less heat transfer and the higher the thermal resistance.

You may also hear the term "U-value," which represents the thermal transmittance at the center of the glass. You want to know the U-factor; this represents heat flow through the whole window, including the frame. The U-factor appears on window labels, so it provides the best basis for comparisons between units.

The core of a modern insulating window is the *insulating glass unit (IGU)*—a sealed *assembly* of two or more layers of glass with one or more coatings. These provide much better insulation than single-pane windows, or even uncoated double-pane windows. Inert *gas fills* (argon or krypton) can be used to further improve insulation. Highly insulating windows, appropriate for very cold climates, may have three, and sometimes even four, layers of glass (or tightly suspended plastic film between layers of glass).

Low-E Coatings

A *low-e* (for *low emissivity*) coating is another important component of the modern IGU. The coating consists of multiple layers of very thin metal or metal-oxide, deposited on the surface of one or more panes, which increase a window's insulating properties. This film is so thin that it barely affects the view through the window.

One type of low-e coating admits the sun's warmth for passive-solar heating while reducing heat loss from indoors to out. Compared to uncoated windows, windows with such a "high-gain" coating have a lower U-factor while maintaining a high SHGC and VT. This type of low-e coating is best suited for cooler climates or windows with good summer shading.

In hot climates where summer cooling is more valuable than passive-solar heating, a low-e coating designed to control solar heat gain may be more appropriate. By selectively blocking wavelengths the human eye can't see, the resulting window can reject more than 70% of the sun's heat without sacrificing much of the daylight or view. Compared to a high–solar-gain low-e product, such a window will have a similar U-factor, a much lower SHGC, and a slightly lower VT.

Use a Compass to Choose Your Windows

For the greatest energy efficiency, you need different window glazing on each side of your house. West-facing windows are generally susceptible to heat and glare from low afternoon sun; east-facing windows in hot climates are similarly vulnerable in the morning. In the northern hemisphere, the solar heat gain through south-facing windows may be welcome in winter; you might select high-SHGC windows for this facade if you also plan to shade these windows in summer. North-facing windows receive no direct sunlight during winter in most of the United States, but they are vulnerable to winter heat loss, so it's worth going for a low U-factor even at the expense of a lower SHGC—which can also help reduce summer heat gain.

TABLE 07.01: BEST GLAZING CHOICES FOR EACH FACADE

Facade	VT	SHGC	U-Factor
West and east	Moderate (0.3–0.7)	Low (0–0.3) (moderate with exterior shading)	Low (0.3 or lower)
South (if passive-solar heat is desired)	High (0.7–1.0) (moderate if not shaded)	High (0.7–1.0) (moderate or low if not shaded)	Moderate (0.3–0.8)
South (if solar heat is never desired)	Moderate (0.3–0.7)	Moderate to low (0–0.7)	Low (0.3 or lower)
North	Moderate (0.3–0.7)	Moderate to low (0–0.7)	Very low (0.15)

By choosing the best windows for each side of your house, you can increase your year-round comfort and lower both your heating and cooling bills. Table 07.01 lists the window qualities that are generally the best for each facade, but always take your local climate and your shading situation into account.

Note that if you choose different glazing for each side of your home, you'll be an unusual consumer. Most window companies want to sell one product for all four sides. Make sure your contractor reads the window labels and installs your carefully chosen windows in the correct locations.

Choosing the right windows is not always enough; you may also need shading devices, especially if you're specifying high-VT, high-SHGC windows. Intercepting direct sunlight before it strikes the window can greatly diminish summer solar heat gain. During hot weather, modest fixed overhangs, awnings, or trellises on the south, and exterior shading devices on the east and west, will produce the best energy performance in most parts of the country.

Window Frames

A window's performance is largely determined by the glazing, but the frames represent 10–30% of the total window area, and frame materials play a significant role in performance. When choosing new windows, consider the thermal, maintenance, aesthetic, cost, and other qualities of the window frames. (See Table 07.02.)

Aluminum

Light weight, durability, and low maintenance made aluminum window frames popular from just after World War II through the mid-1980s. But thermal performance was poor, and aluminum frames were later eclipsed by wood and vinyl. Modern aluminum window frames perform better, thanks to a *thermal break*; the frame consists of two pieces, joined by a less conductive material, such as plastic. Even with a thermal break, however, aluminum frames don't meet current energy codes in very cold climate zones.

COOL AND QUIET IN SUMMER

Jim and Jackie are glad they replaced the windows of their Missoula, Montana, home. The couple replaced their 33-year-old single-pane windows with new, high-performance vinyl-clad wood windows. "It's amazing how quiet the house is," says Jim. "Even better, the lower solar heat gain on the west windows keeps the house cooler during those long, hot summer sunsets."

"We planned it right and were able to take advantage of the 30% federal tax credit along with the Montana energy tax credit," adds Jim. They were able to double the Montana energy tax credit limit on their state income tax using "Married filing separately," allowing them to take a total credit of $1,000.

NATIONAL FENESTRATION RATING COUNCIL

The National Fenestration Rating Council (NFRC) is a not-for-profit organization that rates the performance of windows, skylights, and doors. It maintains databases on hundreds of manufacturers' products, which are accessible to the public (nfrc.org). Participating companies put an NFRC label on their products, listing U-factor, SHGC, VT, air leakage, and condensation resistance (optional). This makes it easier for buyers to collect information about, and compare, window systems.

Air leakage is the flow rate of air through the seams and seals around windows or doors, expressed in cubic feet per minute per square foot (CFM/ft²) of product area. Most products tested by NFRC come in at between 0.1 CFM/ft² (least leaky) and 0.3 CFM/ft² (maximum allowable).

Condensation resistance (CR) is a number between 0 and 100 that expresses how good a window or door is at discouraging condensation. High CR usually means less likelihood of condensation problems. Windows with a high CR also keep the house more comfortable, because the interior window surface temperature is warmer under cold winter conditions.

Look for the NFRC label on a window to understand its properties and evaluate different window systems.

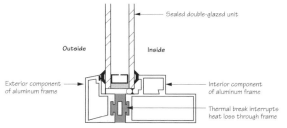

A thermal break in an aluminum frame. Reprinted from *Residential Windows*, 3rd ed., by John Carmody et al.

Wood

Wood frames have long been favored for their aesthetic appeal and good insulating properties. Wood is less durable than other materials, but with regular paint and maintenance, a wood window frame can last a long time. Wood is considered a high-end choice, because competing products tend to cost less. In recent decades, vinyl, enameled metal, or aluminum cladding have been added to the exterior of wood windows to improve their weather resistance.

Vinyl

Vinyl frames have good insulating value; require little maintenance; and are resistant to impact, abrasion, corrosion, air pollutants, and termites. Vinyl frames are more stable and durable nowadays than they once were, but vinyl still expands and contracts with temperature changes more than wood or aluminum does; look for heat-welded joints and/or interior webs (rather than mechanically joined frames) for stress resistance. Insulated vinyl frames offer even greater thermal resistance and are typically used with high-performance glazing.

New Materials

Recent developments have expanded the range of window frame materials:

- Extruded composite frames, incorporating reclaimed sawdust and wood scrap in a polymer binder, are more durable than wood alone.

TABLE 07.02: WINDOW FRAME U-VALUES

Frame Type	U-Value
Insulated fiberglass, insulated vinyl	0.2–0.4
Wood, vinyl	0.3–0.5
Aluminum-clad wood, reinforced vinyl	0.4–0.6
Aluminum with thermal break	0.8–1.3
Aluminum without thermal break	1.7–2.4

Source: *Residential Windows: A Guide to New Technologies and Energy Performance*, 3rd ed. John Carmody, Stephen Selkowitz, Dariush Arasteh, and Lisa Heshong, Norton, 2007, p. 127.

Note: Total window U-factor depends on window dimensions and design details; see NFRC label.

- Fiberglass frames are dimensionally stable and have good insulating value. They are more expensive than vinyl, but less expensive than wood.
- Engineered thermoplastics have some structural advantages over vinyl, but they are more expensive and haven't captured much of the market.

Should You Replace Those Old Windows?

Sometimes there are compelling reasons not to replace old windows. Some old windows are beautiful and repairable. Some are in historic homes, where local ordinances prohibit replacing them. Or you may find the cost of window replacement too high, while less costly projects could save just as much energy. If you choose not to replace old windows, we recommend that you upgrade your windows to make them more airtight, and that you consider adding energy-efficient storm windows tailored to your home's style.

Researchers in Colorado found it possible to improve the overall energy performance of a home's historic, single-pane windows by a factor of 5 without altering their character. They accomplished this by repairing and air sealing the old windows, then installing excellent storm windows with a fiberglass frame and a low-U IGU.

Adding a storm window lets you keep a historic stained-glass window while improving its thermal performance.

Making Informed Window Replacement Choices

In 2010, 41.5 million windows were shipped in the United States—over 71% of them destined for the remodeling and replacement market. Researchers project that this market will reach 36.1 million windows by 2014, and that over 60% of these windows will have vinyl frames.

This growing market leads to fierce competition among manufacturers and retailers, who employ a variety of sales techniques to attract business. These range from newspaper, radio, and TV advertising to e-mails offering "advice" on replacement windows (to sign up homeowners for a home visit by a high-pressure salesman). Home shows aimed at the remodeling market are peppered with purveyors of windows, doors, and skylights.

All of this can be useful, but it's critical to be an informed consumer:

If you love your old single-pane windows and don't want to replace them, you can greatly improve their thermal performance by air sealing and adding storm windows.

- Ask about U-factor, SHGC, and VT, and ask salespeople to distinguish between whole-window and center-of-glass performance. (This signals that you're up to speed on window technology.) If the salesperson cannot or will not answer your questions, find another supplier.
- See if the vendor recommends windows with different properties for different facades. If not, ask why not.
- Ask for the basis of any claims about savings and payback periods. Are they talking about window savings or whole-house savings? How does the house used as a model compare with your house?
- Ask how long the product is expected to last.
- Ask who does the installation, and inquire about the installer's credentials, experience, references, and warranties for the installed product.
- Ask if using your own installer will affect the warranty.

Tubular skylights can be installed without cutting roof framing members due to their small diameter. Solatube International, Inc.

Skylights

Think of a skylight as a window in the roof. Some skylights can be opened for ventilation or for an emergency exit. Skylights have a range of U-factors, SHGCs, and VTs—all of which affect their function and cost. Some skylights include roller-style shades, lowering both SHGC and VT. The most effective shades for this purpose are installed on the outside of the skylight; these intercept sunlight before it penetrates the home's conditioned envelope.

Skylights add natural light and charm, and can replace electric lighting by day (Chapter 11). Install only high-quality skylights, with thermal and optical characteristics appropriate for the climate zone. Install them carefully to avoid water leaks and thermal loss. Moderation in the use of skylights is generally a virtue.

Two kinds of skylight are common in residential structures: conventional and *tubular skylights* (also known as light tubes, *sun pipes*, or *solar tubes*). Their diameter makes it possible to install tubular skylights without cutting roof framing members, and they don't cause as much heat gain or loss as larger skylights. This is important in hot or cold climates; skylights can lose more heat in winter than a window, and are harder to shade in summer.

DOORS

New doors can improve the appearance and functionality of your home, but the best ones can be expensive. To maximize the value of your investment, install doors that are energy efficient and that can be affordably maintained. The quality of a home's doors, and the way they are installed, plays a big role in that home's comfort and energy performance. Because doors are opened and closed frequently, it's important to limit the flow of air around the hinges, doorjamb, door sweep, threshold, and *weather strip*.

There are two kinds of exterior door—the ones like walls and the ones like windows. Wall-like doors are solid; they have little or no glazing, and therefore they transmit little solar radiation. They are usually made of wood and have an R-value of 2 to 2.5. Steel, fiberglass, and composite doors are sometimes filled with insulation; these have R-values of as much as 10.

Window-like doors include sliding glass doors and French doors. These doors have a relatively large *tempered-glass* area and may transmit a good deal of solar radiation. Some of them have IGUs, with low-e coatings and inert gas. Sliding glass doors with an R-value of 3 and a SHGC of 0.3 to 0.5 can be a cost-effective investment; they are more comfortable and more energy efficient than a single-pane glass door.

WINDOW AND DOOR PROJECTS YOU CAN DO TODAY:

- Add shading to windows that get excessive solar heat.
- Add weather strip to doors if what's there now is inadequate.
- Find out in which direction your windows face; think about what improvemeμnts would be appropriate for each facade.

WINDOW AND DOOR PROJECTS THAT TAKE MORE TIME:

- Add storm windows to your existing windows.
- Replace inefficient windows and doors with high-performance models.

Conventional skylights, like windows, now come with an array of energy-saving glazings and built-in shading devices. Photo courtesy of VELUX America Inc.

RESOURCES

Print

"Historic Windows: Problems and Solutions." Larry Kinney, *Home Energy*, November/December 2011, p. 32

Residential Windows: A Guide to New Technologies and Energy Performance, 3rd ed. John Carmody, Stephen Selkowitz, Dariush Arasteh, and Lisa Heshong, Norton, 2007

Window Systems for High-Performance Buildings. John Carmody, Stephen Selkowitz, Eleanor S. Lee, and Dariush Arasteh, Norton, 2004

Online

Door & Window Manufacturer magazine: newsletter@dwmmag.com

Product information related to windows and doors.

The Effects of Energy Efficiency Treatments on Historic Windows. L. Kinney and A. Ellsworth, Center for Resource Conservation: conservationcenter.org/assets/EffectsEnergyonHistoricWindows.pdf

Efficient Windows Collaborative: efficientwindows.org

"Your gateway to information on how to choose energy-efficient windows."

Tips for Daylighting with Windows, Section 5, "Shading Strategy." Jennifer O'Connor et al., Lawrence Berkeley National Laboratory, 1997: windows.lbl.gov/daylighting/designguide/section5.pdf

Includes conceptual designs for overhangs and other shading devices, along with formulas for sizing overhangs.

Window Attachments: windowattachments.org

Designed to help you sort out all the options, features, and functions of a full spectrum of window attachments and treatments.

"Windows and Daylighting": windows.lbl.gov/software/registration/register.asp

Useful software tools from Lawrence Berkeley National Laboratory available for free download.

"Windows and Window Treatments." L. Kinney, Southwest Energy Efficiency Project, 2004: swenergy.org

Search for article title and download pdf.

"Windows, Doors & Skylights" (DOE/EERE): energysavers.gov/your_home/windows_doors_skylights/index.cfm/mytopic=13310

Chapter 8
AIR SEALING: CONTROLLING AIRFLOW BETWEEN INDOORS AND OUT

REMODELING PRESENTS MANY AIR-SEALING OPPORTUNITIES

Include air sealing in your remodeling job if you

- add insulation;
- change any part of an exterior wall (e.g., replacing an old window with a new window);
- make a hole (penetration) through an exterior wall, top-floor ceiling, overhanging floor, or concrete floor;
- turn unconditioned spaces like attics or porches into conditioned spaces;
- add a living space to your home;
- install recessed lights in upper-story ceilings; or
- do work in the attic, crawl space, or basement.

Use Home Energy Saver (hes.lbl.gov) to calculate how much energy and money you can save by reducing your home's air leakage.

What can controlling the flow of air do for you? It can

- make your home a more healthful place;
- increase your comfort;
- reduce your energy bills; and
- increase your home's durability.

Your home's boundary between outdoors and indoors should keep the weather and unwelcome critters outside. The roofing material sheds rain and snow; exterior walls keep the wind from howling through your living room; floors keep critters out. These parts of your house compose the weather shell, the shield that keeps the weather out. That used to be the only boundary between outdoors and indoors that we worried about.

But these days we ask a lot more of our homes. Now we expect them to maintain a constant indoor temperature, not be too humid or too dry, and not be drafty. To enable our homes to do all this, we need to improve the weather shell to make it a really good building envelope. A good building envelope includes insulation and an air barrier, working together—a continuous layer of materials that blocks the movement of air (such as drywall, polyethylene, house wrap, plywood, rigid insulation, dense-pack insulation, and building sealants) and completely envelops the living space. Sometimes the insulation and air barrier are one and the same, as in the case of sprayed-foam insulation (Chapter 9). When the insulation and air barrier are different materials, they'll work best when they are in direct contact with each other.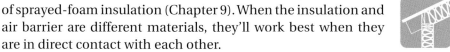

The air barrier is our focus in this chapter. It's one of several layers meant to control the flow of heat, air, and moisture between outside and inside. Our purpose here is to show you

- that a robust air barrier is a good thing;
- how air leakage happens;
- how to measure and reduce air leakage; and
- how to reduce moisture and indoor air quality (IAQ) problems in a tight house.

There are significant health and safety considerations associated with making your home tighter, so it's important that you hire a home energy pro (Chapter 4) to analyze your home's building envelope, identify trouble spots, and develop an air-sealing plan.

WHY YOU WANT YOUR HOUSE AIR SEALED

Whether you're opening walls or adding new ones, working in the attic, basement, or crawl space, air sealing should be part of the job to keep

- **conditioned air inside.** Air leaks waste energy. If you're spending money on air conditioning or heating your home, why would you want to make it easy for that expensive air to escape?
- **unconditioned air outside.** Air leakage works both ways. When a cubic foot of conditioned air goes outside, it must be replaced with a cubic foot of unconditioned air coming inside. That adds to the heating or cooling *load* of your home, costs you money, and can make your home uncomfortably hot, cold, or moist.
- **bad air out and stay healthy.** Not only does the air that leaks in cost you money, but it's probably not the most healthful air. Moldy air from the crawl space, CO and gasoline fumes from the garage, dead animal parts from the attic, pollen from outdoors—none of it's good.
- **moisture out of your walls.** When it's hot and muggy outside, you don't want to pull that moisture into your building cavities and start biology experiments. When it's cold outside, the warm, relatively humid indoor air can condense inside wall cavities and cause materials to rot.

THE CAUSES OF AIR LEAKAGE

Two conditions must exist in order for air to move between outside and inside. There must be

- air leakage pathways; and
- a pressure difference.

You can't turn your house into an ultra-high-vacuum chamber, but you can reduce the amount of air leakage by minimizing pathways. Think of it as closing some big unseen windows and lots of little ones.

Pressure difference is the force that pushes air through the air pathways. If there's an air pathway and no pressure difference, nothing is pushing the air between inside and out. If there's a pressure difference, but no path for the air to travel across the building envelope, again, there's no air leakage.

The Driving Forces behind Air Leakage

We can reduce air leakage by sealing up pathways, but can we do anything about pressure differences? The answer depends on where the pressure difference comes from. The three driving forces behind air leakage are

- wind;
- stack effect; and
- mechanical systems.

DOES A HOUSE NEED TO BREATHE?

Have you heard that you shouldn't air seal your house too tightly because it needs to breathe? It's a common myth, but that's all it is. Houses do need to be able to dry out when they get wet, but controlled ventilation is far more effective and healthful than having a house that leaks air randomly.

This myth probably originates with the supertight, superinsulated houses of the 1970s, when we hadn't yet figured out how to look at the house as a system. Home builders and trade contractors, with the best of intentions, sealed up the houses to eliminate the energy wasted via air *infiltration*, but some of them overlooked one key detail: Tight houses need mechanical ventilation.

A house cannot be too tight. Yes, a very tight house can have problems, but it's not because of the air sealing. The problem is the lack of systems thinking. Here, then, are five appropriate rules:

- People need to breathe, not houses.
- Don't mix combustion air and people air.
- Houses need to be able to dry out.
- Avoid creating cold surfaces where moisture can condense.
- Very airtight houses require a mechanical ventilation system.

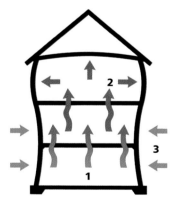

THE STACK EFFECT

1. Heated indoor air rises toward the top of the house.
2. The higher pressure at the top of the house pushes air out through leaks in ceilings and walls.
3. The lower pressure at the bottom of the house pulls air in through leaks in the walls and floors.

Wind

When your window is open, wind blowing outdoors will move air through the window. This causes extra pressure inside the house, pushing air out open windows (or other pathways) at the opposite side of the house.

Stack Effect

Stack effect is what we usually think of as warm air rising. It's mainly a cold-weather phenomenon, because big temperature differences are required to induce this effect. How does it work? Air at 70°F, for example, is a lot less dense than air at 30°F, so the warmer, less-dense air rises and the cooler, denser air accumulates lower in the house. This puts the top of the house under positive pressure and the bottom of the house under negative pressure. Holes at the top and bottom of the house then allow the warm air to leak out at the top and cool air to leak in at the bottom.

If your ceiling has a hole in it—say, through a recessed-can light, a plumbing *chase*, or pull-down attic stairs—that warm, buoyant indoor air will rise through the hole and leak into the attic.

The stack effect depends largely on two factors. These are

- the height of the house; and
- the temperature difference between the top and bottom of the house (which is influenced by the outdoor temperature).

The taller the house and the greater the temperature difference, the greater the pressure difference induced by the stack effect.

Mechanical Systems

The third driving force is created by fans and appliances. When a fan moves air across the building envelope, it can create a pressure difference between inside and out. The fans in your bathrooms and kitchen are obvious culprits. Less-obvious exhaust fans include the one in your clothes dryer or any fireplace fan that draws *combustion air* from inside the house.

The devices listed in Table 08.01 exhaust air from the house to the outdoors. A 200 CFM clothes dryer sends 200 cubic feet of conditioned house air outside every minute it's running, while unconditioned air leaks in to replace it.

Your HVAC system can also create pressure differences, primarily through duct leakage. Let's say your ducts are in the attic and the crawl space, both of which are unconditioned and outside the building envelope. When your furnace, heat pump, or A/C runs, indoor air is drawn into the *return ducts*, travels through the HVAC equipment, and is sent back into the house (with the newly conditioned air) through *supply ducts*. If your house has many air leakage pathways, the return ducts can draw outside air into the house. Meanwhile, supply ducts can push conditioned air through air pathways in the building envelope, which is called *exfiltration*.

The duct system may create interior pressure differences as well. How many air-conditioning vents are in your bedrooms? If each room has one vent, that's a supply vent, sending conditioned air into the room. When the bedroom door is closed the air coming out of those vents builds up, creating positive pressure and looking for a way out. Some of that air will leak back into the house, but some will be pushed outside.

Many homes have only one return vent—a large *grille* located in a central area, like a hallway. When the bedroom doors are closed and the bedrooms develop a positive pressure, the rooms connected to the return vent develop a negative pressure. So the home loses conditioned air from the bedrooms and pulls unconditioned air into the living areas.

To relieve the pressure imbalance, you have a few choices. You could put a return vent in each bedroom. You could undercut the bedroom doors, but research shows that the cut needs to be 4–6 inches—which you probably don't want. Or you could install *transfer grilles* or *jumper ducts*. A transfer grille in a wall or door allows the positive pressure in the bedroom to bleed back into the living areas. A jumper duct is an actual duct connected to grilles in the bedroom and living area (usually the hall outside the bedroom).

TABLE 08.01: AIRFLOW RATES FOR HOUSEHOLD FANS AND APPLIANCES	
Device	**Flow Rate (CFM)**
Bath fan	30–100
Range hood: standard	150–300
Range hood: downdraft	around 600
Range hood: commercial	1,000–2,000
Clothes dryer	around 200
Built-in vacuum cleaner	50–200

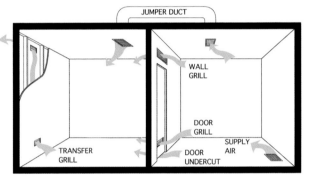

A jumper duct can relieve the air pressure imbalance that can occur when there's no return air grille in a bedroom.

Counteracting the Driving Forces

You can air seal to reduce pathways, but what can you do about the driving forces that create pressure differences?

You can't do much about wind, other than planting or constructing windbreaks. Likewise, you can't eliminate the stack effect; pressure differences will continue to exist. What you can do is seal the air leaks so that the pressure difference doesn't cause an air leakage problem.

With fans, you have some options for reducing pressure differences:

- Avoid installing a high-capacity fan (e.g., a commercial range hood), or provide makeup air to balance pressures (Chapter 12).
- Seal the duct system and/or move the attic air barrier to the roofline to bring the furnace and ducts inside the air boundary (Chapter 10).
- Install dedicated return vents, transfer grilles, or jumper ducts in bedrooms to send air back to the rest of the house.

TESTING THE AIRTIGHTNESS OF YOUR HOME

Before you do any air sealing, have a home energy pro test your home's airtightness and look for air leaks. Your home's airtightness should be tested

- before you start remodeling, to establish the baseline of air leakage in your home and to help locate its sources;

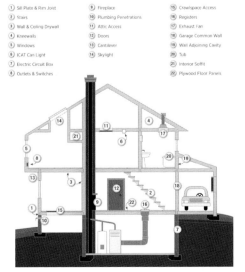

Interior Air Sealing

Conventional construction (and typical retrofits) requires tracking down and sealing multiple penetrations that ultimately lead to or through the exterior shell

1. Sill Plate & Rim Joist
2. Stairs
3. Wall & Ceiling Drywall
4. Kneewalls
5. Windows
6. ICAT Can Light
7. Electric Circuit Box
8. Outlets & Switches
9. Fireplace
10. Plumbing Penetrations
11. Attic Access
12. Doors
13. Cantilever
14. Skylight
15. Crawlspace Access
16. Registers
17. Exhaust Fan
18. Garage Common Wall
19. Wall Adjoining Cavity
20. Tub
21. Interior Soffit
22. Plywood Floor Panels

A smoke pencil or smoke stick, used in conjunction with a blower door, helps identify air leaks.

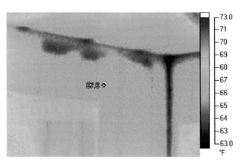

Pictures taken with an infrared camera make thermal differences stand out; in this case, the dark blue areas indicate air leaks and areas with inadequate insulation.

Caulking is often the best way to seal small gaps and cracks. (Sprayed foam works well, too.)

- during the remodeling work, to identify and seal new leaks; and
- after remodeling, document the resulting improvements.

The tool for testing air leakage in your home is called a *blower door*. A home energy pro can use it to quantify the air leakage rate of a house (Chapter 4).

The basic principle of blower door operation is simple. A powerful fan, set temporarily in a doorway, creates a pressure difference between the house and the outdoors, usually by depressurizing the house. All the air the fan blows out of the house is replaced by air coming in through leaks.

So all we need to do is measure the house pressure and the amount of air moving through the fan, and—voilà—we know how much the house leaks at that test pressure. Airflow is measured in CFM, and the pressure normally used for this test is 50 *pascals* (Pa, a measure of pressure differential). Hence, home energy pros in the United States use the notation CFM_{50} or *CFM@50Pa*—which is about equal to the pressure of a 20 mph wind.

A blower door can also be used for diagnosis, by running the blower and walking around the house to find leaks by hand, using a *smoke pencil* or a thermal-imaging (infrared) camera.

FUNDAMENTALS OF AIR SEALING

Let's start with these three simple rules for air sealing:

- Find and seal the big holes first.
- Find and seal the medium-sized holes second.
- Find and seal as many of the small holes as you can.

The size and nature of the hole determine the best sealing material:

- For doors, windows, and access holes: Use weather strip, *gaskets*, thresholds, and door sweeps to reduce air leakage when closed.
- For big holes: Use rigid materials such as plywood, *oriented strand board (OSB)*, drywall, foam board, or sheet metal to fill the hole; then seal edges with caulk or sprayed foam.
- For medium gaps: Fill the gap with *backer rod* and cover with caulk, or use an expanding sprayed foam. *Caution: Use low-expanding sprayed foam around windows and doors. If you don't, you may warp the frame, prevent windows from opening, and void the warranty.*
- For small gaps and cracks: Caulk and sprayed foam work best.

Learning to See the Air Barrier

When designing a remodel, some architects use a simple trick to verify the continuity of the air barrier: On a plan or section, they should be able to trace the air barrier around the entire house without lifting their pencil from the paper. Any gaps where they jump from air barrier material to non-air-barrier material are design flaws that need to be addressed. Do your best to bring ducts inside the building envelope.

Air Barrier Sleuthing

There are many common pathways through which air can leak in or out of your home. Home energy pros are trained to find these holes in your air barrier, but you can look for some of them, too.

- Trouble spots usually occur at transitions: foundation wall to framed floor, wall to ceiling, band *joist* areas, attic knee wall to floor joists to ceiling below, attic knee wall to rafters, and so on.
- Dirty gray or black streaks in insulation usually come from dust left behind as air leaks through.
- Darkened areas on light-colored carpet may indicate where air is leaking through the house perimeter and coming in under baseboards.

Windows and Doors

Window and door openings are major air leakage sites in walls. Whether or not you replace windows and doors, you may have access to the gaps between the window or door frame and the wall framing. Use an air barrier material (not fiberglass or cellulose, both of which allow air passage) to fill those gaps.

Many older windows are themselves leaky. Rebuilding or replacing those windows can further reduce air leakage (Chapter 7).

Diagonal Sheathing

Old homes with diagonal sheathing are very leaky. For the past 60 years or so, builders have used sheet goods—plywood and OSB—for *wall sheathing* and subfloors. Before that, homes were sheathed with diagonal lumber, which is a lot leakier due to gaps between boards. If you close up those walls without sealing those gaps, you've missed a valuable opportunity.

Leaks Around Ducts and Other Penetrations

The photo on the next page (top) shows a house that had a basement mechanical room outside the building envelope. An insulated wall (representing the building envelope) separated the mechanical room from the finished basement.

The joists running across that wall, however, were almost completely unsealed. You can see that someone shot a bit of sprayed foam at the bottom of one duct, but the rest is wide open. Once ducts go in like that and the house is finished, that room is almost impossible to seal. This is a common problem, and may cause a house to perform poorly in a blower door test.

The solution is to seal the joist openings with rigid material (plywood, foam board, or other sheathing) before the ducts go in. Then the duct installer can cut a hole in the sheathing, install a metal collar connector, and attach the ducts to each side. That method will provide a good air barrier between unconditioned and conditioned spaces that are connected by floor joists.

THE AIRTIGHT-DRYWALL APPROACH

Generally, the outer surface of your house should be your primary air barrier, because you don't want unconditioned air getting into your building assemblies. But sometimes you don't want interior air getting into your building assemblies, either. For example, in a cold climate, warm, humid air leaking into the wall cavities can condense when it hits cold sheathing, encouraging mold growth.

The *airtight-drywall approach* seals the interior side of the exterior walls, focusing on the top and bottom of each wall, around all the windows and doors, and wherever there's a penetration through the drywall (at electrical outlets, switches, and light fixtures). By air sealing both sides of the exterior walls, you reduce the total amount of air leakage and reduce the possibility of moisture problems inside the walls.

Homes over 60 years old may have diagonal sheathing, allowing lots of air leakage.

Ducts and joists that cross the building envelope are often unsealed or, as in this photo, inadequately sealed.

Remove abandoned ducts and seal their former location, or you risk a duct-sized air leak, as shown here.

There's often a big, unsealed hole cut for the bathtub drain.

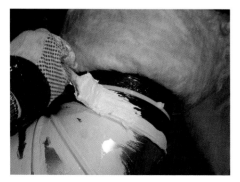

Here you see a duct connection and rigid elbow being sealed with mastic.

Another air-sealing problem related to ducts can appear if a home gets a new duct system and old vents are taken out of use. If the ducts go through the building envelope, they need to be completely removed and the holes sealed. The second photo on the left shows a duct boot that was left in place, which can allow unconditioned crawl space air into the living space.

Look beyond the ducts, as well, and make sure all penetrations—new and old—get air sealed. The biggest hole may be the large opening cut for the bathtub drainpipes, as shown in the third photo on the left. This hole is often left unsealed and can admit not only air but also critters.

Leaks in Ducts

When the ducts in your HVAC system are in unconditioned space, such as an attic or a crawl space, they should be air sealed for two reasons:

- You don't want the ducts to leak when the HVAC system is running.
- Since they form part of the building envelope, leaky ducts will leak even when the HVAC system is not running.

The best way to reduce air leakage from ducts is to bring them inside the building envelope wherever possible. Seal leaky ducts with duct *mastic*, a sticky, paste-like adhesive that can be applied with a brush. Note that the mastic goes on the inner liner of flex duct, not on the outer insulation wrap.

Unsealed Transitions between Old and New

When you add conditioned space, thus moving the building envelope, the old parts of the house don't always connect seamlessly to the new. The photo at the top of p. 65 shows this problem in a house with a recent addition. Notice the gap between the new ceiling drywall and the old ceiling, as seen from the attic. That opening is more than $1^1/2$ inches across (the depth of the 2 x 4 plus a little); it extends laterally for the width of the drywall (4 feet); and it allows unconditioned attic air to go all the way down into the interior wall.

Recessed-Can Lights

Recessed-can lights usually pose problems (Chapter 11). First, they allow air to move across the envelope if the cans are not rated as airtight. Second, if the penetration isn't sealed, air leaks can occur around the perimeter of even airtight cans. Third, can lights displace insulation in the building envelope. They should never be used in vaulted ceilings that are part of the building envelope.

Big Holes Hidden by Insulation

The hole shown in the middle photo on p.65 is not visible on first inspection. To reveal that hole, the home energy pro had to move the insulation aside. How did the pro know to look there? Dirty insulation! A lot of air was moving from inside the living area through that big hole and into the attic. Fiberglass doesn't stop air movement, but it will act as a filter. Hence the dirt you see.

Misguided Vents

See those crawl space vents in the photo at bottom right? It might look like there's a vented crawl space. But appearances can be deceiving. There's actually a finished basement behind that wall, and those vents open into the space above the basement's dropped ceiling. The homeowners basically had open windows into their basement year-round. By sealing those holes and a few others, they were able to reduce their air leakage by 40%.

TIGHT HOUSES HAVE SPECIAL NEEDS

A tight house must be understood as a whole system if you want to avoid problems. Three main problems can occur with tight houses:

- poor IAQ;
- backdrafting of combustion appliances; and
- high humidity and mold growth.

Poor IAQ

Make your house as tight as you can; then add well-designed mechanical ventilation for good indoor air quality (Chapter 12).

Backdrafting

Appliances such as natural-draft gas water heaters or wood-burning fireplaces use air from the space around them for combustion and create a draft for the exhaust gases. If appliances cannot get enough combustion air from the house (which can be the case with a tight house), they may pull air down the flue, preventing exhaust gases from going up the flue. That can introduce deadly CO into the home.

One way to avoid backdrafting is to isolate the appliance from the living space (with insulation and air sealing on all sides) and give it its own combustion air supply. A safer, less costly, more energy-efficient approach is to replace the old water heater with a new power- or direct-vent unit instead of conducting expensive air-sealing and insulating work in the room where these combustion appliances are located.

Have a home energy pro assess your home before you begin remodeling, and address combustion problems before you do any air sealing.

High Humidity

All houses can have problems caused by internally generated moisture. These problems are often addressed by

- installing good mechanical ventilation (Chapter 12);
- sizing the cooling system properly (Chapter 14); and
- using materials that don't trap moisture in the building envelope.

Take special care at the edge between existing and new construction. In this case, failure to do so created a gap between the new and old ceilings that admits unconditioned air into an interior wall.

Dirty insulation can be a clue to hidden air leaks.

When the basement of this house was converted to living space, someone forgot to close off the vent on the right, allowing unconditioned air to pour into the basement ceiling.

AN UNEXPECTED BENEFIT OF AIR SEALING

Perry lives in an 80-year-old house in west Georgia. When he decided to have the vented crawl space sealed, his main goal was to minimize cold floors in winter. The air in the crawl space was as cold as the outdoor air, and his pine floorboards were nailed to the floor joists—with no subflooring. In some places, Perry could look into the crawl space through cracks between the boards.

By sealing the crawl space, Perry expanded the building envelope from the floor to the foundation walls and the ground (Chapter 10). A continuous vapor barrier covered the ground, foundation walls, and supporting piers to keep moisture from getting into the crawl space and house. The foundation vents and band joist were air sealed, and the foundation walls were insulated. Afterward, the crawl space temperature stayed close to the house temperature, and Perry got the warm floors he wanted.

He also got something he wasn't expecting: "I used to wake up every morning and go through a fit of sneezing. I figured it was just allergies, but with the crawl space sealed, I don't sneeze in the morning anymore."

Your mechanical ventilation system should be designed to help remove internally generated moisture.

It's also important not to oversize your heat pump or A/C, for three reasons. First, an oversized heat pump or A/C doesn't have long enough run times to dehumidify well. Second, a properly sized heat pump or A/C that runs for a longer time will be more energy efficient than an oversized one that turns on and off frequently. Finally, the smaller unit will cost less to buy than the larger unit.

Most houses need materials that reduce air leakage without trapping moisture. Unless you're in a cold climate like Minneapolis or a hot-humid climate like Miami, covering your walls with a layer of vapor-impermeable plastic is not a good idea; it can trap moisture. Houses don't need to breathe, but they do need to be able to dry out when they get wet.

Another problem can occur with unvented gas, propane, or kerosene space heaters. In addition to creating toxic combustion by-products, they produce a lot of water vapor and can raise the humidity in your home into the mold-growing range. These devices should be eliminated.

AIR-SEALING PROJECTS YOU CAN DO TODAY:

- Walk around your house, inside and out, and look for air leakage sites.
- Hire a home energy pro to test the home for air leakage.
- Clearly identify where the building envelope is.

AIR-SEALING PROJECTS THAT WILL TAKE MORE TIME:

- Have your home energy pro find and seal air leakage sites.
- Have your home energy pro test the house after air sealing, to document your reduced air leakage.

RESOURCES

"Airtight Drywall." Martin Holladay, *Fine Homebuilding*, September 2010, pp. 86–87: finehomebuilding.com/how-to/departments/energy-smart-details/airtight-drywall.aspx

"Attic Air-Sealing: Products and Materials Overview" (video introduction to air-sealing materials): greenbuildingadvisor.com/attic-air-sealing-products-and-materials-overview

U.S. Department of Energy/Energy Efficiency and Renewable Energy:

- "Air Sealing": energysavers.gov/your_home/insulation_airsealing/index.cfm/mytopic=11230
- *Air Sealing: A Guide for Contractors to Share with Homeowners.* Building America Best Practices Series, vol. 10, 2010: www1.eere.energy.gov/library/default.aspx?Page=2&spid=2
- "Guide to Air Sealing": energy.gov/energysaver/downloads/guide-air-sealing

Chapter 9

INSULATION: KEEP HEAT WHERE YOU WANT IT

What can better insulation do for you? It can

- save energy and lower your heating and cooling costs;
- increase your comfort by making house temperature more uniform;
- reduce the required size of your heating and cooling equipment;
- reduce the risk of wintertime condensation indoors; and
- reduce noise transmission from outside.

When you remodel, you may open up walls, floors, and ceilings. Take advantage of this opportunity to upgrade your insulation; it will almost always be more expensive later.

HOW INSULATION WORKS

Heat travels in three main ways: it is transported via movement of air or water (convection), it radiates from a hotter surface to an unconnected cooler surface (radiation), and it is directly transferred through solid materials (conduction) (see "How Heat Moves" on p. 51). In homes, you reduce unwanted convection by controlling air leakage. You reduce unwanted solar radiation by shading, window selection, and using light or reflective colors for your roof and walls. You reduce conduction by installing insulation (which also reduces convection and radiation in wall cavities).

Heat moves by conduction through walls, floors, and ceilings, from the warmer side to the cooler side. In winter, heat moves from living spaces into neighboring unheated spaces—attics, garages, and basements—and outdoors. In summer, heat moves from outdoors into cooler indoor spaces. A material's ability to slow heat transfer is called its *thermal resistance,* indicated by its R-value. The higher the R-value, the better the insulation.

Insulations like fiberglass, cellulose, and rock wool gain most of their thermal resistance by creating small air pockets that make it difficult for air to circulate and move heat by convection. To perform effectively, these air-permeable insulation materials need to be enclosed with a tight air barrier on as many sides as possible to keep air still inside the insulation, and to inhibit air from passing through the insulation. Wall cavities that are enclosed on the top, bottom, and all four sides (as in standard wood-frame construction) can work well with air-permeable insulations. Any air-permeable insulation will be less effective in floors, ceilings, and open wall cavities, where it is not thoroughly enclosed and may be exposed to air movement.

Sprayed-foam or rigid foam insulation gains its thermal resistance from gases trapped within the insulating material; these types of insulation are not permeable to air.

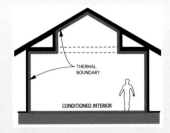

KNOW YOUR THERMAL BOUNDARY

The walls, ceilings, and floors that enclose your living space make up your home's *thermal boundary,* which separates conditioned (heated and/or cooled) and unconditioned space—the boundary within which your conditioned air should be contained. This is where your insulation should be.

Before proceeding, you must understand where this boundary is in your house. It should be clearly defined, well insulated, and aligned with a continuous air barrier. If the air barrier and thermal boundary are not properly aligned, warm moist air—from inside or outside, depending on the climate and time of year—may condense, leaving water in your roof, walls, or floor. This can produce cosmetic or structural damage and encourage mold growth. If there is a question about where the thermal boundary should be—for example, if you're enclosing a porch or considering heating your attic or crawl space—your home performance assessor or architect can help.

Use Home Energy Saver (hes.lbl.gov) to calculate how much energy and money you can save by upgrading your home's insulation levels.

People often confuse insulating a house with air sealing it, but these are not the same thing; you will usually need to do both. Use the air-sealing techniques described in Chapter 8 to stop air leakage. Then use insulation to reduce heat conduction. Only foam-in-place insulation, rigid insulation caulked in place, and dense-pack cellulose insulation allow you to seal and insulate at the same time.

TYPES OF INSULATION

Insulation comes in many forms. Understanding the properties of each form will help you choose the best types for your home.

Loose-Fill Insulation

Loose-fill insulation (also called *blown insulation*) consists of loose fibers or granules of cellulose (recycled newspaper), fiberglass (glass fibers), rock wool (fibers of molten rock or slag), cotton, or other materials. It comes in bags and is usually blown into cavities or attics using special equipment, conforming to the space in which it is installed. Sometimes it is blown at high density *(dense-pack insulation)* to increase resistance to air infiltration.

In existing homes, loose-fill insulation is commonly applied in attics, where it can be blown over existing insulation. It can also be blown into uninsulated wall cavities through access holes drilled from either the inside or the outside (and later plugged). If you are thinking about re-siding your home or refinishing the inside of exterior walls, this is a good time to consider adding loose-fill insulation. If you're opening wall cavities or building new exterior walls, loose-fill insulation can be blown in, and a cover attached to the wall studs to hold it in place (this is called a *blown-in blanket (BIB)* system). In multistory houses, dense packing *rim joists* between floors is an excellent way to insulate and air seal an often overlooked area.

Loose-fill insulation is blown into cavities or attics using special equipment, conforming to the space.

Loose-fill fibers can also be sprayed, mixed with water and sometimes adhesives, into open walls before drywall installation, or to cover irregularly shaped or hard-to-reach areas. This technique—called *wet-spray*—is often used with cellulose. The insulation dries within a few days, then resists settling. Some newer processes *(moist-* or *damp-spray)* speed up drying time by using much less water. Some installers also use drying machines.

Batts and Blankets

Batts and blankets are flexible, bound insulation made from glass, rock wool, or cotton fibers. They come in rolls (blankets) or precut strips (batts). Both come in standard widths (16 or 24 inches) to fit between framing members.

In this attic remodel, the cathedral ceiling is insulated with kraft-paper-faced fiberglass batts, while the knee walls have unfaced cotton batt insulation. Batts should be secured to avoid the gaps you see at the top of some of the cotton batts.

Batts and blankets can fit under floors, in attics, and in unfinished walls. Both are available with or without a *vapor-retarder* facing. This facing is usually not fireproof, so it should not be used where it will be exposed to an open space, unprotected by drywall or other less flammable material.

Good installation is crucial. Avoid allowing batts or blankets to be compressed—as often happens around plumbing and electrical wiring or when squeezing thick batts into narrow cavities. This lowers the R-value. If batts sag within a wall cavity, the resulting gap will also lower the overall R-value. Batts or blankets that come with vapor-retarder facings must be placed in cavities with the vapor retarder in the proper orientation, which depends on your climate (see Vapor Control Layer Recommendations in Resources).

Rigid Insulation

Rigid insulation is made from plastic foam (polyurethane, isocyanurate, or polystyrene) or fiberglass, pressed or extruded into panels. It can provide air sealing when the seams are properly taped, and may have some structural value when used as a continuous layer on exterior structural walls.

Rigid insulation can be applied to the interior of a basement wall; take care to seal joints and seams to avoid moisture penetration.

Rigid foam insulation is commonly used under exterior siding and in foundations. Since it has a high R-value, it is useful where you need a lot of insulation in cramped quarters—for example, in cathedral ceilings. Foam insulation must be covered with finishing material for fire safety, and is not termiteproof unless it's treated or protected.

If you plan to replace your home's siding, this is a great time to improve the wall insulation by applying an inch or more of rigid insulation to exterior walls before the new siding goes on. Such continuous insulation reduces the *thermal bridge* effect that occurs in framed walls.

Another option is all-in-one *exterior insulation and finish systems (EIFS)*. These have a finish similar to stucco, and can be cut in various shapes and placed over standard wood framing. EIFS must be carefully installed to avoid termites and moisture problems.

If you're building an addition, consider using structural insulated panels (SIPs) instead of traditional framing. SIPs consist of a foam core usually moisture-impermeable expanded polystyrene (EPS) or polyurethane foam with structural sheathing glued to both sides.

Foam-in-place insulation provides both air sealing and insulation and can fill very small cavities.

If your addition includes a concrete wall, consider using *insulating concrete forms (ICFs)* (rigid foam form blocks). These are generally made from EPS and are stacked with their hollow centers aligned and then filled with concrete, and sometimes reinforcing bars, to create an insulated structural concrete wall.

Foam-in-Place Insulation

Foam-in-place (or *sprayed foam*) insulations are mixed and sprayed or extruded into wall or other cavities using special equipment. They also provide air and moisture sealing and can fill very small cavities better than batts and other cut-and-fit types of insulation. Foam-in-place insulation is also useful at rim joists. These liquid foam insulations are made from magnesium silicate (cementitious foam), isocyanurate, or polyurethane.

Foam-in-place insulation can be applied to the underside of a roof to bring HVAC ducts into the conditioned space.

TABLE 09.01: CHARACTERISTICS AND USES OF COMMON RESIDENTIAL INSULATIONS

Material	R-Value per Inch	Air Barrier?	Vapor Barrier?	Where Used	How Installed	Environmental and Health Drawbacks	Cost per R-Value	Availability*
Batts and rolls								
Fiberglass	2.9–4.0	No	No†	Wall, floor, and ceiling cavities	Fitted between studs, joists, or rafters	High embodied energy; some products contain formaldehyde; fibers are an irritant; up to 40% recycled content	$	Very common
Rock wool	3.0–3.7	No	No†	Wall, floor, and ceiling cavities	Fitted between studs, joists, or rafters	Fibers may be an irritant; naturally fire and moisture resistant; 75–90% recycled content	$	Not common
Cotton	3.0–3.7	No	No†	Wall, floor, and ceiling cavities	Fitted between studs, joists, or rafters	Can absorb moisture; cotton farming uses lots of water and pesticides; >70% recycled content	$$	Not common
Rigid board								
Expanded polystyrene (EPS)	3.6–4.4	Yes§	Yes‡	Wall, ceiling, roof, foundation	Glued, nailed	Made from petro-chemicals; recyclable; contains HBCD (brominated flame retardant)	$$	Very common
Extruded polystyrene (XPS)	5.0	Yes§	Yes‡	Foundation, subslab, wall, ceiling, roof	Glued, nailed	Made from petro-chemicals; recyclable; contains HBCD (brominated flame retardant); more moisture resistant than EPS	$$$	Very common
Isocyanurate (Thermax, Hi-R)	5.6–7.7	Yes§	Yes	Wall, ceiling, roof	Glued, nailed	Made from petro-chemicals; not recyclable	$$$$	Common
Phenolic foam	4.4–8.3	Yes§	No	Wall, ceiling, roof	Glued, nailed	Uses ozone-depleting blowing agent	$$$$	Rare
Rigid fiberglass	3.4–4.8	Yes§	Yes†	Wall, ceiling, roof, foundation walls	Glued, nailed	See fiberglass above	$$$	Common
Polyurethane	5.6–7.7	Yes§	Yes	Wall, ceiling, roof	Glued, nailed	See polyurethane above	$$$	Not common

* Varies regionally.
‡ Depends on thickness.
† Facing on insulation may provide vapor barrier.
§ Joints and edges must be sealed.

WHERE DO YOU NEED INSULATION— AND HOW MUCH?

Walls, floors, or ceilings without insulation offer the best opportunity for a quick payback on your insulation investment. It's more important to insulate small uninsulated areas (for example, attic and crawl space hatches) than it is to add insulation to large areas that already have some insulation.

The more extreme your climate, the more you can benefit from insulation. See the Recommended Total R-Values map to determine what climate zone you live in and the recommended insulation levels for each part of your house. Consider the low end of each R-value range as a minimum; in the attic, it doesn't cost much to add a few more inches.

Material	R-Value per Inch	Air Barrier?	Vapor Barrier?	Where Used	How Installed	Environmental and Health Drawbacks	Cost per R-Value	Availability*
Loose, poured, blown, or sprayed								
Fiberglass	2.2–4.0	No	No	Ceilings and retrofit walls	Poured or blown	See batts above; loose fibers may create a higher risk of exposure than batts	$	Very common
Rock wool	2.8–3.7	No	No	Ceilings and retrofit walls	Poured or blown	See batts above; loose fibers may create a higher risk of exposure than batts	$	Common
Dry cellulose	2.8–3.7	Partial dense pack	No	Ceilings and retrofit walls	Blown by machine	Can absorb moisture; use chemical fire retardants; heavy metals in ink on recycled paper; >75%; recycled content; very low embodied energy	$	Very common
Wet-spray	3.0–3.7	No	No	Open building cavities	Sprayed cellulose	See batts above; let dry completely before enclosing	$$	Common
Vermiculite (perlite)	2.5–4.0	No	No	Hollow concrete block	Poured	Use only asbestos-free material	$$	Common
Blown fiber with binder (blown-In blanket, BIB)	3.5–4.0	No	No	Walls	Blown dry into cavities faced with mesh screening	See fiberglass or cellulose above	$$	Common
Polyurethane foam, low density (0.5 lb/ft³), open cell	3.6–4.0	Yes	Yes‡	Wall, floor, and ceiling cavities; rim joists, skylight chases	Sprayed into cavities	Made mostly from petrochemicals; not recyclable; low-density products available that use up to 33% soy oil	$$$	Common
Polyurethane foam, high density (2.0 lb/ft³), closed cell	5.6–6.8	Yes	Yes	Wall, floor, and ceiling cavities; rim joists, skylight chases	Sprayed into cavities	More material intensive than low density; not recyclable	$$$$	Common
Isocyanurate foam, open cell (Icynene)	3.6–4.3	Yes	Yes‡	Wall, floor, and ceiling cavities; rim joists, skylight chases	Sprayed into open or closed cavities	Made from petro-chemicals; not recyclable	$$$	Common
Magnesium silicate foam, (Air Crete)	3.9	Yes	No	Wall, floor, and ceiling cavities; rim joists, skylight chases	Sprayed into open cavities	Totally inorganic; no VOCs	$$$	Not common

Roofs and attics. If you plan to reroof, you may want to add insulation to the roof deck first—especially if you have a flat roof or an unvented vaulted ceiling (typically underinsulated). If you have a vented attic, you can add insulation almost any time after air sealing (Chapters 8 and 10).

Before insulating attics, always inspect for the following problems:

- Old knob-and-tube wiring may need to be replaced.
- Venting and baffling may be inadequate. (When there are vents high and low in the roof, have at least 1 square foot of venting for every 300 square feet of attic area. When there is only gable end or ridge venting, have at least 1 square foot of venting for every 150 square feet of attic.)
- Old can lights may not be rated for covering with insulation.
- Exhaust fans may be exhausting air to the attic rather than outside.
- Flue vents must be kept clear of combustible materials (2" minimum).

WHAT IS THERMAL BRIDGING?

Thermal bridging occurs in areas of relatively low R-value in your home's thermal boundary, where heat is conducted more quickly than in other areas. This lowers the average R-value of the entire surface, so it's a good idea to minimize thermal bridging.

In an insulated 2 x 6 framed wall, the area between the studs has an R-value of about 20, but the studs have an R-value of about 6. Therefore, the studs allow significantly more heat loss than the insulated space. An air gap or a properly placed insulating material—called a thermal break—can be used to correct a thermal bridge. For example, heat loss through wood or steel studs can be diminished by sheathing exterior walls with rigid insulation.

An infrared camera makes it easy to see where insulation is gapping or missing. Here, the yellow areas are insulated, while the red areas conduct heat; the red lines are ceiling joists, and the large red ceiling area is missing insulation.

Thermal bridging can play a significant role in the thermal performance of your home. Common examples of thermal bridges include

- wood framing that is part of the thermal boundary of the house;
- masonry chimneys that penetrate the thermal boundary;
- the frames of most high-performance windows;
- uninsulated concrete slabs;
- the reduced R-value at eaves;
- recessed-can lights that penetrate the thermal boundary; and
- uninsulated attic and crawl space access hatches between conditioned and unconditioned space.

Consider a 1,000 ft^2 ceiling insulated to R-38. An uninsulated attic hatch effectively reduces the overall R-value of the entire ceiling to R-27.8—a 27% reduction. To correct for this, you can either add an R-37 cover to the attic hatch or add R-22.7 insulation to the remaining 990 square feet of ceiling.

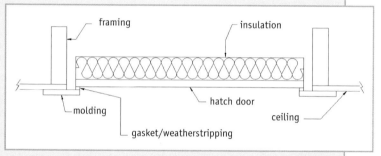

Insulating an attic hatch inexpensively improves the R-value of the whole ceiling.

Attics are usually insulated with batts, blankets, or blown insulation. Blown insulation fills cavities better than batts or blankets, and fits around ducts, wiring, and truss cords. When blowing insulation into a vented attic, use baffles around vents to maintain airflow and keep wind from displacing the insulation.

In uninsulated attics, some installers like to use a hybrid system. This consists of about 1 inch of sprayed foam on the ceiling deck for air sealing and enough of the less-expensive blown insulation on top to make up the desired R-value.

Skylight chases. Skylight chases through unconditioned attics should be insulated to the same level as exterior walls—often difficult with batts or blankets. Consider sprayed foam, or box in the chase with rigid insulation.

Floors. The floors over vented crawl spaces and unconditioned basements can be insulated anytime after air sealing. The hybrid system described above for attics works well. For best performance, floor insulation should be in substantial contact with the floor above and be well supported so it doesn't sag or fall out, diminishing its R-value.

Crawl spaces. If changing from a vented to an unvented crawl space, insulate the new crawl space (Chapter 10).

Concrete slabs. Insulate the perimeter of the slab with rigid foam insulation, down a minimum of 2 feet or to the footings. Protect with a durable material (cement board, stucco, or metal flashing) wherever exposed aboveground.

Basements. In cold climates, insulate walls enclosing conditioned space below ground level (Chapter 10). Exterior insulation is ideal, but excavation is costly, so interior insulation may be your best bet. But if you're excavating for other reasons, consider applying exterior rigid foam insulation board to the outer side of the foundation wall. Protect exposed insulation from sun and weather. If termites are a problem in your area, include a *termite barrier*.

Ducts. Ducts outside conditioned space should be well sealed and insulated with rigid fiberboard, flexible fiberglass, flexible foam, and reflective insulation.

Plumbing. Insulate pipes outside conditioned space to avoid freezing and heat loss (Chapter 15).

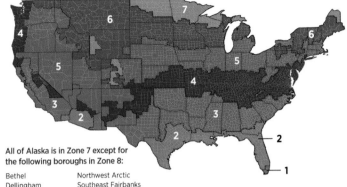

U.S. Department of Energy Recommended* Total R-Values for New Wood-Framed Houses

All of Alaska is in Zone 7 except for the following boroughs in Zone 8:

Bethel
Dellingham
Fairbanks N. Star
Nome
North Slope

Northwest Arctic
Southeast Fairbanks
Wade Hampton
Yukon-Koyukuk

Zone 1 includes:
Hawaii, Guam, Puerto Rico and the Virgin Islands

How Much Insulation Does My Home Need?
For insulation recommendations tailored to your home, visit the DOE Zip Code Insulation Calculator at *ornl.gov/~roofs/Zip/ZipHome.html.*

Zone	Gas	Heat Pump	Fuel Oil	Electric	Attic	Cathedral Ceiling	Cavity	Insulation Sheathing	Floor
1	•	•	•	•	R30 to R49	R22 to R38	R13 to R15	None	R13
2	•	•	•		R30 to R60	R22 to R38	R13 to R15	None	R13
				•	R30 to R60	R22 to R38	R13 to R15	None	R19 - R25
3	•	•	•		R30 to R60	R22 to R38	R13 to R15	None	R25
				•	R30 to R60	R22 to R38	R13 to R15	R2.5 to R5	R25
4	•	•	•		R38 to R60	R30 to R38	R13 to R15	R2.5 to R6	R25 - R30
				•	R38 to R60	R30 to R38	R13 to R15	R5 to R6	R25 - R30
5	•	•	•		R38 to R60	R30 to R38	R13 to R15	R2.5 to R6	R25 - R30
				•	R38 to R60	R30 to R60	R13 to R21	R5 to R6	R25 - R30
6	•	•	•	•	R49 to R60	R30 to R60	R13 to R21	R5 to R6	R25 - R30
7	•	•	•	•	R49 to R60	R30 to R60	R13 to R21	R5 to R6	R25 - R30
8	•	•	•	•	R49 to R60	R30 to R60	R13 to R21	R5 to R6	R25 - R30

These recommendations are cost-effective levels of insulation based on the best available information on local fuel and materials costs and weather conditions. Consequently, the levels may differ from current local building codes.

INSULATION PROJECTS YOU CAN DO TODAY:

- Consider what insulation opportunities your remodel will present.
- Determine the best types and levels of insulation for your climate.
- Evaluate your home's insulation: type, location, thickness.

INSULATION PROJECTS THAT WILL TAKE MORE TIME:

- Have a pro air seal your house and install *moisture barriers.*
- Get new insulation installed.

RESOURCES

Insulation Contractors Association of America (ICAA): insulate.org

U.S. Department of Energy/Energy Efficiency and Renewable Energy: energy.gov/energysaver (search for Insulation)

"Vapor Control Layer Recommendations": buildingscience.com/documents/information-sheets/info-sheet-310-vapor-control-layer-recommendations/files/bscinfo_310_vapor_control_layer_ed3.pdf

ZIP-Code Insulation Program: ornl.gov/~roofs/Zip/ZipHome.html

LEFT: The north side of the Parker-Shepperd house after remodeling. Note from the "before" inset that sloped roof trusses were added to accommodate insulation and PV panels, and that an addition pushed out into the original front porch. RIGHT: Danny Parker on his white-enameled metal roof, surrounded by the new skylights and PV system.

PARKER CASE STUDY

OWNERS: *Danny Parker and Lisa Shepperd*
LOCATION: *Cocoa Beach, Florida*
CLIMATE ZONE: *Hot-Humid*

The Parker house was built in 1958. It originally had 1,300 conditioned square feet, with two bedrooms and two baths, plus a garage, an enclosed south porch, and a swimming pool. When the Parkers bought the house in 1989, it had

- no ceiling insulation;
- mostly uninsulated concrete block walls;
- leaky single-pane aluminum windows;
- an inefficient A/C;
- ducts in the attic, causing high conductive losses; and
- aging gray roof shingles.

Danny is a researcher at Florida Solar Energy Center, seeking ways to dramatically improve the energy efficiency of homes, particularly in Florida's challenging hot-humid climate.

Phase I (1989)

- removed carpet to expose concrete floor for earth-contact cooling;
- insulated the attic to R-19 with blown-in fiberglass;
- relied on natural ventilation and ceiling fans for cooling during spring and fall;
- limited A/C use to June through September, with thermostat set to 79°F;
- lowered thermostat temperature at night in winter months;
- lowered the water heater set temperature, insulated the water heater tank, and installed low-flow showerheads;

- reduced pool pump operation from eight to four hours a day in summer and three hours a day the rest of the year.

Phase I Results

In the first year after they made these changes, the couple used about 10,000 kWh—half the norm for similar Florida households (data weren't available on the previous owners' utility use).

Phase II (1990–94)

- sealed leaky ducts;
- installed a whole-house fan for cooling;
- changed most lighting to CFLs;
- coated the roof with white elastomeric coating (this can cause moisture damage in a humid climate, so they replaced the roofing in the next phase);
- replaced the electric heater, water heater, clothes dryer, and cookstove with gas appliances;
- installed a PV-powered pool pump; and
- installed a PV-pumped solar water heater.

Sealing the leaky ducts reduced A/C use by 19%.

Phase II Results

The elastomeric coating increased roof solar reflectance from 21% to 73%, reducing A/C use by 25%. Sealing reduced duct leakage from 18.2% to 5.3%, reducing A/C use by another 19%.

NEAR RIGHT: The Energy Detective (TED) device helped identify 90 watts of phantom load. FAR RIGHT: The new tankless water heater on the wall receives solar-preheated water from the 80-gallon insulated storage tank in the foreground.

ABOVE: The efficient mini-split heat pump eliminated the need for a furnace, A/C, and ducts. (This outdoor unit was mounted prior to installation of exterior insulation.) RIGHT: The new windows have high-efficiency solar-control low-e glazing; the casements open fully for ventilation.

Phase III (1998–2009)

- expanded the conditioned area to 2,000 square feet (having added two children to the family);
- added roof trusses with a 19-inch overhang on the east, west, and north and a 3-foot overhang on the south to minimize summer solar heat gain;
- reduced daytime electric lighting needs by adding two tubular skylights to the interior bathrooms and a conventional north-facing skylight (with solar-control glass) to the kitchen;
- added low-sone fans to the kitchen range hood and both bathrooms to exhaust warm, moist air;
- insulated the additions to R-4 in the walls and R-19 in the roof;
- swapped out six ceiling fans with high-efficiency models;
- installed a real-time electricity use feedback device, which helped identify 90 watts of phantom load;
- replaced the refrigerator, TV, clothes washer, and dishwasher with the most efficient ENERGY STAR models;
- replaced the water heater with a tankless model; and
- installed a 4.92kW photovoltaic system that produces 20kWh per day.

Phase III Results

The reductions in electricity use, together with the new PV system, made the Parker home a net electricity producer.

Phase IV (2010–12)

Aiming for net zero energy

- installed R-5 EIFS to increase insulation in walls;
- replaced windows with high-efficiency solar-control low-e windows;

- added a 26 SEER mini-split heat pump for heating and cooling, eliminating the furnace, A/C, and ducts; and
- added another 1.1kW of PV modules to cover the daily use of a plug-in hybrid automobile.

Phase IV Results

Window replacement reduced cooling energy consumption by 20–25%. Natural-gas consumption dropped from 221 therms in 2010 to 84 therms in 2011.

Says Danny, "We've transformed an average Florida house to a zero energy home. This means that a zero energy home is available to anyone who is willing to make the investment and effort."

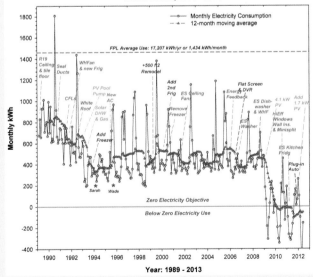

ABOVE LEFT: The concrete block walls were covered with 1 inch of expanded polystyrene insulation, then fiberglass mesh and stucco. ABOVE RIGHT: Before the retrofit, the windows were poorly fitting, single-glazed aluminum awning windows.

For more in-depth information, see D. Parker and J. Sherwin, *Achieving Very High Efficiency and Net Zero Energy in an Existing Home in a Hot-Humid Climate: Long-Term Utility and Preliminary Monitoring Data: Final Report*, DOE Energy Efficiency and Renewable Energy, Building Technologies program, June 2012: osti.gov/bridge.

Chapter 10
IMPROVING YOUR ATTIC, GARAGE, BASEMENT, CRAWL SPACE, OR PORCH

What can improving your home's "surrounding" spaces do for you? It can

- increase your comfort;
- save energy and lower your fuel bills;
- improve your family's health through better ventilation and moisture control; and
- provide more living space without adding on.

Use Home Energy Saver (hes.lbl.gov) to calculate how much energy and money you can save by improving your home's attic, garage, basement, or crawl space.

Attics, basements, garages, *crawl spaces*, and porches can have a tremendous impact on whether your home is too hot, too cold, too damp—or too expensive to operate. However, you can improve these spaces to support your energy efficiency goals, as well as your comfort, space needs, and budget.

Each type of space poses unique challenges. Attics often have hidden air leaks. Attached garages that aren't properly sealed can let toxic fumes seep into the house. Many basements and crawl spaces are damp, and in some areas are subject to intrusion of soil gases, such as *radon*. Porches may have concealed air leaks and poorly sealed windows.

Maybe you're considering converting an attic, basement, garage, or porch into living space. Doing so will change how air, heat, and moisture flow through your home. If you do the conversion right, you will feel warmer in winter, cooler in summer, and happier when your utility bill arrives. Do it wrong, and you could end up with higher bills, uncomfortable spaces, structural damage, and/or poor IAQ. This Chapter will help you do the job right.

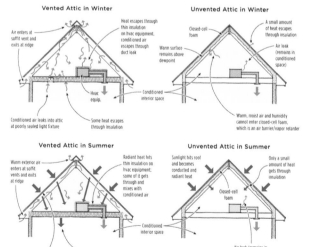

Vented vs. Unvented Attics

In many climates, a vented attic wastes energy and lowers comfort in both summer and winter. An unvented attic brings any attic HVAC equipment into the conditioned space, greatly improving its efficiency. Illustration by Tim Healey. Reprinted by permission of the *Journal of Light Construction* (jlconline.com).

ATTICS

The attic includes everything from the finished ceiling up to and including the underside of the roof. Many attics have air leaks from the house, insufficient insulation, poorly installed heating systems, and inefficient skylights. All of these can waste energy and money, and leave you feeling too hot or too cold.

Because warm air rises, the air high in the house is usually warmer and at higher pressure than the air in the rest of the house. During cold weather, this stack effect constantly drives indoor air up and out the top of the house—especially through attics. In hot weather, colder, denser air sinks to the ground floor and migrates outward, causing a reverse stack effect that can pull in hot air from above. So it's crucial to address attic leaks for the sake of both comfort and energy use. If you plan to convert your attic into a living area, you can improve its performance as part of your remodeling.

First Decision: Go Unvented?

For centuries, homes have been built with vented attics. Screened vent holes under the eaves, a slot vent under the overhang, or louvered openings at the gable ends are part of the attic venting system. This can keep the house cooler in summer and discourage attic moisture build-up. However, it can also allow conditioned air to escape, which wastes energy.

The alternative is an unvented attic, which includes the attic in the conditioned area of your home. Openings between the attic and outside are sealed, and the underside of the roof is insulated. This allows airflow between the attic and the house, and blocks uncontrolled airflow through the roof structure, conserving energy.

Should you change your vented attic to an unvented attic? That depends on your climate zone, the location of your heating and cooling system, and the geometry of your attic. This is a good time to call in a building professional knowledgeable about building science (and to read Chapters 4, 8, and 9).

To go unvented, first determine where your new thermal boundary is (Chapter 9). With attics often defined by knee walls, sidewalls, dormers, sloped rooflines, and flat ceilings, this can be challenging.

Next, air sealing is your most cost-effective step (Chapter 8). Seal any openings, gaps, cracks, or vents at your new air boundary. Take special care when sealing complicated areas, such as knee walls or odd angles. Finally, move the thermal boundary to the plane of the roof deck by installing insulation there.

The Best Place for Mechanical Equipment

In some regions, ductwork and HVAC equipment are often run through attics. Building contractors and developers have recently realized that installing this equipment within the insulated space can improve energy efficiency. If you must have the HVAC equipment in a vented attic, pay special attention to duct insulation (Chapter 9).

Precautions for the Vented Attic

It may be okay to leave your attic vented if

- you don't plan to convert the attic to living space;
- there are no ducts in the attic;
- the attic is well sealed and insulated from the living space; and
- your attic ventilation prevents moisture buildup.

A vented attic does keep the roof cold in winter, reducing the potential for *ice dams*. For this to work, the attic floor and sidewalls must be insulated and sealed to block heat and moist air from the adjacent conditioned space.

It may pay to hire a home energy professional to evaluate whether your attic has sufficient airflow to ventilate properly. In some situations, you may need

DANGER ZONE: RECESSED LIGHTING

If you're adding recessed lighting, avoid penetrations that compromise air barriers and reduce insulation performance (Chapter 11).

A CONDITIONED ATTIC MAKES A DIFFERENCE

In Las Vegas, Nevada, Ron moved from a home with a vented attic to one with an unvented, insulated attic. "Outside temperatures can get over 105°F for many days here in the summer," Ron said. "Our attic could get up to 150°F. In the new home, the attic stays at about 80°F. It takes a lot more energy to cool your living space to 78°F when you've got a 150°F attic than when you've got an 80°F attic."

Converting a vented attic to an unvented attic includes moving the thermal boundary (insulation) to the plane of the roof deck, incorporating the attic into the conditioned space.

Turning attic space into living space can be a great way to gain more room without adding on to your house.

A garage can often be affordably converted to living space, but be careful to improve the floor to avoid moisture problems and heat loss.

a powered attic fan to rid the attic of excessive heat or moisture. Attic fans aren't appropriate for all situations, however; a fan won't help, for example, in a poorly sealed home.

If your attic contains HVAC equipment or ducts, carefully seal all penetrations through thermal or air boundaries to avoid pulling in conditioned air from living spaces, creating drafts and wasting energy. It's difficult to seal complex attic spaces properly; bear this in mind when considering whether to keep your attic vented.

Second Decision: How to Insulate?

Attics can be very hot in summer and cold in winter; insulation helps (Chapter 9). In vented attics, insulation usually goes in any wall or ceiling of adjacent conditioned rooms. Don't allow insulation to cover any vents. In unvented attics, the insulation follows the new thermal boundary, typically at the roofline.

If turning your attic unvented means that your heating and cooling equipment will now be inside the conditioned space, consider investing in insulation beyond the levels recommended for your climate zone. The investment will probably pay for itself in short order.

Converting an Attic to Living Space

Turning your attic into living space involves the same sealing and insulating tasks described for unvented attics. It also involves structural factors. Many attic floors are not designed to handle the added load of furniture and active human bodies. Check with an engineer and your building department to determine whether you need structural improvements. A worst-case scenario could require you to beef up your framing and foundation. If you're lucky, your home is adequately constructed for your planned conversion.

GARAGES

If you don't plan to convert your garage to living space, look carefully at the boundaries between house and attached garage, and between garage and outdoors. Good air sealing and insulation between your garage and living space will minimize unwanted heat transfer and keep vehicle exhaust out of your home, as well as fumes from stored household chemicals.

Regular maintenance will improve your garage's durability and air quality while minimizing the chance of moisture problems.

- Periodically spray-clean the floor.
- Inspect the walls and foundation twice a year for moisture and cracks (and seal any cracks you find).
- Check the weather strip between the interior door and threshold.
- Test the operation of the garage door and maintain all its mechanisms.
- Check for pests, such as termites, ants, or vermin.

Converting a Garage to Living Space

Garage conversion can be relatively inexpensive; the foundation, walls, and roof are already in place. And garages don't have the headroom limitations of attics. The key issue is the floor; the concrete slab is usually sloped and lower than the main living space, and soil moisture may penetrate the slab.

Improve the Floor

You can create a finished floor in your garage by building up the floor or by finishing the concrete floor. Either way, first seal the concrete floor with a moisture barrier to keep any dampness in the slab from reaching the room.

If you plan to raise the garage floor, you can use a continuous layer of 6-*mil* (or heavier) polyethylene over the slab as a moisture and soil-gas barrier, with seams and perimeter taped and sealed. Your contractor can then set 2 x 6s on top of the sealed slab, shimmed or trimmed to level the floor, with moisture-impermeable insulation between them.

If you don't plan to raise the floor, have compression-grade rigid foam insulation installed on the slab, sealing seams with heavy-duty construction tape and leaving a 1/4-inch gap around the perimeter for expansion.

A *subfloor*, usually plywood, goes on top of the insulation (and framing, if any). Make sure your contractor is familiar with the recommended procedures established by the building codes in your area.

Seal and Insulate

If the walls and ceiling of your garage have enough insulation and are covered with *drywall*, make sure all penetrations in the drywall are sealed with caulk or foam. Also seal seams at the ceiling, walls, and floor.

WILL A RADIANT BARRIER HELP?

A *radiant barrier* (often a component of a *cool-roof* system) is a shiny surface that reflects or reduces the emission of radiant energy—usually heat from the sun. The barrier can be a reflective foil, reflective metal roof shingles, or reflective laminated roof sheathing.

In cold climates, radiant barriers are generally not effective or economical. In hot climates, if your roof is not already well insulated, a radiant barrier can save on cooling energy, but it's probably more effective to insulate your attic properly. However, if you're planning to reroof, and if you live in a hot climate, look into ENERGY STAR-rated roofing products, which can reduce cooling demands by reflecting solar heat.

NEW UTILITIES FOR A CONVERTED SPACE

Adding new heating, cooling, ventilating, lighting, and plumbing involves similar issues, whether you're converting an attic, garage, basement, or porch.

Have an HVAC pro determine whether your existing equipment has enough capacity to heat and cool the new room. If you have a forced-air system with adequate capacity, you may only need to add new ducts and fans. Once the new equipment is installed, have a professional balance the airflow for the entire house (Chapters 13 and 14).

If your existing equipment doesn't have the capacity to serve your conversion, it may be cheaper and more effective to add a self-contained heat pump/air handler that can provide heating and cooling in a single, easily maintained unit. For a smaller converted area, a portable A/C or heater, or a ductless mini-split heat pump, may suffice. You might add a baseboard heater or window unit A/C, but the low initial cost may be more than offset by higher energy consumption and operating costs.

If you're adding electrical outlets, consider including a new 20 amp circuit, with wire run as needed. For a bathroom, wet bar, or kitchen, consult a plumber. All wiring, ductwork, and plumbing should be in place before you insulate or finish the walls, floor, and ceiling.

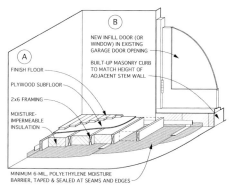

If the garage walls and ceiling have drywall but are not insulated, cellulose can be blown in at little expense. If the garage framing is exposed, you have more insulation options (Chapter 9). Make sure your contractor is familiar with the airtight drywall approach, (Chapter 8).

If the walls between the garage and the outdoors are framed with 2 x 4s, consider adding *furring strips* to the interior of the studs to accommodate additional insulation. In some areas, building codes mandate this.

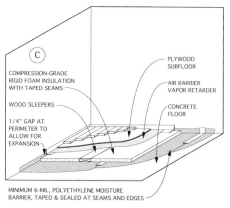

Ⓐ illustrates one way to insulate and finish a garage floor, using 2 x 6 framing to create insulation space.

Ⓑ shows how to build up a curb in the space formerly occupied by the garage door.

Framing

The existing garage door opening is a good place for a new door and windows, avoiding the expense of cutting new openings. You'll need to have a new curb installed at the base of the former garage door, built up with concrete or masonry blocks to the same height as the adjacent foundation *stem walls*. This curb will raise the infill framing above ground moisture, keep water from running in at floor level, and allow the new siding to blend in with the rest of the home.

BASEMENTS

Being underground, basements tend to be damp. Whether or not you plan to convert your basement to a living space, it's crucial to identify and resolve all moisture problems. Moisture can damage stored items and interior finishes, and mold or mildew can form on damp surfaces.

Ⓒ illustrates how to insulate a garage slab by laying down rigid insulation between wood sleepers.

Proper drainage and maintenance on the outside of your house will minimize moisture intrusion. Keep gutters clean, downspouts clear, and rainwater flowing away from the foundation. Subterranean drainage cures, such as *perimeter* or *French drains,* can be more expensive, but may be well worth it to avoid moisture damage. A sump pump may also be helpful. If you have a high water table or an adjacent stream, it may be difficult to control basement moisture enough to convert basement space to living space.

To remove moisture from inside the basement, focus on controlling potential moisture sources. Check that there are no plumbing leaks from the floor above. Moisture could be coming from a poorly exhausted shower, so install a fan to increase air circulation. If your dryer is in the basement, make sure its exhaust vent doesn't leak and has a direct path to the outside. If you have an energy-saving switch on the exhaust, use the outdoor setting.

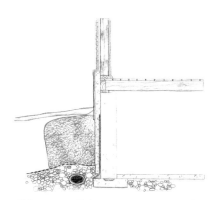

When possible, excavate around a basement to add a perimeter drain, exterior insulation, and moisture-proofing.

Finally, any basement should be insulated and have sufficient lighting installed (Chapters 9 and 11).

Converting a Basement to Living Space

Basements can be ideal for remodeling into usable space. They are quiet, private, and cool—and often already have plumbing and HVAC equipment. Insulating, air sealing, and moistureproofing are vital, and it's important to identify potential problems with basement HVAC equipment.

Air Sealing Your Basement

A seamless barrier keeps moisture and soil gases from entering the new living space (Chapter 8). In the United States, radon is prevalent throughout mountain zones and the upper Midwest; test for radon if you think it may be a hazard. You can purchase a radon detector at most hardware stores, and there are radon remediation contractors in most parts of the United States.

Before adding finish materials to the floor and walls of your basement, make sure all cracks in the concrete are caulked. You may also want to build up the floor, as described under "Garages," to keep the finish floor from being in contact with the damp, cold concrete floor.

Peeling paint on the inside of the basement walls indicates moisture seepage from outside. If you're not in a position to excavate to improve the drainage from outside, masonry sealer and paint may help. If seepage is frequent, the entire wall may need to be resurfaced with a concrete coating. If you plan to add interior wall finishes, apply a rigid foam moisture barrier to the concrete walls before adding framing, to minimize condensation from interior humidity.

Insulation

Your home performance assessor can check your basement's current insulation values and identify areas that need attention. The best materials for interior basement insulation are rigid foam with sealed seams or sprayed polyurethane foam (SPF). Both can provide unbroken air and vapor barriers that won't be damaged by moisture.

Although SPF is expensive, it has several advantages over rigid foam: it controls moisture better, saves more energy, and makes a basement more comfortable—and it may allow you to downsize the mechanical system. It also provides more design flexibility, since the necessary R-value is fitted into small framing cavities. Note that SPF can't be installed without sufficient access. The applicator must be able to get close enough to the sheathing to spray from 16 to 24 inches away as straight on as possible.

Basement Lighting

Basements can be dark, so lighting is an important factor (Chapter 11). First, maximize natural light; if the basement is at least partly aboveground, add windows. If you add window wells, make sure they have waterproof covers to avoid leaking. If you're concerned about break-ins, install glass bricks rather than windows.

For electric lighting, recessed lights can create a more open feeling than light from surface fixtures. As long as the basement is part of the conditioned space, there won't be a problem with disturbing ceiling and floor insulation. You may want to use occupancy sensors to turn on lighting for hands-free ease when carrying objects downstairs.

DANGER ZONE: PROVIDE ENOUGH COMBUSTION AIR

Any fossil-fueled appliance in a garage or basement (space heater, water heater, clothes dryer) produces combustion gases that must be managed for health and safety. Remodeling tends to change the way air flows, which could change the way gases are exhausted.

If your project will enclose a formerly unenclosed combustion appliance, provide combustion air from outside or through a louvered connection to a large interior space. If you air seal the space, this may decrease the amount of air available to the appliance. In either case, the equipment may *backdraft*, with serious health consequences. Have a service person check how the equipment operates in the remodeled space and check for depressurization under worst-case conditions.

If you have a ducted forced-air system, seal leaks in return ducts in the new space. If the equipment backdrafts, you can install a powered exhaust system to pull out combustion gases, or you might upgrade to high-efficiency sealed-combustion equipment.

You may want to isolate mechanical equipment in a room outside the conditioned space, with vents to provide air to combustion appliances.

A basement can be converted to a cozy living space, but be sure to address moisture, insulation, and air-sealing issues.

When exterior insulation isn't feasible, you can insulate and moisture seal interior basement walls. This Chicago basement has four kinds of insulation (left to right): polyisocyanurate, two types of encapsulated batts in frame wall, and fiberglass blankets.

A damp crawl space can lead to condensation, warped flooring, mold, and termite damage.

CRAWL SPACES

If your house has a raised floor and no basement, the crawl space is the area between the floor framing and the ground below. This space can be either vented (the most common practice until recently) or unvented (sealed).

Although codes have encouraged *vented crawl spaces* for decades, recent evidence shows that in humid climates, vented crawl spaces can be subject to mold, decay, condensation on ductwork, and termite damage. Hardwood floors above a vented crawl space can cup, and radon levels in the crawl space may be elevated.

Newer building codes (e.g., IRC, Section R408.3) allow unvented, conditioned crawl spaces. *Unvented crawl spaces* are generally drier than vented spaces. Extending the conditioned space may increase winter heating demand, but the cost is minor compared to the cost of moisture damage.

Climate Zones and Crawl Space Venting

Unvented crawl spaces work best in the midwestern, southern, and eastern United States, where hot, humid summer conditions encourage condensation and cold, moist winters can freeze water in pipes and moisture in ducts.

Vented crawl spaces generally perform well in most of the western United States, where condensation is rarely a problem in the hot-dry and marine climates. Make sure that the floor is insulated above the crawl space, that the insulation is properly supported, and that there is no space between the insulation and the floor.

In the West, homes with vented crawl spaces tend to use less energy than those with sealed crawl spaces, even in the Pacific Northwest. Although vented crawl spaces in western climates may have higher average humidity levels, this is not likely to be a problem if condensation risks are low (when the average ground temperature is above the average seasonal dew point).

Outside the dry and marine climates west of the Rockies, a vented crawl space may work best in an extremely cold climate, where warm conditioned air in a sealed crawl space can melt the permafrost beneath the home, causing the home to sink.

In cold climates, insulate all plumbing pipes in vented crawl spaces to keep the water in them from freezing. Heat tape can also help where insulation isn't sufficient to avoid freezing.

In a flood zone or an area with a high water table, it can be useful to install operable vents in an unvented crawl space to allow for drying after flooding.

Sealing a Crawl Space

When sealing an unvented crawl space, place insulation around the perimeter walls rather than in the floor above. A fan or air blower provides conditioned air to the crawl space via ducting, coupling the house with the cooler ground temperatures (helpful in hot-summer climates).

Work with a building science professional to make sure your crawl space upgrade addresses potential problems with moisture and air pressure. Make sure your contractor

- Covers a dirt or cracked-concrete floor with 6-mil polyethylene sheeting. Attach and seal the sheeting at least 6 inches up the walls, overlapping and taping the seams to ensure sealing along the full perimeter.
- Seals perimeter walls and access doors to prevent infiltration of outside air. Seal at joints between the top of the foundation wall and the *mudsill,* between the mudsill and the rim joist, between the rim joist and the subfloor, and at any penetrations through walls or rim joists, such as ducts or pipe conduits. (Chapter 8)
- Insulates perimeter walls and/or foundation walls according to applicable building codes, using fire-rated, water-resistant rigid foam board or sprayed-foam insulation. Do not use fiberglass batts or spray-on cellulose insulation, which are air permeable.

For the greatest energy savings, all ductwork should be brought into the conditioned space. Seal any ductwork located in the crawl space, and ensure that ducts and appliance vents do not terminate inside the crawl space. Any ductwork in the crawl space should be well supported.

If there is insufficient air exchange with the house above, consider ventilating the crawl space via mechanical exhaust or conditioned-air supply. If radon is a concern in your area, make sure that the crawl space is properly vented.

PORCHES

If you have a roofed porch and you want more indoor space, it may be cost-effective to enclose the porch. You can convert a small back porch to a mudroom, laundry, or utility room. A bigger porch could become a bedroom, study, or dining room. If the porch is adjacent to the living room, it can be used to enlarge that room.

For porch conversions, structural factors are more likely to come into play than for other converted spaces. Pay attention to whether the porch footings can support the greater weight of the fully enclosed space. You may need a new concrete slab, additional footings, or stronger beams. The roof must be able to carry the added load of insulation and ceiling finishes, and the walls must be strong enough to carry not only a heavier roof but also the added weight of windows, insulation, drywall, and additional framing.

If you expand an existing room into a porch, an exterior house wall must be removed and a new beam installed to handle the weight previously carried by the removed wall. It's less expensive to keep the converted porch as a separate room, leaving the exterior wall intact.

Your porch conversion will need air sealing, insulation, and HVAC (Chapters 8, 9, 12, 13, 14). Start with the floor; porch floors are rarely insulated or sealed. Then pay particular attention to the juncture of the porch roof and the house wall. In most cases there is no wall sheathing on the part of the exterior wall adjoining the porch roof cavity. This allows conditioned air to flow between

An unvented crawl space is insulated, air sealed, protected from moisture, and included in the conditioned space of the home.

the porch ceiling and the porch roof and escape. Seal this juncture with rigid material and sealant, or with dense-packed cellulose.

PROJECTS YOU CAN DO TODAY:

- Check for air leaks between surrounding and conditioned spaces.
- Hire a building professional to get a better sense of what your project could entail, and of how much energy it could save.
- Determine whether you really need extra space (Chapter 6).
- If you need more space, decide which part of your home is the best to expand into.

PROJECTS THAT WILL TAKE MORE TIME:

- Work with design, energy efficiency, and engineering professionals to plan your project.
- Work with your building department and a building contractor to carry out your project.

RESOURCES

Print

Air Conditioning and Ventilation of Garages. Darcee A. McAninley, Wojcieszak & Associates, Technical Bulletin No. 16, February 16, 2004

Closed Crawl Spaces: Top Performers Nationwide. Applied Building Science Team of Advanced Energy, December 2009

Conditioned Crawl Space Construction, Performance and Codes. Joseph Lstiburek, Building Science Corporation, Research Report 0401 2004-11-02

"The SCARY Crawl Space." David Hales, *Home Energy,* Jan/Feb 2011, pp. 38–42

Online

"How to Insulate Your Attic" (Madison Gas and Electric Company, Madison, Wisconsin): mge.com/images/PDF/Brochures/Residential/HowToInsulateAttic.pdf

"Turning a Basement into an In-Law Suite: Six Elements of Successful Conversions." Mike Litchfield, *Fine Homebuilding,* January 9, 2011 blog: finehomebuilding.com/item/15284/turning-a-basement-into-an-in-law-suite-six-elements-of-successful-conversions

U.S. Department of Energy/Energy Efficiency and Renewable Energy:

- Radiant Barriers: energysavers.gov/your_home/insulation_airsealing/index.cfm/mytopic=11680

U.S. Environmental Protection Agency:

- Consumer's Guide to Radon Reduction: epa.gov/radon/pubs/consguid.html
- EPA Map of Radon Zones: epa.gov/radon/zonemap.html
- Indoor airPLUS Construction Specifications (for controlling radon, moisture, pests, combustion products, etc.): epa.gov/indoorairplus/construction_specifications.html#1.2

Chapter 11
LIGHT YOUR HOME WISELY

What can good lighting do for you?

- Save money on your electrical bills
- Improve safety
- Create the mood you want in every room
- Minimize headaches and eyestrain when reading, sewing, or performing other close work
- Prevent distracting glare on TV and computer screens

LIGHT IT RIGHT

Some experts estimate that lighting represents 20% of all residential electrical energy use. Through thoughtful design and selection, you can cut that amount in half.

Your home's lighting could stand improvement if

- your electricity bill is high
- you turn on electric lights during the day
- you have to squint to read a book
- you cast a shadow on your kitchen counter or work bench
- you avoid rooms that feel "gloomy"
- glare, shadows, or lack of contrast cause people to trip

Simple lighting changes—many of them inexpensive—can make your home not only more energy-efficient, but also safer and more comfortable.

Think through how you want to use each room in your house and identify any lighting problems. Then you can develop a plan to address problems and make your lighting system meet your needs.

Designers categorize lighting in terms of three basic functions:

- *General lighting*, also known as *ambient lighting*, illuminates space so you can see people and objects clearly and move about safely.
- *Task lighting* shines directly on visually demanding activities, such as reading, knitting, or chopping vegetables.
- *Accent lighting* is used for decorative purposes, usually to highlight art objects or architectural details.

TOP: Ambient lighting is provided here by the corner torchiére, the cove lighting in the ceiling, and sunlight; it is often of lower wattage than task or accent lighting. BOTTOM: Accent lighting is a decorative element that picks out art objects or interesting textures. LEFT: Task lighting is more intense, letting you use higher-wattage bulbs only on items you need to see clearly.

For example, if you turn your spare bedroom into a home office, you might put a desk lamp at the workstation (task lighting), place a *torchiere* in the corner (ambient lighting), and focus a *halogen* light on your diploma (accent lighting).

START WITH SUNLIGHT

Daylighting means using the sun as your main light source during the day. You may be able to increase the amount of free light you get from the sun by making a few basic changes. Start by looking at your furniture arrangement: Could you move a desk or reading chair closer to a window?

Daylighting offers too many benefits to pass up:

- Sunlight is free.
- Daylighting decreases your dependence on the power grid.
- When you use less electrical lighting, you lower your contribution to greenhouse gas buildup.
- Sunlight is dynamic, constantly changing in direction, intensity, color, and warmth.
- Sunlight makes you feel good. It links your internal clock to the sun's cycles. Regular, prudent exposure to sunlight may even improve your health and mood.

Because the sun follows a predictable path, you can plan your daylighting based on your family's schedule. You might turn a dark corner of your kitchen into a cozy breakfast nook that catches the morning sun, or put a window in a solid door to light up a dark foyer.

Pay attention to where the sun shines into your house, and how that shifts throughout the day and the year. Are some rooms too dark, and others too bright? Make notes on how you'd like to change the daylighting in each room.

Now explore ways to add, remove, block, or treat windows to let in more sunlight where you want it (see Chapter 7). If you live in a hot climate, you'll be glad to know that you can choose windows or apply special treatments to keep out the sun's heat while letting in its light.

Look around the outside of your house. Are your landscape plantings supporting your daylighting schemes? Trimming, adding, or removing vegetation can significantly change the daylighting in a room. Roof overhangs, shade trees, plants, and the ground surface outside your home also affect how light comes through your windows.

If you're planning an addition, you have the opportunity to design for daylighting from the start. Be sure to also take into account how the addition will change the way sunlight falls into existing rooms.

Plan Your Daylighting

To best use daylight, think about how each room will be used:

- Is it a space for paying bills or reading? Place desks and reading chairs near windows, but facing away from them if glare is a problem.

Moving furniture closer to a window is a double-win: you get the pleasures of sunlight, and you save on your electrical bill.

The deciduous trees outside this room admit plenty of winter sun, then provide shade when they come into leaf during hotter seasons.

Having windows on more than one wall gives a room more depth and dynamism.

- Will people gather there? If sunlight will shine directly into people's faces, install blinds that direct light toward the ceiling, hang curtains to diffuse the light, or simply rearrange the seating.
- Does your family watch TV, play video games, or use computers there? Position fixed screens so they don't reflect a window (or an electric light), and consider where people will sit to use portable items. Test the reflection by holding a mirror where the TV or monitor will be situated. If you see a window or a light in the mirror, there will be a reflection on the screen.

Designing Windows for Light

Windows are the key to sunlit rooms. Here are some helpful rules of thumb for designing and using windows to admit light:

- An unobstructed glass area equal to 5% of a room's floor area should provide adequate ambient light.
- Windows on more than one wall make a room feel lighter and more dynamic.
- The higher the window, the farther sunlight can reach into the room.
- *Clerestory* windows (a series of windows high in a tall wall) can light spaces directly, or indirectly by reflecting sunlight off walls and ceiling.
- Unobstructed north windows provide relatively glare-free lighting.
- *Borrowed light* makes use of glazed interior openings to transmit light from a sunny room to a darker room or hallway. To maintain privacy, use textured glass or glass block.

Selecting Skylights

Sunlight from above makes a space feel open and lively while reducing the need for electric lighting. Skylights needn't be large; a skylight can illuminate a room twenty times its size.

Tubular skylights have a highly reflective inner surface that bounces sunlight into the living space. A tubular skylight can be a good choice for a small, dark space, such as an interior hallway or a windowless bathroom.

If you choose a conventional skylight, you can distribute sunlight more broadly into the room by angling the walls of the light well through the attic. For either type of skylight, make sure the light well or tube penetration is insulated where it passes through the attic, and that it is well sealed against air and moisture from the attic and outside. (See Chapter 7 for more on skylights, and Chapters 8, 9, and 10 for air-sealing, insulation, and attic options.)

Balancing Daylight and Solar Heat

Too much sunlight may make your house too warm. Here are some ways to avoid this problem:

A daylit kitchen can be delightful, as long as glare isn't a problem. Use adjustable blinds or sheer curtains if there are times of day when sunlight shines straight into your eyes.

A "skylight well" should be carefully sealed and insulated. Splaying the walls of the well allows broader sunlight distribution.

A tubular skylight admits abundant sunlight without the need to cut roof framing members.

Light outdoor surfaces and furniture will bounce more daylight into a space.

- Install rollup shades inside or outside the window; exterior retractable shading blocks solar heat more effectively than interior.
- At south-facing windows, add an awning or overhang to block direct sunlight.
- Apply reflective film to window panes.
- If your winter heating costs are low and your summer cooling costs are high, choose window glass with a low solar heat gain coefficient (SHGC—see Chapter 7).
- Plant *deciduous* bushes and trees outside east- and west-facing windows—or train a vine up a vertical trellis—to filter hot summer sunlight and admit winter sunlight.

If you want both solar heat and light, see Chapter 13.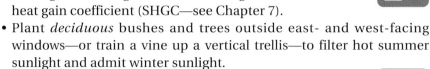

Daylighting on a Budget

If the daylighting in your home isn't ideal—and your budget doesn't include new windows—try some of these low-cost tricks:

- Light-colored walls and floors bounce light around a room and make the space feel bigger and brighter.
- Semisheer curtains or glare-reducing window treatments diffuse intense sunlight.
- Blinds or plantation shutters let you control how much light gets in. For large, wide windows where horizontal blinds would be heavy and difficult to manipulate, try vertical blinds.
- Light surfaces outside your windows (such as a light-colored patio or path) will reflect sunlight into a room, while vegetation or dark surfaces will absorb light.

SUPPLEMENT DAYLIGHT WITH ELECTRIC LIGHT

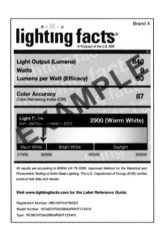

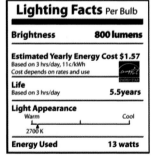

TOP: The LED Lighting Facts label (U.S. Department of Energy) helps you identify the best LED products for you. BOTTOM: The FTC Lighting Facts labels appear on the package of all medium screw-base bulbs.

Most of us learned to select our lighting by choosing an *incandescent light bulb* that we considered "bright enough." That brightness is roughly indicated by *wattage (W)*—a measurement of how much energy the bulb uses. Comparing wattage has been a pretty good way to choose a good incandescent light bulb for the desired illumination level (usually a 40W, 60W, or 75W bulb).

However, new developments in lighting products give us many more choices than we had ten years ago—and knowing how much energy a bulb uses doesn't tell you much about the appearance of the light it casts. Fortunately, more precise information is available on Lighting Facts labels, found on all new lighting products.

Here are some terms to look for:

- **Lumens (Lm):** light output. High-efficiency bulbs supply more lumens per watt than lower efficiency bulbs. In other words, they use less energy, so you get more light for less money.
- **Color Temperature:** the hue of seemingly "white" light, ranging from "cool" (bluish) to "warm" (reddish), expressed in degrees *Kelvin (K)*.

In general, cooler light is best for visual tasks, while warmer light enhances flesh tones. For most uses, you'll probably want a color temperature of 2700K to 3000K. (Table 11.01.)

- **Color Rendering Index (CRI)**, also referred to as color accuracy: a measure of how faithfully a given light source reproduces particular colors in relation to an ideal or natural light source. As a reference point, sunlight and incandescent light bulbs have a CRI of 100. When buying *compact fluorescent lights (CFLs)* or *light-emitting diodes (LEDs)*, look for a CRI of 80 or more to get good color rendition. With a CRI below 80, some colors may shift in tone or lose saturation.

You may also come across the term *foot-candle* in relation to lighting levels. While "lumens" describes the output of a light source, "foot-candle" refers to the intensity of light falling on a given surface.

Also consider the way the bulb and fixture distribute light and where the unit is placed in the room. Overhead fixtures and bulbs that cast light in all directions are commonly used for ambient light. *Cove lighting* is a type of *indirect lighting* that involves incandescent or fluorescent lights concealed in a reflecting trough near the ceiling; the light is usually reflected off the ceiling or wall. *Directional lighting* is designed to cast a narrow beam; it's good for task and accent lighting. Using the right fixture for the job puts those lumens where you need them.

What Kind of Electric Lighting Is Best?

There is no one right type of lighting for all applications; each type has its own strengths and weaknesses (see Table 11.02).

Incandescent light bulbs have been the dominant technology for most residential lighting since they were introduced in the late 1880s. They supply light that resembles sunlight early or late in the day. Ninety percent of the energy used by an incandescent bulb is lost as heat. New incandescent bulbs are markedly more efficient and longer lasting than the older ones, but as efficiency standards rise and competing technologies improve, their predominance is fading.

HOW MANY LUMENS DO YOU NEED?

The answer depends on the size of the room and the color of your decor. Here are some rules of thumb (Lm/sf = lumens/square foot):

- Dining: 5–20 Lm/sf
- Living: 5–20 Lm/sf
- Kitchen: 5–50 Lm/sf
- Bathroom: 5–50 Lm/sf
- Office: 10–50 Lm/sf
- Outdoor: 0.3–1.5 Lm/sf

Apply the lower end of the range for ambient lighting and the higher end for task and accent lighting. Older occupants generally require more light, especially for close visual tasks—as much as 100 Lm/sf for sewing or reading.

Light bulb styles. From left to right: incandescent, compact fluorescent, and light-emitting diode.

TABLE 11.01: COLOR TEMPERATURES OF LIGHT SOURCES

Source	Hue	Degrees Kelvin
Candle flame	Orange/red, warm	1,850–1,930
Sun at sunrise or sunset	Orange/red, warm	2,000–3,000
Incandescent light bulb	Orange/yellow, warm	2,700–3,000
White fluorescent	Wide range of options	2,700–7,500
Sun at noon	Blue, cool	5,000–5,400
Partly cloudy sky	Blue, cool	8,000–10,000

A HAPPIER KITCHEN

The *can lights* in Marc and Jill's New England home cast a pale, unpleasant light of 12-15 foot-candles at countertop level. The 23W CFLs were fairly energy-efficient, providing 1640 lumens at a CRI of 82 and a color temperature of 3000K. However, little of the CFL's light could escape the can. Marc and Jill wanted more light, better color, and even more energy-efficiency. Without changing the can light fixtures, Marc replaced the CFLs with 10.5W LEDs that provided 575 lumens at a color temperature of 2700K and a high CRI of 92.

"The difference in lighting quality is profound," says Marc. "The kitchen feels brighter and cleaner— well worth the upgrade. Interestingly, the light levels are *barely* higher—maybe 15 to 17 foot-candles. This shows that the lumen output of the light doesn't tell the whole story; what matters is how the *system* of the light and the fixture moves the light to where we want it."

Halogen lights are a longer lived, more efficient type of incandescent bulb. They emit a very bright, white light and come in many shapes and sizes; some provide an intense beam appropriate for accent lighting.

Fluorescent lights use electricity to produce light more efficiently than incandescent bulbs do. A *ballast* regulates the current through the light, making fluorescent lights more costly than incandescent bulbs. Four-foot fluorescent tubes have been common in commercial settings, as well as in some residential kitchens and garages. Smaller tubes are often used in kitchens as under-cabinet lighting.

Compact fluorescent lights (CFLs) are a type of fluorescent designed to fit in a standard incandescent bulb socket. They are 3 times more efficient than incandescent bulbs, and generally last 2 to 3 times as long. Ask people about their experiences with CFLs, and you're likely to hear anything from "I will never buy them again" to "Why would anyone still buy incandescent lightbulbs when you can buy CFLs?" The "never again" people may be remembering older or low-quality CFLs that flicker, buzz, interfere with the radio or TV, render colors poorly, or fail early.

Fortunately, newer fluorescent products (both tubes and CFLs) solve many of the problems that gave them a bad name in the past. Many provide high-quality, appealing light. Most fluorescent lights today have *electronic ballasts*, which don't cause flickering the way the old *magnetic ballasts* did. You can realize substantial savings from a small investment if you upgrade from incandescent lights to CFLs—and you probably won't need to change your light bulbs nearly as often.

When a CFL burns out, it's important to dispose of it safely. Contact your local waste management company or recycling center to learn their preferred procedures.

Light-emitting diodes (LEDs) are a relative newcomer on the lighting scene, and promise to become an even more energy-efficient option. They are currently much more expensive than incandescents or CFLs lighting, so use them wisely.

LEDs are very efficient at focusing light into a small area, and therefore have been successfully used to replace other types of directional lighting. Unlike fluorescents, they can be turned on and off frequently without shortening their life, which also makes them well suited to use in hallways and in fixtures controlled by motion sensors.

Maintenance Makes the Light

A ceiling fixture that looked bright and cheery with 60W incandescent light bulbs when it was new may require 150W incandescent bulbs to look cheery once it gets dirty. This is not just a waste of energy; it can be hazardous if you use bulbs of a higher wattage than the fixture was designed for.

Cooking grease makes kitchens especially susceptible to this problem. Keeping kitchen light fixtures clean will maximize light levels.

It may not be obvious just how dirty a light fixture is, so be sure to take a close look periodically—and run your finger over the fixture if it's not too hot. Most light fixtures can be cleaned with a little soap and water, but make sure everything is dry before you turn the lights back on.

You're in Control

Lighting controls turn lights on and off or adjust the level of light. They allow you to optimize your use of light in a space while minimizing waste. Here are some ideas for making the best use of lighting controls. Some of the following suggestions are easy retrofits; others may only be practical if you're building an addition or doing major electrical work.

Switches

- Install individual switches on light fixtures so that people can use what they need without having to turn on lights for the entire room.
- If you're rewiring or adding on, locate switches in obvious and convenient places. Install two-way wall switches at every entrance to hallways, staircases, and large rooms.
- Use separate switches to control lights in areas that are used for different purposes, such as the counter, island, and ambient lights in a kitchen.
- For safety, make switches near stairs and other critical areas easy to see, with switch plates that glow in the dark or large toggles on pull cords.

Dimmers

- Use *dimmers* to change the mood of a room instantly.
- Use one light for many purposes with a simple adjustment of the dimmer.
- Buy a cord dimmer or a socket adapter to dim plug-in lamps.
- Replace dimmers installed before about 1960 if they dim the light by increasing electrical resistance (released as heat), rather than by decreasing the flow of electricity. Not sure? If the dimmer itself is warm, you're wasting energy and money.
- Use dimmers with incandescent lights (including low-voltage systems) or with fluorescents or LEDs labeled as dimmer compatible. (Most CFLs aren't dimmable, and can be damaged by dimmers.)
- Don't buy bulbs for dimming that provide more light than you need. You save more energy by replacing a 100W bulb with a 60W bulb than you do by dimming the 100W bulb to the lower light output.
- Operate halogen incandescents at full power from time to time. Otherwise, they will become less efficient and may burn out sooner. (Even undimmed, older halogens that contain diodes may flicker noticeably. Dimming the light makes the flicker more pronounced.)

IS FULL-SPECTRUM LIGHTING AS GOOD AS SUNLIGHT?

Full-spectrum lights (typically fluorescent) are designed to simulate the color appearance of sunlight at noon—an intense, slightly bluish light. Full-spectrum lights can make colors appear vibrant. However, replacing a regular light with a full-spectrum light does not replicate the essential range of daylight. Claims that full-spectrum lighting is more "natural" than other lighting are largely marketing hype.

Full-spectrum lighting is appropriate

- in an art studio, where it can help you perceive color more accurately;
- in a windowless room, where it can make the area feel more "natural" and less confining;
- during winter at high latitudes (Alaska) or in cloudy regions (the Pacific Northwest); and
- anywhere you find its effects appealing.

TABLE 11.02: COMPARING LIGHT SOURCES

Type	Description	Pros
Incandescent	Produces light by heating a tungsten filament, which then glows.	Light appears natural to the eye. Inexpensive. Easily dimmed. Inexpensive timer and occupancy control. Intensity and direction easy to control. Most fixtures accept a range of wattages and light outputs. Lamps and fixtures widely available.
Halogen (incandescent)	An incandescent with a gas fill tungsten filament and gases that cause a chemical reaction that returns spent tungsten onto the filament.	Slightly more efficient and longer lived than other incandescents (typically 3,000 hours). Maintains stable light output over product life.
Fluorescent (including CFLs)	Contains mercury vapor that produces short-wave ultraviolet light, which strikes a phosphor, causing it to emit visible light.	Provide more lumens per watt (46–100) than incandescents. Longer lived than incandescents (6,000 to 20,000 hours for CFLs; 20,000 hours or more for many linear lamps). Many high-quality products are available. Available in a variety of color temperatures (3,000–10,000°K) and CRIs (51–98). Most states require spent lamps to be recycled. Available in colors (red, green, blue, yellow).
Light-emitting diode (LED)	Consists of tiny light bulbs that fit into an electric circuit and are powered through a semiconductor.	Much longer-lived than fluorescent or incandescent (35,000–50,000 hours or more). Moderate to good output (20–60 Lm/W). Intensity and direction easy to control. Excellent colored lights available.

THE ENERGY INDEPENDENCE AND SECURITY ACT (EISA)

The Energy Independence and Security Act (EISA) states that by 2014, all types of common household light bulbs that use between 40 and 100 watts must be 27% more efficient than comparable incandescent bulbs manufactured in 2007. These new standards will be phased in between 2012 and 2014.

CFLs and many LEDs already meet these standards, but manufacturers have also found a way to make incandescent halogen lights that meet the standard. These improved incandescent bulbs have a small halogen-filled bulb within the outer bulb, while the evacuated space between the inner and outer bulbs blocks heat losses. These lights cost more than the older bulbs, but they last longer and are more efficient.

Cons	Typical Uses
Over the life of the bulb, filament material coats the glass, and the bulb gets dimmer. Inefficient: about 12–17 Lm/W. Relatively short lived: typically 750 to 1,500 hours. Illegal in new construction in California, unless coupled with dimmer or occupancy control.	Indoor lighting for almost any room. Flood- and spotlighting, indoors and outdoors.
Relatively inefficient: about 20–24 Lm/W. Some halogen lamps require special fixtures and sockets.	Indoor and outdoor lighting, especially flood- and spotlighting and low-voltage systems.
Older technology gives off light that looks unnatural or is unflattering. Costs more than incandescents. Linear and circular lamps don't fit fixtures designed for incandescents. Low-quality lamps may be short lived and inefficient. Lamps suitable for enclosed fixtures cost more and are difficult to find. Dimmable CFLs are more expensive and do not dim as well as incandescents. Most states require spent lamps to be recycled. Some lamps slow to start, or take time to come to full brightness. Frequent switching may shorten life.	Gradually replacing incandescents for most residential applications. Indoor and mild-climate outdoor applications. CFLs can be used in most places where incandescents are used. Often used for cove lighting.
Technology is new and may not be well tested. Manufacturers and distributors may not be well established. Relatively expensive. Variable quality.	Outdoors as spotlights, floodlights, and security lighting. Indoors as spotlights, track lighting, decorative lighting, under-cabinet lighting, and general lighting.

FLUORESCENT LIGHTS AND MERCURY

Mercury is used to produce light in a fluorescent tube or CFL. It's also toxic. But mercury is present as a contaminant in coal and other fuels used to produce electricity. Consequently, more mercury escapes into the environment from operating an incandescent bulb than from operating and landfilling an equivalent CFL.

In the last several years, the amount of mercury in a fluorescent light has been reduced to about one-tenth of what it was in the past. Today, breaking a new CFL indoors does not create a major hazard. If you remove the broken CFL and ventilate the area for an hour, your mercury exposure will be about the same as from eating a bite of tuna fish. See epa.gov/cfl/cflcleanup.html.

TABLE 11.03: ROOM-BY-ROOM LIGHTING

Room	Lighting Concepts
Kitchen	Position overhead and undercabinet fixtures to avoid shadows. Use fixtures made for moist environments. Consider allowing the task lighting to provide your ambient lighting. Install separate switches for range, countertops, island. Consider cove lighting to provide ambient light, possibly mounted on top of cabinets.
Bathroom	Provide adequate ambient lighting for safety while bathing. Use warm task lighting to enhance flesh tones for grooming. Install fixtures made for moist environments. Consider a small night-light for middle-of-the-night visits.
Living	Look at the room in sections and choose flexible lighting that supports several uses at once. Avoid creating glare on TV and computer screens.
Home office	Provide cool task lighting for visual work. Use accent lighting to highlight displays such as artwork, whiteboards, or framed certificates. Consider daylighting if you use the office only during the day.
Dining room	Create a relaxed mood for nighttime dining with warm ambient lighting. Encourage a more active mood with cooler lighting at breakfast or lunch.
Bedroom	Set the stage for relaxation with warm, low-level ambient lighting in the early evening, mimicking late-day sunlight. Use individual reading lights (task lighting) to allow one person to read while the room lights are off so another person can sleep.
Outdoors	Use yellow lights to avoid attracting moths. Focus lights downward to curb "light pollution" in the night sky. Aim a motion detector so it doesn't "see" small animals and windblown bushes. Use photovoltaic path lights to increase safety without increasing your electricity bill.

This kitchen has daylighting via windows; general lighting from ceiling fluorescents and cabinet-top cove lighting; task lighting on countertops; and accent lighting from ceiling-mounted spots.

Timers

- Save money and energy by using timers to switch lights off if you tend to forget to do this yourself.
- Increase your safety while you're away by using light timers to give the appearance that someone is home. (CFLs or LEDs will cost less to operate and burn cooler than incandescent bulbs.)

Motion Detectors

- Save energy by using *motion detectors* or occupancy sensors to turn a light on when you enter the room, and off when the room is unoccupied. (Once used primarily in security systems, these sensors are now available for home use.)
- Install motion detectors in bathrooms and bedrooms, where lights are frequently left on.

- Be sure your bulbs are compatible with the sensors (some CFLs should not be used with motion detectors).

Photosensors

- Install *photosensors* to turn lights on when it gets dark.
- Use photosensors to adjust electric lighting levels in daylit areas.
- Install photosensors at lights you want to keep on all night and turn off automatically when the sun comes up, such as outside lights that illuminate a garden or path.
- Combine photosensors with motion detectors for security lighting.

Central Controls

Central controls monitor lighting and operate switches, sensors, and dimmers throughout the home.

The term can refer to many different technologies, from computerized systems you manage remotely to equipment that lets you adjust the lighting or appliances in one room from another part of the house.

Central controls may be integrated with security systems, telephones, and cable TV. They are common in commercial buildings, but may be overkill in your home. Assess how much time and energy you would actually save by installing central controls. Consult a professional to see if the system you want to install calls for upgrading your wiring.

GET THE MOST BANG FOR YOUR BUCK

- Make the best use of daylighting before buying any electrical lighting.
- Participate in programs subsidized by your utility company, such as instant rebates on CFLs.
- Buy Energy Star-qualified fixtures and bulbs.
- Design your lighting well; if a task light enables you to stop using inefficient ambient lighting, you may not need to spend money retrofitting an overhead fixture.

LIGHTING PROJECTS YOU CAN DO TODAY:

- *Move some furniture* closer to windows for better daylight.
- *Replace inefficient lights* with more efficient models.
- *Trim a shrub* that blocks daylight from a room.
- *Don't light up the whole room* if all you need is task lighting; bring in new light fixtures if needed.
- *Move light sources* or computer and TV screens to reduce glare and reflection on the screens.

LIGHTING PROJECTS THAT WILL TAKE MORE TIME:

- *Add a new skylight or window* to improve daylighting.
- *Paint walls and ceilings* in lighter colors to bounce light around the room.
- *Add dimmers, motions sensors, or timers* to save electricity.
- *Redesign and install new lighting* in each room to better match the lighting to your needs.

DANGER ZONE: CAN LIGHTS

Can lights (also known as *recessed lights* or *downlights*) fit well with modern design. They provide local, focused lighting with minimal glare, but they're inefficient for wide-area ambient lighting.

They can also cause problems, largely because they're installed in a hole cut into the ceiling. Older can lights installed in cathedral ceilings or below an attic may allow air and moisture to pass from the room into the roof structure, increasing heating and cooling bills and encouraging mold growth. Finally, insulating around the can may create a fire hazard.

If you want can lights, buy new, insulated, airtight models that have been pressure tested for low air leakage and rated for insulation contact. Use reflector-type bulbs; most of the light from a regular bulb will get trapped inside the can, making the fixture extremely inefficient. If you use CFL or LED reflector bulbs, make sure they're designed for enclosed fixtures or they may become very hot, making them run inefficiently and shortening their life.

Consider using surface-mounted fixtures instead of can lights—perhaps *track lighting* or wall sconces.

RESOURCES

Print

Lighting Design Basics, Mark Karlen and James Benya, Wiley, 2004. Also available as an ebook.

Residential Lighting: A Practical Guide to Beautiful and Sustainable Design, Randall Whitehead, Wiley, 2008.

Online

"Coloring Your Room With Energy-Efficient Lighting," Alliance to Save Energy: http://ase.org/efficiencynews/coloring-your-room-energy-efficient-lighting

"GE Energy Smart® CFL Savings Calculator" (General Electric: estimates energy savings from replacing incandescent bulbs with CFLs): gelighting.com/na/home_lighting/products/pop_lighting_calc.htm

Energy Star:

Interactive guide to choosing lights: drmedia server.com/CFLGuide/index.html

Qualified light bulbs: energystar.govindex.cfm?fuseaction=find_a_product.showProductGroup&pgw_code=LB

Qualified light fixtures: energystar.govindex.cfm?fuseaction=find_a_product.showProductGroup&pgw_code=LF

Overview of CFLs: energystar.gov/index.cfm?c=cfls.pr_cfls_about# how_work

U.S. Department of Energy:

"Energy Savers: Lighting and Daylighting": energysavers.govyour_ home/lighting_daylighting/index.cfm/mytopic=11970

"Energy Basics: Lighting and Daylighting": eere.energy.gov/basics/buildings/lighting_daylighting.html

Chapter 12

VENTILATE RIGHT FOR INDOOR AIR QUALITY, HEALTH, AND COMFORT

What can good ventilation do for you? It can

- improve air quality by diluting pollutants;
- help control moisture and thereby mold; and
- provide fresh air in an affordable, energy-efficient manner.

Ventilation is about bringing fresh air into your home, with the dual goals of controlling moisture and maintaining good IAQ. The simple formula for avoiding trouble when building or remodeling is: Build tight, ventilate right. Building tight is covered in Chapter 8. Ventilating right means controlling where your ventilation air comes from, as well as how and when it enters your home.

MOISTURE

If you get only one thing under control in your remodeling, it should be moisture. Most houses don't have major moisture problems, but when those problems do occur, the consequences can be serious. High moisture levels cause building materials to rot. (The term "dry rot" is a misnomer; all fungal growth requires moisture.) If the moisture content in the air becomes too high, mold, mildew, dust mites, and other microorganisms thrive. Mold and mildew make your house look and smell bad, and they may trigger allergic reactions in susceptible people.

In summer, moisture can enter a house via humid outdoor air; dehumidification may be an appropriate solution. In winter, with the house closed up, moisture can come from human activities such as cooking and bathing; good *spot ventilation* is the answer here.

You also want to avoid more serious sources of moisture, such as

- leaks in the roof, plumbing, or around windows;
- runaway humidifiers; and
- wet crawl spaces.

Even the best ventilation system won't make up for these sources of moisture; you need to control them at their source.

Cold temperatures cause another kind of moisture problem. When warm air strikes a cold surface, the water vapor in the air will condense. An obvious example is condensation on windows. This condensation can lead to mold growth and the decay of the sash and framing. Another common condensation spot is air-conditioning supply grilles and nearby ceilings.

HEAT RECOVERY AND ENERGY RECOVERY VENTILATORS

In winter, heat recovery equipment recovers "waste" heat from air on its way out of the house. It transfers this heat to incoming air by passing it through a simple *heat exchanger*. Up to 70% of the heat in the air being exhausted out of the house can be recovered.

In a hot climate, an HRV can also be used to precool outdoor air, reducing the air-conditioning load. The cooler outgoing exhaust air absorbs heat from the warmer incoming air, cooling it as it enters. But an HRV recovers only dry heat, not humidity.

An ERV can go one step farther. It will transfer not only the heat between the two airstreams, but about half of the humidity, as well. For this reason, an ERV is superior in humid climates. If you live in a hot and humid climate, however, an ERV alone will not dehumidify incoming air sufficiently. You will probably still need to consult with your HVAC contractor about adding dehumidification.

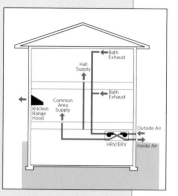

A heat recovery ventilator or energy recovery ventilator allows you to exhaust moist or stale air and bring in fresh air while capturing much of the heat from the exhaust air in winter via a heat exchanger.

The heat exchanger, where warmth is transferred from exhaust air to incoming air, is a central element in a heat or energy recovery ventilator.

An HRV or ERV can reduce the cost of cooling or heating your ventilation air. The equipment has a high first cost, and it requires proper installation, but it is highly energy efficient. It is most likely to be cost-effective in cold or harshly cold climates, or in very hot, humid climates, especially where fuel costs are high. In milder climates, there is less of a temperature difference between incoming and exhausted air, so an HRV or ERV is less likely to be cost-effective.

If you install an HRV or ERV, you will still need a separate range hood in the kitchen and an exhaust fan in the bathroom.

What's the best way to ventilate? Do you need mechanical equipment to control humidity? That depends on the climate zone you live in. The right thing to do in Minneapolis is the wrong thing to do in Houston. Climate zones range from dry to very humid. In the North, Northeast, and West, the air is generally dry most of the year. In the South, it's typically very humid. However, in any given region, humidity can vary greatly depending on the season.

In drier climate zones, exhaust ventilation in the kitchen and bathrooms can keep moisture under control most of the year. If you live in an area where summers are hot and humid, consult your air-conditioning contractor to discuss mechanical means to control moisture.

No matter where you live, you should build tight to help control where moisture flows (Chapters 8 and 9), line your crawl space with a vapor barrier (Chapter 10), keep up with maintenance, go easy with the humidifier, and install a ventilation system that's appropriate for your climate.

INDOOR POLLUTANTS

The first rule for a healthy home is to control indoor pollutants at their source. If pollutants aren't created or brought into the house in the first place, you won't need to get rid of them.

Sources of indoor pollutants include toxic household cleaning supplies, furniture, new carpets, paints and finishes, cabinets, cosmetics, smoking, pets, car exhaust, and pests. Many furnishings and interior finish products *outgas* (or off-gas) pollutants, sometimes for several months or years.

Combustion appliances—fueled by propane, natural gas, kerosene, oil, or wood—are another source of indoor pollutants. They produce toxic gases and tiny particles that pollute indoor air. Unvented combustion appliances (e.g., a gas range or unvented space heater) can have ventilation added to reduce the concentration of pollutants. Combustion appliances that have a chimney or vent pipe can also cause trouble if the exhaust air is sucked back down into your living space (Chapter 8).

THE NEED FOR VENTILATION

When you tighten your house to conserve energy, natural ventilation is likely to be too low to exhaust moisture and dissipate indoor pollutants. Leaving ventilation to chance and thinking, "We'll just open the windows," is a thing of the past. This is where *controlled ventilation* comes in.

Effective ventilation exchanges fresh outdoor air for stale, particle- and chemical-laden indoor air. Air exchange occurs consistently, every day, throughout the year, and pollutants are exhausted from wherever they are produced.

Standards for good ventilation are set by the *American Society of Heating, Refrigerating, and Air Conditioning Engineers (ASHRAE)*. All ventilation recommendations in this book meet or exceed ASHRAE Standard 62.2.

There are two main types of home ventilation:

- Spot exhaust ventilation
- Central ventilation

Both are important for a healthy, durable home.

SPOT EXHAUST VENTILATION

Cooking and showering introduce a lot of moisture into the home. Spot exhaust ventilation quickly removes moisture (as well as odors and pollutants) at the source, such as over the stove or in the bathroom. In order to truly remove the moisture, all ventilation ducts must terminate outdoors—never in the attic, basement, or garage. (This requirement is spelled out in the International Residential Code; see Chapter 16.)

If possible, install the exhaust fan directly above the source of whatever you want to get rid of. These fans should be turned on whenever you cook or whenever the bathroom is occupied, and they should stay on until

CONTROL INDOOR AIR POLLUTION

Ventilation can improve your indoor environmental quality, but many indoor air pollutants need to be addressed more directly. Check out the following resources to help keep you and your family safe.

Combustion Equipment Safety, U.S. Department of Energy (DOE): apps1.eere.energy.gov/buildings/publications/pdfs/building_america/26464.pdf

Improving Home Indoor Air Quality, University of Texas Indoor Environmental Science and Engineering: engr.utexas.edu/attachments/Improving%20IAQ% 20in%20the%20home%20(2).pdf

"Indoor Air Quality and Personal Exposure Assessment Program," California Environmental Protection Agency Air Resources Board: arb.ca.gov/research/indoor/INDOOR.HTM

U.S. Environmental Protection Agency (EPA):

- An Introduction to Indoor Air Quality (IAQ): epa.gov/iaq/ia-intro.html
- Citizen's Guide to Pest Control and Pesticide Safety: epa.gov/oppfead1/Publications/Cit_Guide/citguide.pdf
- A Brief Guide to Mold, Moisture, and Your Home: epa.gov/mold/moldguide.html
- Radon: epa.gov/radon
- Where You Live (local radon information): epa.gov/radon/whereyoulive.html
- Volatile Organic Compounds (VOCs): epa.gov/iaq/voc2.html
- Asbestos in Products and Buildings and How to Manage It: epa.gov/oppt/asbestos
- Lead: epa.gov/oppt/lead
- An Introduction to Indoor Air Quality: Formaldehyde: epa.gov/iaq/formaldehyde.html

FAN NOISE RATINGS

Fan technology has come a long way since the days of annoying fans that rattle your ears. There are now many superquiet, very efficient fans on the market.

Sound levels are measured in sones. The higher the sone level, the noisier the fan. A fan has to be turned on in order to work, and it won't be turned on if it's noisy.

Many spot exhaust fans are rated at 1.0 sone or less; others may be rated at 5.0 sones or more. Fans rated at 1.5 sones are very quiet, and low-capacity fans rated as low as 0.3 to 1.0 sone are nearly inaudible.

Since central ventilating fans run for extended periods of time, ASHRAE Standard 62.2 says they can be no louder than 1.0 sone if they are mounted in the living space.

the room is free of moisture and odors. Because warm air rises, place exhaust fans above the stove or shower; a fan placed off to the side works much harder to pull air across the room, wasting your electricity dollars.

A new generation of fans has become available in the past few years. These fans are ultraquiet, and supercheap to operate (under $30 a year in most areas), and they exhaust air more effectively than the old fans did. They also have controls that do the work for your family. Ever tried to get some people to turn the exhaust fan on and off? These new controls automatically turn the fan on when the humidity in the bathroom goes up during a shower, and then turn the fan off when the room is dry. Other controls have occupancy sensors, turning on or off when anyone enters or leaves the room. It's much easier to use these fans than to change your family's old habits.

MAXIMUM FAN SOUND RATINGS

New Replacement Fans	Existing Retained Fans*	Maximum Sound Rating
Local bath, on-demand		3.0 sones or 50 dbA[†]
	Local bath, on-demand	N/A
Local bath, continuous		1.0 sone or 30 dbA[†]
	Local bath, continuous	N/A
Local kitchen, on-demand		3.0 sones or 50 dbA[†]
	Local kitchen, on-demand	N/A
Local kitchen, continuous		1.0 sone or 30 dbA[†]
	Local kitchen, continuous	N/A
Whole-building		1.0 sone or 30 dbA[†]
	Whole-building	1.0 sone or 30 dbA[†]

©ASHRAE, ashrae.org. ASHRAE Standard 62.2-2010.
* Valid only if Appendix A, 62.2-2010, is used.
[†] A-rated decibels measured at 5 feet from fan grille.

Installation can also affect a fan's noise level. Until recently, a low-sone fan attached to a duct that twists and turns, or is kinked or too small, could be just as noisy as the noisiest model. But many newer fans are able to adapt to high static pressure by increasing fan speed, which increases sone rating only slightly.

Consider the quality of the fan's sound, too. Different sound frequencies produce different tones, even at the same sone level. Try to listen to the fan yourself before you buy it, to make sure that it's acceptable to you.

For quiet operation, install either a fan with a low *sone* rating (see "Fan Noise Ratings" sidebar) or a remote-mounted fan. With the latter, the grille is located above the pollution source, and is ducted to a fan in an attic or other remote location that vents to the outdoors—never into the attic. Make sure the remote-mounted fan is well secured so it doesn't vibrate.

What Size Exhaust Fan Do You Need?

ASHRAE Standard 62.2 is the national standard for sizing exhaust fans. ASHRAE recommends that the bathroom exhaust fan be able to move at least 50 CFM if it is user controlled, 20 CFM if it operates continuously. Most new bathroom fans can do this.

For the kitchen exhaust hood fan, ASHRAE recommends 100 CFM for intermittent use. For continuous use, have an HVAC professional size the exhaust fan based on your kitchen's size. Avoid getting a fan that's too powerful; it can cause negative pressures and backdrafting. If your exhaust fan exceeds 400 CFM, the new building codes require that you provide makeup air, via a hard-wired fan, to prevent this from happening.

A bathroom exhaust fan (seen here in the ceiling) is crucial for removing moist air after showering or bathing.

It's important to have an exhaust fan above a gas range in order to avoid indoor air pollution from combustion products. Be sure to follow the range manufacturer's recommendations for fan size.

People with a kitchen range in an island sometimes don't want a range hood, so they use a range-level fan. But since a range-level fan must pull hot air both across and down, it must be very powerful. Some of these fans can depressurize the house enough to backdraft combustion appliances—and they don't do well at removing odors and pollutants.

Don't get a *recirculating fan* (sometimes called a *ductless range hood*). All they do is take the greasy, smoky air, concentrate it, and blow it back into the room—a poor way to improve air quality. These fans are supposed to filter the air before returning it, but they don't remove heat or moisture, and they remove less cooking grease and odors than ducted fans. They are much cheaper to install than ducted fans, but at the expense of performance.

An exhaust fan over the range helps remove cooking odors and moisture—and combustion products in the case of a gas range.

Any time you replace a combustion appliance, seal ducts, do air sealing, or in any way change how your house system works, contact a local energy rater—preferably one with *BPI* (Building Performance Institute) or *RESNET* (Residential Energy Services Network) certification—to test and make sure that all combustion appliances inside the home work properly.

CENTRAL VENTILATION

Ventilating your whole house is especially important if your remodeling job will tighten up the house, as most do, or if you already have poor IAQ. In humid climates, consult an air-conditioning professional; it is often a good idea to mechanically control humidity along with temperature and ventilation.

There are three basic types of central ventilation system. You could install a system that

- exhausts air out of the house (a central exhaust system);
- brings fresh air into the house (a central supply system); or
- does both (a balanced central system).

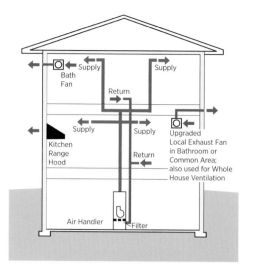

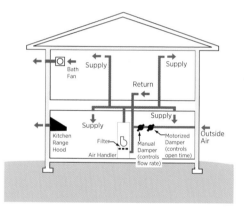

A central exhaust system pulls air out of the house at one point or several, depending on the design.

A central supply system pulls outdoor air into the house, giving the indoor air a slight positive pressure.

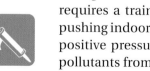

Central Exhaust System

A central exhaust system pulls air out of the house. It differs from a *whole-house fan* in that it is not intended to cool the house, but only to cause enough air exchange to maintain good IAQ. It may consist of a single fan centrally located in a hallway or at the top of the stairs.

The simplest kind of central exhaust system is an upgraded bathroom fan with a motor built to run for long periods of time, and sized to ventilate the whole house. You can simply replace your old, noisy bathroom fan with a new one (making sure it's appropriately sized), then remember to turn it on and let it run when needed—or install a continuously operating model. In the latter case, use a two-speed fan that can be operated continuously at low speed to provide general ventilation and switched to high speed when the room is being used. (Other bathrooms still need their own spot exhaust fans.) See Table 12.01 for the ASHRAE 62.2 standard for the amount of air the fan should exhaust when operated at low speed.

The new generation of bathroom fans we've been discussing almost always have *permanent-magnet motors* that are rated for continuous duty. They are inexpensive to run; they are rated at under 1.0 sone; and they last between 12 and 20 years in continuous duty—unlike many bathroom fans, which have a short life and make lots of noise.

Another central exhaust strategy is to install a remote multipoint exhaust fan. Usually located in the attic, a remote fan is ducted to several exhaust grilles that take air from locations throughout the house, including each bathroom. This system replaces several noisy, inefficient bath fans.

Exhaust ventilation was once recommended only for homes in cold climates, but in tightly built homes with low airflow, it can be used in any climate. In humid climates you may need to add a small dehumidifier or opt for a variable-speed blower with a humidistat control on your A/C to help control indoor humidity. In cold or dry climates, the very slight negative pressure (about 3 pascals or less) in the house helps keep warm, humid indoor air from pushing into the walls, where it might lead to condensation and moisture problems. To allow air circulation, interior doors should be under-cut or jumper ducts should be installed between rooms.

Central Supply System

A central supply system pulls outside air into the house. It is a good option for tight homes in hot and humid climates; proper installation usually requires a trained contractor. The system slightly pressurizes the house, pushing indoor air out through small openings in the building. This is called positive pressure (Chapter 8), and it helps prevent outside moisture and pollutants from getting in through these openings.

Adding a central supply system is not recommended in cold climates, where you don't want to force warm, moist air into cold walls or ceilings. This can quickly lead to condensation, mold, and rot.

With a central supply system, install an air filter on the supply fan to clean the air coming into your house. Even if the air around your house isn't highly polluted, it is likely to contain particulates that should be filtered out.

Using Your Furnace Fan for Central Supply

When contractors add supply ventilation to an existing house, they often run a duct from outside and connect it to the return duct of an existing forced-air heating-and-cooling system. This brings in outdoor air and distributes it around the house through the heating and air-conditioning ducts.

An air filter added at the intake will remove particles from incoming air—recommended if you have a central supply system.

This method is appropriate only if your furnace fan or blower is a newer unit with a permanent-magnet motor, *electronically commutated motor (ECM), integrated control motor (ICM),* or *variable-speed motor* (all names for the same kind of motor). These are far more energy efficient than blower motors of a few years ago and allow airflow to be set to much lower levels when outdoor humidity is high and you want the fan for ventilation only.

If your *air handler* or furnace fan is one of the old-fashioned models, using it to ventilate can significantly increase energy use because it moves much more air than is needed. This can also cause uncomfortable drafts.

An ECM fan will operate efficiently at lower than typical furnace speeds. This allows a reduced airflow for ventilation when heating or cooling is not needed. These new fans use far less electricity than the old ones, and fan speed can be varied, which can be a big help in controlling indoor humidity. If you are replacing your furnace or A/C as part of your project, you should consider buying a unit with such a fan. However, retrofitting your existing furnace air handler with an ECM is expensive (about $1,000). If you are not replacing the unit as part of the project, it's better to get a fan specifically dedicated to ventilation, keeping it separate from the heating-and-cooling system.

Balanced Central System

A balanced central system uses two fans. One fan exhausts stale air out of the house; the other fan brings the same amount of outside air into the house. This system creates a *neutral,* or *balanced, pressure,* and and is particularly appropriate if you want to use a heat recovery system (see "Heat Recovery and Energy Recovery Ventilators").

There are two ways to go, depending on your climate:

- *Heat recovery ventilators (HRVs)* are best suited for heating-dominated, less humid climates.
- *Energy recovery ventilators (ERVs)* are best suited for locations with humid summers.

Heat/energy recovery is most likely to be cost-effective in severe climates. Be sure to have a skilled pro install and maintain your HRV or ERV.

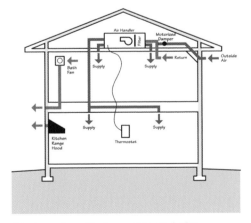

A balanced ventilation system includes both supply and exhaust fans, and allows the inclusion of a heat or energy recovery ventilator.

There are inexpensive balanced systems that use two wall-mounted fans of equal capacity—one for supply and one for exhaust—in two different rooms. However, this may cause poor distribution and uncomfortable drafts, because the single supply dumps all the fresh air in one spot, and the single exhaust takes all the stale air from a different spot.

The best method is to supply air to the common living areas, such as living rooms and bedrooms, and to exhaust air from the rooms where pollution is high, such as the kitchen and bathroom. This can be done with ducts and remote fans. (Keep the kitchen range hood separate.)

To minimize drafts from supply fans, a diffuser can be used to mix the air. A diffuser is a grille that has a smaller open area than the duct attached to it. The reduced airflow forces air moving through the grille to speed up and move farther into the room, where it can better mix with indoor air. Placed high on a wall, a diffuser allows air to mix before it reaches anyone. This makes the room more comfortable, especially in harsh climates where entering air may be unpleasantly hot or cold.

Sizing Central Systems

You can determine the best size for a central system based on the volume of your house and the desired ventilation rate. Table 12.01 will help you pick the right ventilation rate for your home based on floor area and occupancy level, represented by the number of bedrooms. Note that this table gives minimum requirements; you may want greater fan capacity if you want more fresh air or believe you have allergies to something inside your home. Your home performance assessor should be able to guide you in this decision.

TABLE 12.01: MINIMUM VENTILATION AIR REQUIREMENTS (CFM)

Floor Area (ft²)	0–1 Bedroom	2–3 Bedrooms	4–5 Bedrooms	6–7 Bedrooms	>7 Bedrooms
<1,500	30	45	60	75	90
1,501–3,000	45	60	75	90	105
3,001–4,500	60	75	90	105	120
4,501–6,000	75	90	105	120	135
6,001–7,500	90	105	120	135	150
>7,500	105	120	135	150	165

©ASHRAE, ashrae.org. ASHRAE Standard 62.2-2010.

A fan's capacity in CFM can be found on its label. However, these labels can be misleading. They assume an ideal installation, with short, straight duct runs and a prescribed *pressure drop*. Most real-life installations involve long duct runs with droops and elbows that increase airflow resistance and lower the actual capacity of the fan. Start with a good fan, make the installation as simple as possible, then have your home performance pro verify whether you've achieved the desired CFM.

If your installation is complex, have your contractor determine the overall pressure drop over the ventilation duct system and pick a fan that will deliver the desired airflows at that pressure drop. Consulting with a certified home performance pro who has the equipment to actually measure pressure drop and airflows can also be a good idea.

When to Use Your Central System

If people are home all day, you might want to ventilate 24 hours a day, as most IAQ programs recommend. ASHRAE recommends, at the minimum, ventilating whenever people are home. For healthier air, ventilate at least 8 to 12 hours a day by using a 24-hour timer set for two or more different periods. One of these periods should be when people are sleeping. The single longest time period during which our homes are usually at full occupancy is during the night, so this is when we really need to ensure good IAQ.

You can trade off fan size and operating time. For intermittent ventilation, size the fan larger. For continuous ventilation, use a smaller fan.

CHOOSING THE RIGHT EQUIPMENT

Installing a good mechanical ventilation system means getting an energy-efficient, quiet fan; designing and installing the ducts properly; and choosing appropriate accessories and controls for your system.

The Home Ventilating Institute (HVI) rates and certifies equipment and provides sizing recommendations. Look for the HVI-Certified label, and refer to the HVI's online rating and sizing information (see Resources).

The Home Ventilating Institute (HVI) rates and certifies home ventilation equipment.

Fan Efficiency

With the quality of the air your family breathes at stake, it's worth spending a little extra money to get a really good fan. Inexpensive fans are not intended for continuous use. The motor largely determines how well a fan will work, and how much it will cost to run over its lifetime.

Fans with *shaded-pole motors* are the least expensive to buy. These are the fans that builders usually install, especially in bathrooms. But these fans generally don't last long when operated for extended periods; they make so much noise (5.0 sones or more) that you won't want them on for long; they're inefficient; and they cost a lot to run.

Fans with permanent *split-capacitor motors* will cost more, but their motors are about twice as efficient as shaded-pole motors, and should last much longer. These fans are usually rated for continuous operation and often have squirrel cage blowers that are designed to make 90% less noise than fan blades. Some of these units are rated as low as 0.3 sone.

If your ventilation system is part of a heating-and-cooling system, you can improve it somewhat by using a highly efficient fan motor. The most efficient motor on the market is the ECM. It doesn't lose efficiency when it runs at low speeds. This is important if you want to be able to run the fan at low speed for central ventilation and turn it to high speed for heating and air conditioning.

Look at the wattage of the fan you want to buy, and divide this by its capacity in CFM. For higher-capacity spot fans, you want one that uses less than 1 watt/CFM. Low-capacity fans (50 CFM) should use less than 0.4 watt/CFM. If the wattage isn't on the label, get the information from the manufacturer or the Home Ventilating Institute. If you shop for ENERGY STAR-labeled fans, you'll find they've done the watts/CFM calculations for you.

Ventilation Ducts

Well-designed and properly installed ductwork ensures that the fan will operate at peak capacity, and that moisture and indoor pollutants will actually be taken out of the house. Duct runs should be as short, smooth, and straight as possible. Bends lower the fan's capacity, increase noise, and create a place for moisture to condense. According to the International Residential Code and ASHRAE 62.2, all ducts should terminate outside the building—not in an attic, soffit, or crawl space.

Most ventilation systems use either *smooth-metal* or *flexible duct.* Smooth metal (galvanized sheet metal) has about half as much resistance to airflow as flex duct, but it's harder to route through the house because it's rigid. For kitchen range hoods, use only smooth-metal ducts; the fan is typically not strong enough to overcome the friction loss of flex duct. Flexible duct is prefabricated metal, polyvinyl chloride (PVC), or Mylar on a metal frame. Metal flex is better for ventilation systems because it is more rigid, making it less likely to sag or kink. Flex duct almost always requires hangers or other supports every 3 or 4 feet to keep it from sagging or kinking.

Ducts must be sized correctly to produce the desired rate of airflow. Your installer must carefully calculate resistance to airflow in order to determine the correct duct and fan sizes. Because flexible duct has more resistance to airflow, it should be sized larger than smooth-metal duct. Manufacturer's specifications for duct size are too small in most installed conditions. (See Chapters 8, 9, and 10 for information on properly sealing and insulating ducts.)

Grilles and Dampers

Grilles are openings through which ventilation air enters and exits rooms. *Dampers* inside ducts allow airflow to be adjusted. *Mechanical* or *gravity dampers* are set at the time of installation (though they can be reset if needed). A motorized damper is operated by controls that open it when the fan is on, and close it when the fan is off. *Backdraft dampers* keep air from moving the wrong way through a duct system; their use is required by national building codes.

Timers and Other Controls

There are many kinds of ventilation controls. *Programmable timers* allow you to ventilate at scheduled times. Controls that detect high humidity, motion, and pollution activate the ventilator when needed. Variable-speed controls allow you to adjust the amount of ventilation to your needs. Manual overrides can allow intermittent spot ventilation or halt ventilation if outdoor air is polluted by a nearby wildfire, for example.

If your heating-and-cooling fan is one of the efficient ones described above, you can link ventilation with the system's thermostatic control, or with devices that remember when and for how long the ventilator recently ran. Some inexpensive new controls can be retrofitted to your existing furnace or A/C. They operate the fan regularly even when the thermostat doesn't call for temperature control. They can even halt ventilation if the outdoor air is too hot, cold, or humid and resume it when conditions moderate.

Including a good timer and damper control on your system can make it much more efficient, and easier to maintain. No matter what type of control you select, make sure it is easily accessible, and keep the instructions in your Homeowner's Manual (Chapter 17).

A programmable ventilation timer allows you to ventilate your house at scheduled times.

VENTILATION PROJECTS YOU CAN DO TODAY:

- Minimize toxic household products.
- Have combustion appliances checked for proper functioning.
- Check the age and type of fans you currently have in your bathroom, kitchen, and central ventilation system.

VENTILATION PROJECTS THAT WILL TAKE MORE TIME:

- Meet with an HVAC professional to determine the best ventilation system for your home, family, and climate.
- Select and install new ventilation fans.

RESOURCES

American Society of Heating, Refrigerating, and Air-Conditioning Engineers: ashrae.org

- ASHRAE 62.2 Ventilation Standard: techstreet.com/standards/ashrae/62_2_2010?product_id=1703549

"Healthy Air at Home" (American Lung Association): lung.org/healthy-air/home

Home Ventilating Institute (fan rating and sizing information): hvi.org

National Center for Healthy Housing: nchh.org

U.S. Department of Energy/Energy Efficiency and Renewable Energy:

- Energy Renovations: *HVAC: A Guide for Contractors to Share with Homeowners.* Building America Best Practices Series, vol. 14, 2011: buildingamerica.gov
- Moisture Control: energysavers.gov/your_home/insulation_airsealing/index.cfm/mytopic=11750
- Ventilation: energysavers.gov/your_home/insulation_airsealing/index.cfm/mytopic=11830

"Ventilation for Homes" (U.S. Environmental Protection Agency): epa.gov/iaq/homes/hip-ventilation.html

Chapter 13

HEATING: STAY WARM IN WINTER

What can a better heating system do for you? It can

- eliminate drafts and cold areas in your home;
- allow the sun to give you free heating;
- improve the quality of the air you breathe; and
- help you stay warm in winter—while putting money in your pocket.

Wondering why your thermostat is set on low, but your heating bills come in high? If you've already sealed up air leaks (Chapter 8) and beefed up your insulation as needed (Chapter 9), the problem could be a poorly functioning heating system, very leaky ducts, or even a faulty thermostat.

The four basic approaches to heating are

- using the sun to heat rooms;
- installing a central forced-air system;
- installing a central hydronic radiant system; and
- using room-by-room solutions.

Sunshine warms you on cold sunny days, and it's free. Forced-air distributes heated air throughout the house. A central *hydronic* (fluid-based) system keeps your feet comfortable. A room-by-room system allows you to maintain lower temperatures in less-used spaces. You can combine any or all of these approaches.

HEATING YOUR HOME WITH THE SUN

In most of North America, sunlight can help heat your home on winter days, if you let it in and hold on to its heat. This simple, direct use of the sun's heat is called *passive-solar heating* and requires two things: south-facing windows to admit sunlight and interior *thermal mass* materials to store that solar warmth. Insulating window shades will help keep heat indoors at night, and shading those windows in summer will prevent overheating.

This tile floor and the concrete slab below it act as thermal mass, storing and releasing the sun's heat to warm the space.

The winter sun rises in the southeast and arcs low through the southern sky to set in the southwest. So the best place for windows to let in solar heat is the south side of the house, where winter sun can reach deep into the living space. Even if your home wasn't designed for solar heat, if the midday winter sun shines on your south walls, you've got a chance of improving your passive-solar heating.

Next, consider thermal mass. If you've ever leaned against a sun-warmed brick wall on a cool evening, you've experienced the power of thermal mass. Brick, stone, tile, and concrete can store the sun's heat and release it in the evening when air temperatures drop.

South-facing glass and thermal mass work together for your winter comfort. The more glass you have, the more surface area of thermal mass you need to soak up the solar heat. Even with a good balance of south glass and thermal mass, a long run of sunny winter days could overheat your south-facing rooms. You can spread the warmth to north-facing rooms by opening an interior door or window, or by installing a quiet fan.

Windows

If your south-facing glass area is less than 8% of the room's floor area, don't expect to get much heat from the sun unless you add windows. If it's more than 24%, the room might overheat on a sunny winter day.

Choose south-facing windows with a SHGC of 70% or more to admit solar heat, and a U-factor of .33 or less, so you'll lose less of that heat (Chapter 7). Many codes now require a low SHGC for all windows, which works well for west, east, and north windows. But for passive-solar heating, you may need to make the case for high-SHGC windows with your building department.

Incorporating Thermal Mass

"Thermal mass" refers to materials with a high capacity for storing heat, like masonry or stone. The darker their surface color, the more heat they absorb. Without thermal mass, your house will get too hot during the day and too cold at night. Thermal mass helps even out those temperature swings.

Designers of passive-solar homes typically specify 6 times as much thermal mass area as south glass area, with thermal mass about 4 inches thick. Concrete slabs and brick walls can meet these specifications, but what about readily available thinner mass—such as mortar-set tile floors, granite countertops, or thickly plastered walls? Those will work too, but you'll need more area. If most of your interior mass is significantly less than 4 inches thick, aim for 9 times the area of the south glass.

Remodeling gives you a chance to expose masonry or stone already built into your house to direct sunlight, and to add new thermal mass. If your house has an insulated slab foundation, exposing the slab floor near south windows by removing carpets or wood flooring may provide all the mass you'll need. (If you have an uninsulated slab, you may not want to remove that insulating carpet.) Or maybe you have a brick fireplace, and can add a south window to let the sun shine onto it.

If your house sits over a crawl space or a basement, you can still add thermal mass. Concrete floors can be attractive, durable, and easy to build. Some house structures can't take the added weight, so consult a structural engineer.

Don't cover thermal-mass floors! Leave them as bare as possible to soak up and release heat. You can polish or otherwise finish the concrete surface, or cover it with paving bricks, slate, quarry tiles, or dark ceramic tiles.

Another strategy is to replace a wood-framed interior wall that receives direct sunlight with a thermal-mass wall. Dark surfaces are best, as light colors

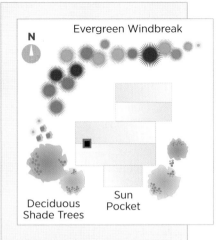

Evergreen Windbreak
N
Deciduous Shade Trees
Sun Pocket

MAINTAIN SOLAR ACCESS

Do hills, trees, or buildings keep that midday sun from falling on your south walls? Any obstructions in your home's solar access zone—from about 30° east to 30° west of due south—can block the winter sun when it is strongest, between 10:00 am and 2:00 pm.

If your home has good solar access, modifying your landscaping might help you get more winter sun. Keep trees out of the solar access zone; even the bare branches of deciduous trees can block some sun, and trees that hold on to their leaves through January are really a problem. When selecting new plants, be sure to take their mature dimensions into consideration—and don't plant evergreen trees on the south side of your house!

reflect much of the sunlight the wall could otherwise absorb. Such mass walls are particularly effective when they run perpendicular to the south wall; the east side gets morning sun, and the west side gets afternoon sun.

Active-Solar Heating

Unlike passive-solar heating, *active-solar heating*—also known as *solar thermal*—requires a large solar collector, a pump, a large storage tank, and a distribution system. The solar collector heats a liquid, which can provide both space heating and domestic water heating, saving you the cost of a separate water heater and *boiler*. This approach is best suited to a cold, sunny climate and a well-insulated home.

It's also possible to have solar forced-air heating. You can use a fan to blow air through *coils* that are heated by water from a solar storage tank. Or you can use a collector that heats air, which is then blown into your heating-duct system.

THE SUN SPACE: A PASSIVE-SOLAR ROOM

This sun space collects solar heat to warm the rest of the house. The overhang provides summer shade, and the vent windows and operable skylight release excess hot air in summer.

A *sun space* is a tightly constructed, windowed enclosure facing south that provides heat, light, and ventilation for the house. It can be an entryway, a sitting room, or a hallway. Sun spaces are not recommended in hot climates, where summer overheating outweighs any winter heating benefits.

Sun space heat is distributed to the house through connecting doors and windows, sometimes via a fan. The space will get much warmer than the rest of the house on sunny days, and much colder on winter nights. Between these extremes, there are times when the sun space is comfortable.

A sun space is also a great location for anything that prefers a hot setting, such as a passive-solar water heater, a hot-water storage tank.

Windows. A sun space should have as much south glass as possible. For most climates, the best sun space windows are low-e double-pane units with a SHGC above .70 and a U-factor at least as low as that of the windows in the rest of the house. If the sun space exists mainly to provide heat, the low-e coating should be on the inner pane, because the coating itself heats up when exposed to the sun, warming the glass. If the sun space is in a warm climate, the windows should have a low-e coating on the outer pane and a low SHGC—around .25 (Chapter 7). Sun space windows should be shaded in summer (Chapter 14).

Some sun spaces also have sloping glass walls and overhead windows, but sloping glass is harder to shade from summer sun; it loses more heat at night and in winter; it can be covered by snow; and it breaks, leaks, or fogs up more readily than vertical glass. If you do use overhead or sloping windows, get specially designed very low-e glass made to handle the strains of horizontal placement.

Walls. The sun space should be separated from the main house by an insulated wall; a wall of thermal mass material, such as brick or concrete; or a combination of the two. To retain heat, the east wall, west wall, and floor should be insulated, moisture sealed, and

Active-solar systems are usually expensive to maintain, so seek simple solutions that have been used successfully in your area for a long time. Consult local solar water-heating contractors and your utility company for a locally appropriate design.

Solar thermal probably won't meet all your heating needs year-round, so couple your solar-heating system with a backup mechanical system.

These solar collectors provide active-solar heating to warm both the house and the domestic water supply.

SHOULD YOU UPGRADE OR REPLACE YOUR CURRENT HEATING EQUIPMENT?

If your present system is unsatisfactory or won't serve a planned addition, you can upgrade or replace it. Ask yourself the following questions.

air sealed. If the sun space is an addition or a porch conversion, carefully air seal and weatherproof its junction with the main structure (Chapters 8 and 10).

Thermal mass. If you want many hours of comfort in your sun space, provide thermal mass to keep it from overheating. If you want a lot of very warm air for the house toward the end of a sunny day, use little or no thermal mass so the sun space will overheat and act as a temporary furnace. As long as the sun space can be sealed off from the main living space, you can keep it from overheating the house by day or cooling it too much by night.

Plenty of south-facing glass in the walls and thermal mass in the floor make this sun space a solar heat collector for the whole house.

Ventilation. For winter warmth, the sun space should have openings to the main house. Locate vents (with dampers) high and low on the common wall, separated by at least 8 feet if possible. For every 100 square feet of south glass, there should be about 3 square feet of unobstructed vent area near the ceiling and an equal amount near the floor. Close these vents any time the sun space is cooler than the adjacent rooms, or you risk losing more heat than you gain. Temperature-controlled motorized dampers and fans may be helpful.

You may prefer to ventilate the sun space using operable windows or French doors. Open double-hung windows at top and bottom to provide airflow high and low. For this type of ventilation, you need 10 square feet of free vent area for every 100 square feet of south glass.

For summer cooling, the sun space should have closable, airtight vents to the outdoors (operable windows work).

A low-wattage fan can help distribute sun space heat to the rest of the house in winter; an exhaust fan will help evacuate unwanted heat in summer.

Greenhouses. It's easy to imagine using a greenhouse attached to the house as a heat source. But a greenhouse rarely provides a house with much solar heating or cooling. Many plants have a limited temperature tolerance; they shade the floor; they need year-round direct sunlight; and they release moisture into the air. In addition, they need light from at least two directions. Greenhouses tend to develop mold because the plants give off moisture, so a greenhouse doesn't make a good living space. It won't help heat your house, either, since the plants absorb much of the heat and cool the space.

Use Home Energy Saver (hes.lbl.gov) to calculate how much energy and money you can save by changing your heating system and fuel choice.

Are Your Heating Bills Too High?

If you have high heating bills, you may be thinking about switching fuels—say, from electricity to gas. Resist that itch until you have investigated your home's insulation and airtightness (Chapters 7, 8, and 9). A new furnace or heat pump will waste energy if your home is poorly insulated and/or sealed.

Does Your System Keep the House Warm Enough?

If not, start by asking yourself these questions:

- Do you change or clean your furnace filter every one to three months? Some systems have a second filter near the unit that is rarely cleaned.
- Has someone mistakenly closed the damper on some supply *registers*?
- Is something partially blocking the return air register?
- Are cracks or gaps visible when you remove the registers and look inside? Can you see dirty duct insulation, which indicates leakage?

Next, closely inspect the air ducts. They should be sealed and insulated, unless they are within your house's conditioned space. Sometimes—usually near the furnace—air ducts have internal dampers. Make sure these are fully open.

Are There Cold Areas?

Get a home performance assessment and upgrade your insulation and air sealing as needed. If you still have cold spots, ask your home energy or HVAC pro if your existing heating system can be extended to warm those cold spots. If not, you may be able to install a separate system for a small area.

Do You Really Need a Whole New System?

If you have extensive ductwork or hydronic tubing in good shape, you might just replace the central unit with a more efficient model. But if the ducts or tubes are in bad shape, or if insulating and repairing them is difficult, you may want a different type of system. If you have one of the following systems, you should seriously consider replacing it.

Electric radiant-ceiling heat. This system yields cold feet, stagnant air, and high humidity. Hot air stays at the ceiling, and cold air lingers at the floor, providing little warmth. The one advantage is that each room usually has its own thermostat, which encourages *zoning*, allowing you to set the temperature of each room individually. If you aren't ready to replace an electric radiant ceiling, emphasize air sealing, insulation, passive-solar heating, and room-by-room heating, so you won't need this inefficient heat source often.

Electric baseboard heaters. If you're doing a deep energy retrofit (Chapter 4), you'll have little need for heating; electric baseboards may be appropriate because they cost so little. Otherwise, you can do better. The high energy use, the smell of frying dust, the ticking sound of a warming heater, the fire danger if a toy or blanket contacts the heating coils—all can be avoided.

✖ DANGER ZONE: IS YOUR HEATING EQUIPMENT WORKING CORRECTLY?

Any heating device needs occasional maintenance, but some cases are urgent. Furnaces and boilers that burn gas, propane, or oil need reliable combustion air and unimpeded exhaust of combustion products. Burners need cleaning to avoid producing deadly CO. A cracked furnace heat exchanger can introduce CO into your home. If you smell natural gas, propane, or heating oil in your furnace room, call your utility or fuel supplier immediately.

Consider scheduling annual system tune-ups until you are confident your equipment is working correctly and safely. Your utility company or a BPI-certified heating inspector can provide good advice.

Open fireplace. Unless you've installed a duct to carry outdoor air to your fireplace, you're sending heated indoor air up the chimney. Even with a special duct, an open fireplace is not for serious heating. Fireplaces are delightful, but they waste energy and pollute your neighborhood. If you want to keep the chimney and hearth, install a highly efficient woodstove, pellet stove, or *direct-vent* (outside intake and exhaust air) gas insert.

Oil furnace. Replace an oil furnace with a higher-efficiency condensing gas furnace or heat pump. Have your HVAC contractor determine whether any part of your duct system is salvageable. Be sure to include ductwork to bring outdoor combustion air directly to your new furnace. You'll get better fuel efficiency and cleaner furnace exhaust.

Electric furnace. Replace with a heat pump to reduce winter electric bills and provide summer air conditioning.

TO SELECT A NEW HEATING SYSTEM

If you are replacing an existing heating appliance with a new one of the same type, invest in the most efficient model available to minimize energy use and operating cost. If you're considering a new type of heating system, compare systems for up-front cost, energy efficiency, noise, space requirements, and other important features, as shown in Table 13.01.

The cost of a heating system includes the cost of the unit, installation, and upgrading or repairing the distribution and ventilation systems, as well as operating cost. Over the life of the equipment, the highest of these is usually the operating cost. Long after you've made the last payment on the system, energy bills keep coming in as fuel costs rise.

Consider how much heating capacity you really need. If you're adding on to your house, don't assume you'll need a larger system. If you're not adding on, don't just get the same-size equipment you now have. Many contractors put in oversized equipment to compensate for leaky, poorly insulated houses. Insulate and air seal before you have your heating system sized, or you'll pay more than necessary—up front and every month.

To avoid buying a too-big system, get a home performance assessment (Chapter 4) to decide which improvements to make *before* choosing a new heating system. Then have an HVAC professional calculate how much heat your house needs. Ask to see the load calculations, and look for *Manual J* and *Manual D* on these sheets—the industry standards for calculating heating and cooling loads and designing duct systems.

THE THERMOSTAT IS IN CONTROL

A faulty thermostat may be making your home uncomfortably cold or hot, adding to your fuel bill. Old thermostats can lose their accuracy, misreading temperature settings and turning the heat on or off at the wrong time. A service representative can recalibrate and clean your old thermostat, but it might be smarter to buy a new one with a few extra energy-saving controls.

A programmable thermostat lets you automatically heat the house only when needed, potentially saving fuel.

Setback and *programmable thermostats* let you set a daily or weekly schedule for your heating system. You can warm the house only when needed, and turn down the heat when you're sleeping or away. Some more-expensive models can be programmed for every day of the week. A weekday/weekend setting may be enough to suit your family's lifestyle, but look for a model with a manual override so you can change it easily when you are home unexpectedly. Choose one that reverts to the programmed setting after the override period, in case you forget to reset it. Note: Turning a thermostat higher than the desired temperature will not warm the house faster and will probably overheat it.

Placement is important. Mount the thermostat about 5 feet above floor level, in the main living area and away from the kitchen. Do not place it near an incandescent light, a TV, or another heat-producing appliance. Avoid any spot that can trick the temperature sensors: in a draft or direct sunlight; behind a door or in a closet; by a radiator or a warm-air supply grille; or on an uninsulated exterior wall, a wall covering pipes or flues, or a wall near an exterior door or beneath stairs, where vibrations can interfere with accuracy. If you have a central return duct on a forced-air system, look above or near this return duct for a good spot.

TABLE 13.01: COMPARING RESIDENTIAL HEATING SYSTEMS

System	Space and Equipment Required	Zones	Air Quality Control	Air-Conditioned Cooling	
Central Forced-Air	Extensive ductwork[†] and interior unit, including fan	1 per unit[†]	Can have air filtration added, disperses humidity	Compatible	
Furnace (gas or propane)	Plus combustion air, flue, condensate drain	1 per unit	Same as above	Requires separate adjacent unit	
Electric airsource heat pump	Plus outdoor unit needs breathing space, drain, refrigerant loop to indoors	1 per unit	Same as above	Includes cooling	
Electric ground source heat pump	Plus extensive network of piping loop to trenches or wells	1 per unit	Same as above	Includes cooling	
Central Hydronic	Boiler, pump, manifold, and loop of pipes or tubing	Multiple	None	Separate A/C system required	
In-floor	Tubes in or under floor	Multiple	None	Separate A/C system required	
Baseboard	Pipes to/from baseboard radiators	Multiple	None	Separate A/C system required	
Room-by-Room	Varies with unit; see below				
Portable electric radiator	Standard electrical outlet	1 per unit	None	NA	
Direct-vent gas wall heater	Small wall area	1 per unit	None	NA	
Gas direct-vent fireplace	Vent to outside, includes combustion air	1	None	None	
Woodstove or pellet	Flue, combustion air vent, hearth, wood storage	1	None	None	
Ductless mini-split heat pump	Outdoor unit needs breathing space, drain, refrigerant loop to indoors	Multiple	Filters air, disperses humidity	Includes cooling	
In-wall gas heater	Vent to outside	1	None	None	
In-wall *electric-resistance* heater	Space within wall; 240V circuits	1	None	None	
Electric-resistance baseboard	240V circuits	Multiple	None	None	
Passive solar	South windows, extensive interior thermal-mass surface	1 per room	None	None	

*These are estimates. The specifics of your home will determine actual cost. †Ductwork can be minimized by insulating and tightening the envelope

Heating Speed	Noise	Relative Purchase Cost*	Relative Energy Efficiency
Fast	Fan, through ducts (minimized by good design)	See below	See below
Fast	Same as above	Medium	Medium
Medium	Outdoor unit noisy (except for newer high-performance units)	High	High
Medium	Fan, plus compressor	Very high	Very high
Medium	Pump, water hammer	See below	See below
Medium	Pump, water hammer	High	Medium
Medium	Pump, water hammer	Medium	Medium
Fast	None	Low	Medium
Fast	Low, depending on fan type	Medium	Medium to high
Medium	Fan in room	Low	Low
Medium	Crackling fire, possible stove circulating fan	Medium	Medium
Fast	Outdoor unit noisy (except for newer high-performance units); indoor fans somewhat noisy	High	High
Fast	Fan in room	Low	Medium
Fast	Fan in room	Low	Medium
Fast	Tick-tick	Low	Medium
Slow	None	Medium	High

and by reducing the number and size of ducts.   ‡Motorized dampers can serve more than one zone.

WARMTH FOR A COOL BASEMENT

Cathy and Vaughan's Portland, Oregon, home has two floors and a full basement, where a natural-gas furnace provides some warmth at one end. The other end of the basement was recently converted to a guest room with a carpet, couches, and a TV. It was quiet, cool in summer, but cold in winter.

To heat the guest room, Cathy and Vaughan installed a direct-vent gas fireplace on an exterior wall, between the guest bed and the TV area. The guests flip a wall switch beside the fireplace and flames spring up. Once the heat builds, a fan automatically circulates heat within the room. Guests must remember to turn off the switch, at which point the flames die; but the fan continues to run until there is little residual heat left. The cozy warmth from the gas fireplace turned an area seldom used in winter into an inviting space.

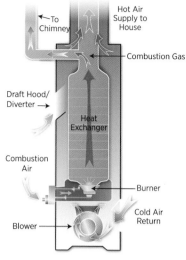

Conventional Gas Furnace

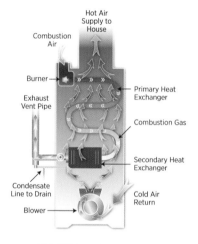

High-Efficiency Gas Furnace

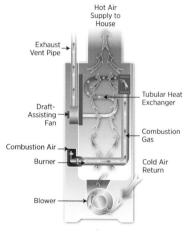

Mid-Efficiency Gas Furnace

WHY SELECT A FORCED-AIR SYSTEM?

A forced-air heating system includes a heat source (usually a furnace or heat pump), a fan, and a duct system with openings serving every room. It also needs a duct to return air to the heat source for reheating. A forced-air system requires considerably more space than most other heating systems.

The fan forces air through ducts and supply grilles. Registers are grilles with dampers that can be closed. After the warmed air disperses and cools, it must be returned to the heat source, which requires separate return air ductwork and usually one or two large return grilles.

Where winter heating is more demanding than summer cooling, supply registers are usually located in the floor, because warm air rises naturally. The supply ductwork is thus often contained in a crawl space or basement.

Forced-air systems have several advantages: the fan and ducts distribute heat, minimizing cold spots. Water vapor from cooking, bathing, and perspiration can be dispersed. And air filtration can be added.

For your heat source, consider whether a furnace or a heat pump better meets your needs. Furnaces supply only heat, while heat pumps provide cooled air in summer as well. Furnaces are usually fired by either natural gas or propane. Electric furnaces are inefficient; a heat pump is a better choice if gas is unavailable.

Furnaces

Gas, propane, or oil furnaces require an exhaust flue, and should have a duct to supply outdoor combustion air. While it's thermally advantageous to place the furnace within the house's heated space, this is sometimes prohibited by the building code. Look for a *sealed combustion* furnace; these draw air from and expel combustion products to the outside.

Ask your contractor for high-efficiency equipment. A condensing furnace with about 95% *AFUE (annual fuel utilization efficiency)* is top-drawer; it recaptures some of the heat wasted in traditional systems by condensing water vapor from the combustion gases before they go up the chimney.

The filter at the furnace should be cleaned or replaced regularly, preferably monthly. Forced-air systems can be expensive to maintain if you don't keep up with routine preventive maintenance.

Heat Pumps

A heat pump works like an A/C in reverse; it extracts heat from the outdoor air, earth, or water to warm your house. Even in winter, there is always some heat to be extracted. Efficiency is given as *HSPF (heating seasonal performance factor)* or *COP (coefficient of performance)*. The higher the number, the greater the efficiency; aim for an HSPF of 9 or higher. The most common complaint about heat pumps is that they need periodic maintenance.

There are two types of heat pump: air source and ground source (also known as geothermal or water source). Air source heat pumps are far more common. They consist of an outdoor unit that extracts heat from winter air and an indoor unit that delivers the heat.

A ground source heat pump has an extensive underground pipe loop through which fluid circulates to pick up heat from the earth. That heat is then extracted from the fluid and delivered into the home. The underground loop is laid out either in horizontal trenches or in a series of vertical wells, making the system prohibitively expensive for many homeowners. Ground source systems are often plagued by installation and sizing errors, and their rated performance does not include the energy required for ground loop pumping, making them appear to be more efficient than they are.

Air source systems are far less expensive to install, but the outdoor unit can be noisy, so be careful where you locate it. Newer high-end heat pumps are much quieter; ask your contractor for the sone rating on the pump you're considering. A heat pump must work harder to glean heat from very cold air than from the ground, so expect lower efficiency from an air source system. Where winters are very cold, a ground source heat pump may be better.

If you live in a very cold climate, you will need a backup heat source. One common choice is electric-resistance coils integrated with the system, but these can cause electricity consumption to skyrocket in really cold weather. A more energy-efficient option is an inline "gas pack" or "dual-fuel" system, which adds a gas coil to the duct system. Consult your HVAC pro.

The ductless *mini-split* is a type of heat pump that can be appropriate for an addition or a whole house (see room-by-room systems).

Ducts

Ductwork must be sealed and insulated. Provide enough space for duct insulation and for access to check on the condition of duct insulation and sealing. If you can incorporate the ductwork within the heated space (for example, in a dropped ceiling or by insulating at the roof rather than the attic floor—Chapter 10), you use less insulation. Ducts gather dust and debris, so they should be cleaned by professionals every few years (especially true for return ducts in the floor).

WHY SELECT A HYDRONIC SYSTEM?

A central hydronic system is one type of radiant-heating system. It includes a heat source (a boiler or a heat pump), a pump, a *manifold,* and a distribution loop to carry hot fluid throughout the home and back to the heat source. Hydronic systems generally cost more than forced-air systems, but they're low maintenance; they lose less heat than ducted systems; and they don't take up a lot of space.

The outdoor unit of an air source heat pump can be noisy; locate it with care.

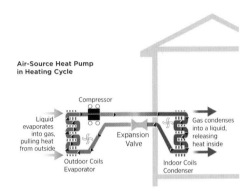

Air source heat pump.

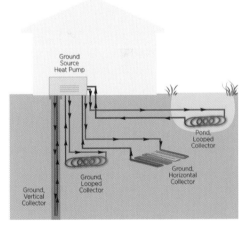

Ground source heat pump system.

Getting It Hot

The boiler that heats the circulating fluid can be fired by gas, propane, or oil; by a heat pump; via solar preheating; or by (highly energy-inefficient) electric resistance. The pump forces hot fluid from the boiler to a manifold, which separates the delivery system into zones. Each zone is controlled by its own thermostat, making it possible to fine-tune heat delivery.

Gas, propane, or oil boilers require an exhaust flue, and should be provided with combustion air ducted directly from the outdoors; aim for a sealed-combustion unit. Ask your contractor for a high-efficiency boiler. As with a furnace, it is a thermal advantage to place the boiler within the house's heated space, but codes sometimes prohibit this.

Tubing

Today it's common to use cross-linked polyethylene (PEX) tubing to circulate the heated fluid, turning the whole floor into a radiator. This keeps the residents' feet warm and gently induces air movement. The tubing can be within a concrete slab or beneath a wood floor. Because a concrete slab has thermal mass, the heat from the tubes lingers longer, but the concrete also takes longer to heat up. Tubes within concrete are extremely expensive to repair, unlike tubes beneath wood floors. Wood flooring, however, slows the heating response, and repairs to wood floors can damage the tubes.

Some flooring materials aren't warrantied over radiant-heating systems. Heated floors must be especially well insulated from below and along any edges exposed to the outdoors.

Baseboard Radiators

If wall-to-wall carpeting is a must, consider hydronic baseboard radiators instead. These will affect furniture arrangements (if you block a radiator, you won't feel the heat) and will need periodic cleaning. Installing baseboard radiators is less complicated than replacing an entire floor.

WHY SELECT A ROOM-BY-ROOM SYSTEM?

The biggest advantage of the room-by-room approach is easy zoning; each heating device is individually controlled. It can also be a good choice for an addition if extending your existing system isn't an option.

With room-by-room systems, there is usually no distribution heat loss, and they don't have energy-consuming fans or pumps. They are flexible and easily adapted to new layouts—and if one unit fails, you still have heat elsewhere.

Portable electric radiators can be a cheap, quick way to heat a room. The best ones are filled with fluid, so they heat up and cool down slowly. They don't need a special outlet, but they will put a big demand on an electrical circuit; if you need the radiator on full-time, a built-in solution is better. There are also gas-, propane-, and kerosene-fired portable heaters, but these must be vented to the outside or the CO they can produce will be a deadly threat.

Direct-vent gas wall heaters may be appropriate for a one-room addition if your central system can't easily be extended. These sealed-combustion units mount on an outside wall, need no ductwork, and can be very energy efficient. Some come with fans, and some provide air conditioning.

Natural-gas fireplaces are not particularly energy efficient. The energy-saving models are direct-vent, meaning they're ducted to the exterior, have exterior air intake, have sealed glass doors, and are controlled by an electric switch. A fan moves the warmed air into the room.

A **woodstove** is a good choice for sensory appeal, and a well-built stove is fairly efficient. But it's also very high maintenance, and the chimney, outdoor air ducts, hearth, and firewood storage take up space.

As is true of other radiant-heat sources, wherever you can see the stove, you can feel its heat; the closer you are, the warmer you feel. But if you can't see the stove, you can't feel the heat, which influences furniture placement. Woodstoves also present a significant fire hazard. That said, adding a very efficient wood-burning insert (with external combustion) to an old fireplace is an excellent choice, provided you have easy access to firewood. Correct installation is crucial for safety and efficiency.

Ductless heat pumps, or mini-splits, have an outside unit, often called the *condenser*, and as many as four inside units that deliver winter heat and summer cooling. Each room can have its own thermostat, and they save a lot of space by eliminating ducts. However, a separate indoor unit must be installed in each room. Mini-splits are highly visible, they take up space, and the fan is audible—probably more audible than the central fan of a ducted heat pump system. Having several units places limits on where you can put the furniture. Mini-splits can be hung from the ceiling, recessed in a suspended ceiling, or mounted on walls or floors. The controller and installation are currently the weak links in a mini-split system. Make sure the installer *commissions* the control system in both the heating and the cooling mode.

In a hydronic radiant-floor heating system, PEX tubing carries the fluid heated by the boiler from the manifold in the wall to the various heating zones. In this case, a lightweight concrete slab will be poured over the installed tubing.

This direct-vent gas wall heater mounts against an outside wall and needs no ductwork; it can be an efficient heat source for an addition or a cold room.

A ductless heat pump eliminates the heat loss and space use of ducts, but each room must have its own unit.

For a natural-gas fireplace, look for a direct-vent model with exterior air intake, sealed glass doors, and an electric switch.

HEATING PROJECTS YOU CAN DO TODAY:

- Maintain your current heating system properly: clean registers, baseboards, or indoor units; clean or change filters.
- Get a home performance assessment (Chapter 4).
- Consider how you can improve access to winter sun.
- Install a programmable thermostat.
- Start searching for a good HVAC contractor.
- Turn down your thermostat and wear a sweater.

HEATING PROJECTS THAT WILL TAKE MORE TIME:

- Add windows and thermal mass for passive-solar heating.
- Upgrade insulation and air sealing.
- If you have ducts, have them cleaned, sealed, and insulated.
- Select and install a new high-efficiency heating system.

A woodstove takes up space, requires a source of fuel, and places constraints on adjacent decor and furniture placement—but there's nothing quite like gazing into the flames.

RESOURCES

Print

Forced Hot Air Furnaces: Troubleshooting and Repair. Roger Vizi, McGraw-Hill, 1999

Modern Hydronic Heating: For Residential and Light Commercial Buildings. John Siegenthaler, Delmar Cengage, 2012

Passive Solar Architecture: Heating, Cooling, Ventilation, Daylighting and More Using Natural Flows. David A. Bainbridge and Ken Haggard, Chelsea Green, 2011

The Passive Solar Energy Book. Edward Mazria, Rodale Press, 1980

Online

ENERGY STAR: energystar.gov/index.cfm?c=heat_cool.pr_hvac

Heating Help: heatinghelp.com

Sun Path Chart Program: solardata.uoregon.edu/SunChartProgram.php

Tree Guide: arborday.org/trees/treeguide/index.cfm

U.S. Department of Energy/Energy Efficiency and Renewable Energy:

- *Energy Renovations: HVAC: A Guide for Contractors to Share with Homeowners.* Building America Best Practices Series, vol. 14, 2011: buildingamerica.gov
- Heating Systems: eere.energy.gov/basics/buildings/heating_systems.html
- Heat Pump Systems: eere.energy.gov/basics/buildings/heat_pump_systems.html
- Passive-Solar Design: eere.energy.gov/basics/buildings/passive_solar_design.html
- Supporting Equipment for Heating and Cooling Systems: eere.energy.gov/basics/buildings/supporting_equipment.html

Chapter 14

COOLING: DON'T SWEAT IT IN SUMMER

What can a better cooling strategy do for you? It can

- keep the sun from overheating your home in summer;
- optimize nature's cooling with breezes and shade; and
- provide mechanical cooling without burning up your budget.

If you need AC to feel comfortable in summer, you may wonder:

- Is there any way to make air conditioning cost less?
- How can I choose the best A/C for my house?
- Do I have to feel so cut off from the outdoors?
- Is it possible to feel cool without air conditioning?

Before we had air conditioning, people got by with well-placed insulation, shade, access to breeze, pleasant outdoor rooms, and doing heavier work during cooler hours. If your area has moderate summer temperatures, you could be comfortable without air conditioning by applying these principles.

To save money on cooling, first consider the need for a well-insulated envelope (Chapter 9) and adequate ventilation (Chapter 12). Cooling and heating often involve similar mechanical systems, so also read Chapter 13.

If your climate requires mechanical cooling, apply the principles of natural cooling to lower your cooling bills.

WORK WITH NATURE FOR COOLING

The primary goal in cooling is to avoid experiencing heat. Keep the sun out, let cool breezes in, turn off your lights and appliances, and seek the coolest spot indoors or out. The summer sun heats your house on the east side in the morning; the south side at midday; the west side in the afternoon and evening; and the roof all day long.

Stay Cool in the Shade

Shading is one of the best ways to avoid the sun's heat. Windows are more vulnerable to summer sun than walls or roofs; they account for 40–50% of a home's unwanted heat. Shading outside these windows stops the sun before it strikes the glass (Chapter 7).

COOLING BY CLIMATE ZONE

The climate where you live will determine the best cooling strategies for you:

- In **hot-humid** areas, moist air slows the evaporation of sweat, making it difficult for our bodies to lose heat. Mechanical air conditioning using the refrigeration cycle is the main solution. Natural, non-mechanical strategies may help in spring and fall, and lessen your need for mechanical cooling in summer.

- In **hot-dry** areas, evaporative coolers and natural strategies might keep you comfortable most of the time. Refrigerative air conditioning can take you through the worst periods, such as more humid spells.

- In **moderate** and **mixed** areas, all cooling strategies are options. The more moderate your summer, the more the natural strategies will work for you.

Use Home Energy Saver (hes.lbl.gov) to calculate how much energy and money you can save by changing your cooling system and house features.

Overhangs, Awnings, Blinds, Screens

At south windows, awnings or long roof overhangs can block the high-noon summer sun. For east and west windows, awnings, exterior roll blinds, or shade screens can be effective. If you also have a roof overhang, you might be able to preserve the view by installing a shade screen over the lower half of the window, while the overhang protects the upper part. Exterior blinds and screens will probably need to be secured against strong winds, and should be easily removable for cleaning.

Interior blinds provide some shading, but when the sun penetrates the glass, its heat has already entered your home. However, interior blinds are easier to maintain, aren't buffeted by winds, and stay much cleaner. They are also easy to control from inside, and they bounce sunlight up toward the ceiling rather than into your eyes. The exterior side of the blind should be white, to reflect the sunlight outward.

Plants

Shrubs and trees are a beautiful way to shade windows. Keep in mind:

- Shrubs will block the very low sun in the morning or evening, but they may block views and breezes as well; weigh your options.
- The farther a shrub is from the window, the taller it must be to shade that window. The closer it is to the house, the more likely it is to damage the foundation or the plumbing.
- Shrubs on the south side will block some reflected light, but they will not block the high, intense noonday sun.

Trees can cast shade over a wide area, creating a cooler *microclimate* below them. Deciduous trees allow some winter sun to penetrate. Trees and shrubs emit water vapor, which lowers the air temperature near them while raising the humidity (not desirable in humid climates).

It's usually easier to add an awning to block the midday sun's heat than to extend an overhang.

Deciduous trees help to create a cool zone by providing shade and emitting water vapor.

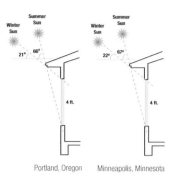
Sun angle and overhang recommendations for windows in representative cities

Portland, Oregon   Minneapolis, Minnesota

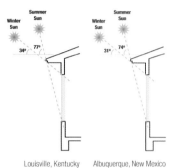
Louisville, Kentucky   Albuquerque, New Mexico

COOL ROOFS

Midday summer sun shining on the roof is a major source of unwanted heat, but insulation and a radiant barrier can reduce your roof's contribution to your energy bill. Roof insulation reduces the conduction of solar heat into your house (Chapter 9). A radiant barrier is a very shiny surface that reflects radiant heat; it can be effective in hot climates, but it is often difficult to install in an existing attic (Chapter 10).

If you don't have wide, spreading shade trees near your home, consider installing a white or very light roofing material next time your roof needs to be replaced. However, if your winters are far worse than your summers, this will be counterproductive, because it will also reflect away desirable winter warmth.

Trellises

Trellises act like living awnings and are especially effective for shading. They can support deciduous vines that keep their leaves until autumn's cool weather, then stay leafless until spring's warm weather. This is especially important for shading south windows; the sun's path is identical at the equinoxes, but September is usually warm, while March is usually cool.

A trellis can't be adjusted on a daily or hourly basis, while an awning can. A hot spell after leaves have fallen in October, or a cold spell after leaves have appeared in May, can leave you without the shade or sunshine you want.

A trellis shading south windows needs to be high enough to allow winter sun to fully strike the window, and deep enough to fully shade the window in summer. This also applies to roof overhangs. Table 14.01 shows the dimensions necessary to provide complete south window shading.

A trellis can support a deciduous vine for shade, beauty, and even food.

A Refreshing Breeze

Cool breezes are often welcome—as long as they don't carry pollen or fumes. Moving air is beneficial in summer, because it helps our bodies lose heat by evaporating sweat, and by removing heat buildup from our homes.

Getting the breeze through your home is a four-step process:

1. Confirm that outside temperature is lower than inside. (Use a shaded indoor-outdoor thermometer at the window you use most often.)
2. Open windows on the wind inlet side.
3. Open windows on the opposite, or outlet, side.
4. Open any interior doors that restrict the flow between these openings.

Openings

How much window area do you need? Generally, both the windward side of your home (the side the wind hits) and the opposite (leeward) side should have a total openable window area of about 7% of the total floor area. Internal walls should have a similar open area to avoid obstructing airflow. (Close down your exterior openings as the wind speed increases or the outdoor temperature drops.) This type of cooling is called *cross-ventilation*.

It's good to have some ventilating windows high in the wall and some low. High windows let out the hot air that collects near the ceiling. Low windows allow the breeze to cool you directly.

Window type matters, too. Casement windows cranked entirely open admit nearly all the breeze. Double-hung, single-hung, and sliding windows admit about half the breeze, and awning windows admit about three-quarters. Screens reduce breeze velocity, so wash them often.

Landscaping

Does the wind usually come from one direction in hot weather? (If unsure, see Climate Consultant in Resources.) If so, you can use shrubs to direct

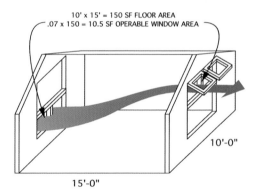

10' x 15' = 150 SF FLOOR AREA
.07 x 150 = 10.5 SF OPERABLE WINDOW AREA
10'-0"
15'-0"

For good cross-ventilation, the windward and leeward sides of your house (and intervening interior walls) should each have openings that are 7% of the floor area of the house.

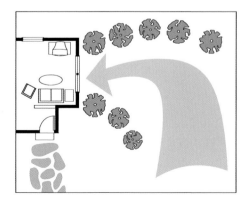

If the wind blows right past your windows, you can landscape to direct breezes for better natural cooling.

TABLE 14.01: SOUTH WINDOW SHADING: TRELLIS OR ROOF OVERHANG

Mild-Winter Climates (complete shade from March 26 to September 18)		
North Latitude	Bottom of Trellis Distance above South Window	Edge of Trellis Distance beyond South Window
28° (Corpus Christi, TX; Tampa, FL)	0.63x*	0.79x
32° (Tucson, AZ; El Paso, TX; Shreveport, LA; Savannah, GA)	0.66x	0.95x
36° (Las Vegas, NV)	0.66x	1.12x
Cold-Winter Climates (complete shade from May 12 to August 2, and complete sun from November 17 to January 25)		
North Latitude	Bottom of Trellis Distance above South Window	Edge of Trellis Distance beyond South Window
32° (San Diego, CA)	0.26x	0.33x
36° (Fresno, CA; Springfield, MO; Nashville, TN; Raleigh, NC)	0.30x	0.42x
40° (Reno, NV; Denver, CO; Peoria, IL; New York City, NY)	0.32x	0.54x
44° (Boise, ID; Rapid City, SD; Traverse City, MI; Burlington, VT)	0.33x	0.65x
48° (Seattle, WA; Duluth, MN; Montreal, QC	0.33x	0.76x

Table by John S. Reynolds, based on data from the National Renewable Energy Laboratory.
*x = height of south-facing window.

If you have a high window or an operable skylight, you can use the stack effect to exhaust hot air and pull in cooler air from nearby shaded outdoor areas.

breezes toward your windows. They can be planted in a V shape, spreading out from the windows that admit the breeze. If the wind strikes the opening at a diagonal, the shrubs just downwind of the opening can divert flow into the window.

No Breeze?

Warm air rises, so to let it out, open the windows highest in your house. Then open the lowest windows. The resulting airflow uses the stack effect, whereby outgoing hot air is replaced by incoming cool air from below. The highest opening should not face into the prevailing summer wind, or the warm air may be blown back down into the house.

IF YOU NEED MECHANICAL COOLING

When natural cooling just isn't enough, you have several options:

- simple fans to move room air or exhaust hot air;
- cooling units for individual rooms; and
- central A/C with a distribution system.

If your objective is to cool some spaces some of the time—a home office or living room by day, bedrooms by night—then smaller units may be a good choice. If the whole house needs long-term cooling, a central system is better.

Cooling with Fans

Sometimes a fan is all the boost you need to stay cool—and fans generally use much less electricity than A/C.

Why does moving air on your face feel so cool? In hot weather, our bodies try to dissipate heat by evaporation. The more we sweat, the faster we want that sweat to evaporate, and moving air aids evaporation. Because we're acutely conscious of anything that accumulates on our face, especially sweat, that fan on our face is especially sweet. Many ceiling fans are reversible, allowing you to choose whether to feel the moving air directly on your skin (downward flow) or more indirectly (upward flow).

Smaller desk fans are affordable, portable, and easy to direct. They can't cool an entire room, but they can make a personal workplace more comfortable, and they use very little energy. Variable-speed desk fans give you finer control, and can be set to rotate their direction of flow.

Exhaust fans can be set in an open window, surrounded by barriers to avoid readmitting the exhausted air. Avoid facing exhaust fans into the prevailing summer wind (Chapter 12).

Evaporative Coolers

If you live in a very dry climate with hot summers, the *evaporative cooler* (or *swamp cooler*) is a simple, relatively inexpensive way to cool. They use far less electricity than A/C. They also provide warmer, wetter, fresher air than A/C, so they must deliver more air to do the same job.

Most evaporative coolers blow air into the house via a single *diffuser* in the hall ceiling or a modest duct system in the attic. If you live in a mild, dry climate, this system can meet all your home's cooling needs.

An evaporative cooler consists of a fan, a water source, and a wet pad. A small pump circulates water from a built-in water reservoir to keep the pad wet. The fan draws hot, dry outside air through the wet pad, cooling and humidifying the air. This air is blown into the house, forcing the warmer house air out through open windows or a vent into the attic.

There are two basic types of evaporative cooler. Direct evaporative coolers move outside air through a wet pad directly into the house. Two-stage (also called indirect/direct) evaporative coolers are like two evaporative coolers in one. The first precools the air indirectly, so no humidity is added. The air then travels through the second cooler, where it is directly cooled. Because the precooled air can't hold much moisture, the result is cooler, drier air. Two-stage coolers are more expensive than direct evaporative coolers, but they perform better during extremely hot, dry days.

When the weather is warm, a fan can cool you down by creating a gentle breeze while using less electricity than an A/C.

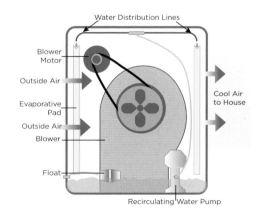

FANS COOL PEOPLE, NOT ROOMS

Fans cool us by increasing the evaporation of sweat, which in turn cools our skin. They should be turned off when no people are present, because their electric motors give off heat. The exception is an exhaust fan, which sends its motor heat out along with the hot air.

An evaporative cooler draws outside air through a wet pad to provide cooler, moister air—appropriate in hot, dry climates, and more energy efficient than an A/C.

TABLE 14.02: COMPARING RESIDENTIAL COOLING SYSTEMS

System	Space and Equipment Required	Zones	Air Quality Control	Humidity Control	Heating	Cooling Speed	Noise
Central Air, Using Refrigeration Cycle							
Electric air source heat pump	Extensive ductwork and indoor unit; outdoor unit needs breathing space, drain, refrigerant loop to indoors unit	1	Filters and recycles most of indoor air	Dehumidifies when high humidity	Compatible	Fast	Outdoor unit noisy, indoor central fan
Electric ground source heat pump	Extensive ductwork and indoor unit; extensive network of piping loop to trenches or wells	1	Filters and recycles most of indoor air	Dehumidifies when high humidity	Compatible	Fast	Outdoor unit noisy, indoor central fan
Cooling coils added to furnace	Extensive ductwork; space needed at supply outlet of furnace; outdoor unit needs breathing space, drain, refrigerant loop to indoor unit	1	Filters and recycles most of indoor air	Dehumidifies when high humidity	Furnace provides	Fast	Outdoor unit noisy, indoor central fan
Ductless mini-split heat pump	Outdoor unit needs breathing space, drain, refrigerant loop to each indoor unit	Multiple	Filters and recycles most of indoor air	Dehumidifies when high humidity	Compatible	Fast	Outdoor unit noisy, fan in each room
Room-by-Room							
Room air conditioner	Sits in window or in exterior wall; needs drain	1	Filters and recycles most of indoor air	Dehumidifies when high humidity	No, unless it's a heat pump	Fast	Very noisy, fan and compressor
Evaporative Cooler							
Direct	Outdoor unit needs breathing space, drain, water supply line	1	All fresh air, mild filtering	None; raises humidity	None	Medium	Fan
Indirect	Outdoor unit needs breathing space, drain, water supply line	1	All fresh air, mild filtering	Little or none	None	Medium	Fan
Low-Tech Alternatives							
Whole-house fan	Fan discharge opening, with protective cover	1	All fresh air, mild filtering	None	None	Slow	Fan
Breeze	Window openings on opposite exterior walls, and openings in all appropriate interior walls	1	All fresh air, no filtering	None	None	Slow	Outdoor sounds
Ceiling fan	Electric line to fan	1	No fresh air, no filtering	None	None	Slow	Fan

Evaporative coolers use much more water than refrigeration A/Cs. Using water heavy in minerals means frequently replacing the pads. Unfortunately, the best climates for evaporative cooling are usually the ones with the least available water, and that water is often mineral rich. In some water-starved cities, evaporative coolers for residences are illegal.

Evaporative coolers also use water to flush out mineral buildup. This can be done in one of two ways. A bleed-off can drain a small amount of water from the cooler whenever it is running. Or a sump dump can evacuate the water from the reservoir every half hour or so; this is more effective than a bleed-off system, because it discharges not only brackish water but also some of the dirt that collects in the reservoir.

Most evaporative coolers are mounted on the roof and have a blower that discharges cool air out the bottom. However, foot traffic and water leaks can damage the roof. Rooftop coolers also produce slightly warmer air, because they are directly exposed to sunlight. The easiest installation to maintain is a ground-mounted cooler that discharges out the top or the side. Put the cooler on the north side of the house for shade.

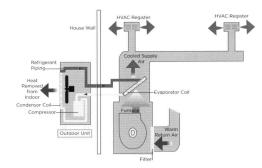

A central A/C functions much like a refrigerator, transferring heat from indoors to outdoors for greater indoor comfort in hot weather.

Air Conditioners

In areas with hot, humid summers, the A/C excels. It transfers heat from the air inside the house to the air outside. An A/C consists of a *compressor*, a condenser, an evaporator, refrigerant lines, a blower fan, and, for a central A/C, ductwork to distribute cooled air through the house. A refrigerant transports the heat from the evaporator coil inside to the condenser coil outside. In fact, an A/C functions much like a refrigerator.

Heat pumps and A/Cs have identical components, but the heat pump has a reversing valve that allows it to supply either heating or cooling. If your home is heated by a heat pump, your A/C is built into that system.

A mini-split is a type of heat pump in which refrigerant loops connect an air handler in each zone with the outdoor compressor/evaporator, eliminating the need for ducts (Chapter 13).

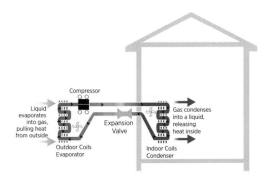

HEAT PUMP IN HEATING MODE

Ready for a New A/C?

The efficiency of a room A/C is measured by its *energy efficiency ratio (EER)*—the ratio of the energy the unit removes from the air to the electrical energy it uses. A system with a high EER may cost more, but your bills will be lower. Look for the ENERGY STAR label (Chapter 4).

The efficiency of a central A/C is measured by its *seasonal energy efficiency ratio (SEER)*. SEER indicates the cooling output in Btu during a typical cooling season, divided by the total electric energy input in *watt-hours* during that same period. A/Cs sold in the 1970s and early 1980s had SEERs of about 6. Today you can buy an A/C with a SEER of 18 or higher. The higher the SEER rating, the more energy efficient—and the purchase price will be offset by lower electric bills. Again, look for the ENERGY STAR label.

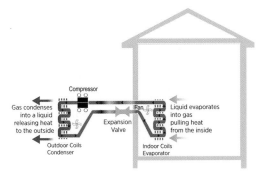

HEAT PUMP IN COOLING MODE

A heat pump behaves like an A/C in summer, but can reverse its function and also provide heat in winter.

EVAPORATIVE COOLER TIPS

- Get a model with a two-speed blower, allowing the cooler to operate often in more-efficient low-speed mode.
- Be sure the cooler inlet is 10 feet away from, and 3 feet below, plumbing vents, gas flues, clothes dryer vents, and any exhaust fan vents.
- On cool evenings, turn off the water supply while running the fan. It will then serve as a whole-house fan.
- Leave a high window or large vent open so that hot air can escape while the cooler is operating.
- Replace the pads every year or two. Provide a minimum of 3 feet of clearance on any side of the cooler that requires access for maintenance, such as for cleaning and replacing pads.
- Provide a ground-level, accessible water shutoff for rooftop installation. If your cooler leaks, you won't have to run around looking for a ladder.
- Provide an electrical disconnect near the cooler to facilitate safe maintenance (better units come with one).

Air-conditioning capacity is expressed in *tons*. A ton equals just a little more than 12,000 Btu per hour of A/C capacity and is approximately the amount of cooling you'd get from melting a ton of ice.

Chris and Emily Boniface planted a dogwood tree to the southwest of their house for future natural cooling.

Contractors often size A/Cs 0.5–1.5 tons larger than necessary, to make sure you have plenty of cooling power. But correctly sizing an A/C can save you money, because running a smaller unit steadily for a longer time is more energy efficient than running a more powerful unit that turns on and off frequently. Having a correctly sized unit can also reduce demand on the *electrical grid* during the hottest afternoons (Chapter 17).

To avoid buying an oversized A/C, have your contractor measure your house, take into account the window area and the direction the house faces, and measure insulation levels. These data are entered into formulas to calculate the needed cooling. Ask your contractor to show you his or her ACCA *Manual J* calculations, and make sure the A/C recommended by the calculations is the same size as the one the contractor wants to sell you.

Another important consideration is the A/C's ability to remove moisture from the air. If you have hot, humid summers, ask your contractor for an A/C with an evaporator coil that has a *sensible heat ratio (SHR)* of 0.75 or lower. This means that 25% of the coil's capacity is used for humidity control. The lower the SHR, the more of the coil's capacity is being used to control humidity.

THINGS TO KEEP IN MIND ABOUT COOLING

- For strong, healthy people, cooling is a comfort issue. For vulnerable people, it can become a survival issue.
- Climate change means that cooling strategies that work in your region now may not be adequate in the future. With temperatures expected to increase and hot-dry and hot-humid climate zones expected to expand, you may want to be prepared to handle greater cooling challenges.
- Most economic projections predict increasing energy costs in the future, so you'll want to be especially careful to cool your home in energy-efficient ways.
- Because much of our electricity is generated by burning fossil fuels, which contribute to greenhouse gases, energy efficiency can also lessen your contribution to climate change.

It's also important that the condenser and the evaporator coil be matched in capacity. Some firms install mismatched equipment—for example, a 3-ton condenser (outdoor unit) with a 3.5- or 4-ton evaporator coil (indoor unit). This is not advised; the air delivered is likely to be warmer and more moist than you want it, since it will not be sufficiently dehumidified.

Troubleshooting and Maintenance

If your A/C isn't old enough to replace, but it isn't working well, there are several ways to increase its efficiency. If some rooms cool fairly rapidly, and others never cool, your problem is probably in the ductwork; fix leaks and insulate. Replacing equipment won't fix this problem.

Another straightforward fix is to increase the flow of return air to the A/C by adding a second return air grille and duct. Many A/Cs don't get all the return air they require, decreasing efficiency.

If cooling is inadequate throughout your home, look at maintenance. Do you clean the filters on the manufacturer's recommended schedule? A leaky or inefficient compressor is also a possible culprit. Another problem might be leaking refrigerant; have your contractor check to make sure your refrigerant level is where it should be.

Extending an Existing Air-Conditioning System

If you have central air conditioning, and you're adding space to your house, perhaps you can simply add another duct run to the addition. Duct additions—even those as simple as a single new run—require an understanding of duct geometry and airflows, proper installation, sealing, and balancing, so have an HVAC contractor figure out what will work for you.

Using a Room A/C in an Addition

Some of the cooling energy in central systems is wasted via air friction in ducts, making the fan work harder. Room A/Cs don't have ductwork, but the units themselves are generally less efficient than central A/Cs. The strength of room A/Cs is that they let you cool just the area you're using. Look at the EnergyGuide label to compare the energy efficiency of different models.

If you get a window A/C, take it out of the window and store it in winter to prevent air from leaking in and out around it. If you get a wall A/C, insulate it and cover it inside and out for the winter, sealing the cover to the wall.

Adding an A/C to Your Furnace

If you have a furnace and want to add an A/C, check to see if you have sufficient space next to the furnace. The indoor portion of the A/C needs to sit between the furnace and the supply ductwork. This will probably require a clearance of about 3 feet. You will also need a new heating-and-cooling thermostat. The outdoor unit needs room to discharge hot air and should be located where the noise it creates will cause the least annoyance. If you

WILL A WHOLE-HOUSE FAN HELP?

Until recently, whole-house fans were considered a good way to cool a house at night by exhausting indoor warm air, to be replaced by cool night air. However, whole-house fans turn out to be a net negative factor because the cool night air often introduces humidity, causing the dehumidifier to work harder. Even in dry climates, the large hole cut for the fan is less insulated than the surrounding roof or wall and often leaks air, causing greater heat transfer than the fan itself justifies.

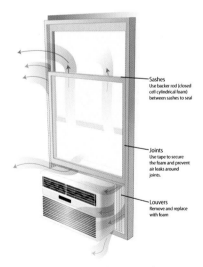

Sashes
Use backer rod (closed cell cylindrical foam) between sashes to seal

Joints
Use tape to secure the foam and prevent air leaks around joints.

Louvers
Remove and replace with foam

Be sure to seal air leaks around a room A/C to increase comfort and keep cooling costs down. Illustration by Marjorie Schott, National Renewable Energy Laboratory.

also plan to replace your furnace and space is tight, you could consider buying a shorter low-boy furnace—or a heat pump.

COOLING PROJECTS YOU CAN DO TODAY:

- Do your basic cleaning and maintenance.
- Provide shade for your windows, preferably on the exterior.
- Check windows and interior openings for access to breezes.
- Get a home performance assessment.

COOLING PROJECTS THAT WILL TAKE MORE TIME:

- Add or remove plantings to improve shading and redirect breezes.
- If needed, shop for a fan, evaporative cooler, or A/C.
- Investigate control systems for windows, shades, fans, and other equipment.
- Follow through on your home performance assessment.

RESOURCES

Print

Homeowner's Guide to Window Air Conditioner Installation for Efficiency and Comfort, DOE/GO-102013-3920. June 2013. nrel.gov/docs/fy13osti/58187.pdf

Passive Solar Architecture: Heating, Cooling, Ventilation, Daylighting and More Using Natural Flows. David A. Bainbridge and Ken Haggard, Chelsea Green, 2011

Online

"Central Air-Conditioner and Heat Pump Efficiency 101" (The Consortium for Energy Efficiency): ceedirectory.org/Content/ CentralAirConditionerandHeatPumpEfficiency_2.aspx

Climate Consultant: energy-design-tools.aud.ucla.edu/ (scroll down to Climate Consultant)

Free, user-friendly software package that provides information about sun and wind for use in your remodeling design.

Cool Roofs: coolroofs.org

ENERGY STAR: energystar.gov/index.cfm?c=heat_cool.pr_hvac

"Swamp Cooler/Evaporative Cooler": alternative-heating-info.com/ altcool_swamp_evaporative.html

U.S. Department of Energy/Energy Efficiency and Renewable Energy

- Cooling Systems: eere.energy.gov/basics/buildings/cooling_systems.html
- *Energy Renovations: HVAC: A Guide for Contractors to Share with Homeowners.* Building America Best Practices Series, vol. 14, 2011: buildingamerica.gov
- Heat Pump Systems: eere.energy.gov/basics/buildings/ heat_pump_systems.html
- Space Heating and Cooling: energysavers.gov/your_home/ space_heating_cooling/index.cfm/mytopic=12300
- Supporting Equipment for Heating and Cooling Systems: eere.energy.gov/ basics/buildings/supporting_equipment.html

Chapter 15
WATER: HEAT IT AND USE IT EFFICIENTLY

What can an efficient, well-maintained water system do for you? It can

- lower your water bill;
- save energy on water heating;
- deliver hot water safely and quickly; and
- grow beautiful landscaping without wasting water.

Water is an essential and limited resource, not to be wasted. Treating and pumping water to your home consumes energy. Heating that water consumes even more energy; it takes 30 times more energy to heat a gallon of water than it takes to treat and deliver that water to your house.

Water heating accounts for 15–40% of a household's energy bill. Often you can substantially reduce your energy use simply through water conservation. Your first thought might be to go buy the most efficient water heater you can find. But the price tag may be high—and it may not even get you what you want: enough hot water, quickly, safely, and inexpensively.

So let's look first at other parts of your water system. You may be able to use the equipment you already have, with some modifications or with better maintenance. You'll probably need to work with a plumber. Reading this chapter will help you communicate with your plumber to get what you want.

Equip yourself to ask the right questions. If you take the time to understand the process, you'll save yourself from

- replacing your water heater when a bit of maintenance would have kept it serviceable much longer;
- buying the fanciest, most efficient water heater available, but not getting enough hot water when you want it;
- spending a lot for a new *tankless water heater* that's not appropriate for your needs;
- buying a solar-thermal system before reducing water waste—and then finding that the system is oversized for your new, reduced needs;
- making requests your contractor doesn't understand;
- trying to do the work yourself; or
- not trying to do the work yourself.

If you take steps in the right order, you'll save resources, money, and time—and wind up with the hot-water system you want. Here's the right order:

1. Wring out the waste.
2. Install water-saving devices.
3. Select a water heater that is compatible with your needs.

Water is a precious resource to be enjoyed, not wasted. Treating, pumping, and heating water consume energy—also not to be wasted.

HOW MUCH WATER AND MONEY CAN YOU SAVE?

The average American family spends about 18% of their total energy bill on hot water—about $400 per year to heat water with natural gas, or about $650 with an electric water heater. In warmer states, about half the gas bill is for heating water. The average American household could save as much as 50% on both its water bill and the water-heating bill by making its water system more efficient. Fewer than 1% of American households use *solar water heating*, which might handle up to 75% of the remaining water-heating load.

Use Home Energy Saver (hes.lbl.gov) to calculate how much energy and money you can save by choosing different water-heating equipment.

DANGER ZONE: WATER HEATER SAFETY

Hazards of working on a hot-water system include scalding water, flammable gas, combustion gases, and electricity.

If the relief valve is gushing steaming hot water, don't turn the water off; if the water is above the boiling point, you risk an explosion. **Get out of the house quickly** and turn off the gas at the meter or the electricity at the breaker box. Water heaters can fly 500 feet when they blow up.

Follow manufacturer's warnings. Don't take things apart unless you are sure you know what you're doing. If you are coming close to electric, gas, oil, or propane lines, turn off the supplies to the areas you are working on, or have a plumber do so.

For a good discussion of precautions, see waterheaterrescue.com.

STEP ONE: WRING OUT THE WASTE

First, figure out how much water (and water-heating energy) your household currently uses. Establishing this *base load* makes it easy to quantify how much you save.

To establish a water use base load, look at your water bills, month by month and over a whole year. If you don't water your landscaping in winter, compare your winter and summer water bills for a good idea of how much water you use for irrigation (assuming the rest of your water consumption remains fairly steady year-round).

To establish a water-heating energy use base load, subtract all non-water-heating energy uses from your total energy use. Begin by comparing your summer utility bills with your winter utility bills. If your furnace and water heater are both gas fired, your summer utility bills will indicate your gas usage minus the energy used for winter heating. If your range and oven are also gas fired, you can read your gas meter; not use the stove for a day; then read the meter again to subtract cooking gas usage from your total.

If you have electric water heating, start with a year's worth of utility bills. Then use a *Kill A Watt meter* to measure refrigerator electricity use over a week or two. Multiply this out to represent a year's use and subtract the result from your total annual electricity use. If you have electronics like TVs that use a lot of power, use the Kill A Watt meter to measure their electricity use. In the same way, remove any other large loads from your total annual electricity use. The amount that remains is your water-heating energy use base load.

Time-to-Tap: What Are You Waiting For?

When you turn on the hot-water faucet, you have to wait for the hot water to arrive. What flows first through the pipe from the water heater to the tap (and then down the drain) is the cooled-down water that's been sitting in the pipe—the water you heated last time you turned on the hot water. How much water are you running down the drain? You can measure it by collecting it in a bucket. Let's say it's 2 cups. If so, you're in pretty good shape; the distance between your water heater and the faucet is probably short. If you're wasting more than 2 cups, there's plenty of room for savings.

Let's look more closely at that water sitting in your pipes. When you turn off the tap, all the water in the pipe between the water heater and the tap begins to cool. If your pipes are uninsulated, that water can cool down pretty quickly. But if your pipes are insulated or are in a hot attic, the water cools more slowly.

You may be able to cut the amount of cool water that is wasted while you're waiting for hot water by insulating any uninsulated distribution pipes. But how much you can save depends a lot on when hot water is used in your home. If you use hot water only for an hour or so in the morning and a couple of hours in the evening, insulating your distribution pipes probably won't save you much. That's because, even with insulation, the hot water in your pipes will eventually cool down to match the surrounding temperature. So water that was hot in the morning will be cool again by evening. On the other hand, not too much heat will be lost if the times when you use hot water are clustered together, even if the distribution pipes are not insulated. If your hot-water use is spaced throughout the day, your potential savings from insulation will be greater.

You might also be able to save energy by reconfiguring the routes from hot source to tap, or by installing a *recirculation system,* as described below, but these are both fairly expensive options.

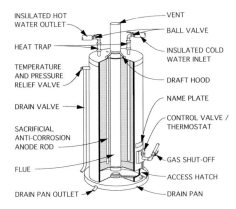

GAS-FIRED WATER HEATER

Maintain Your Water Heater to Maximize Its Efficiency

If you decide to keep your current water heater, set up a maintenance schedule so that it will last longer and function more efficiently:

- Test the *temperature and pressure relief valve* annually. Have a plumber do this the first time. After that, you can test the valve once a year.
- Check the *sacrificial anode rod* every three to five years in normal water, every two years in softened water. Have the plumber install a curved *dip tube* in the tank for easier tank cleaning, install *thermal traps* (also called heat traps) on the water lines, check and replace the sacrificial anode rod, and get rid of sediment in the bottom of the tank. Have the plumber add a second anode rod to the tank if possible, so the tank will be protected twice as long.
- You may also want the plumber to install a *brass ball valve* on the water heater drain. Plastic valves are delicate and are likely to fail when used.
- If you have a gas- or oil-fired unit, also have the plumber check the air supply and venting.

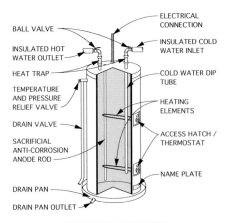

ELECTRIC WATER HEATER

A curved dip tube lets you clear out sediment every six months:

- Hook up a hose to the end of the *drain valve.*
- Open the drain valve. The dip tube should deliver a stream of water that stirs up the sediment and flushes it out.
- Leave the valve open until the water runs clear (three to five minutes).

Once your plumber has demonstrated these tasks, you can continue to do maintenance yourself.

Now and then, just stop and look at the heater. Is rain coming down the vent pipe? Did the cat knock the vent pipe loose? If so, call your plumber.

Insulate the Storage Tank

If your tank-style water heater was purchased after the mid-1990s, it probably has tank insulation built in; it's not worth adding more.

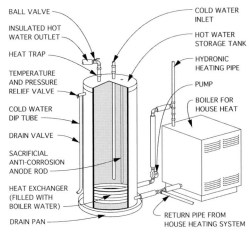

COMBINED SYSTEMS

But if your water heater is older than that, it might not have adequate insulation. If you place your hand on the tank and it feels warm, it needs more insulation. Insulating your water heater is an effective, inexpensive *do it yourself (DIY)* task, especially if the tank is in unconditioned space (garage, basement, outdoors).

Add-on water heater tank insulation is cheap and readily available at home improvement and hardware stores; look for an R-value of 12 or greater.

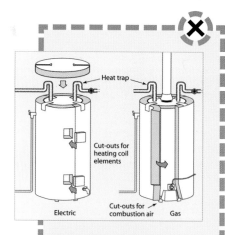

Electric   Gas

Heat trap

Cut-outs for heating coil elements

Cut-outs for combustion air

DANGER ZONE: INSULATE IT RIGHT

Add insulation to your water heater—but carefully. For gas water heaters, blanket insulation can slip down and choke off the combustion air supply. Wrap plumber's tape around the top edge of the insulation and secure it with self-tapping screws. This will hold the blanket to the top edge of the tank. Everywhere else, you can just use more tape if the insulation comes off.

With an electric heater, don't add insulation over the access hatches to the elements. It's okay to insulate the top of an electric water heater tank, taking care not to cover any valves. But insulating the top of a gas or oil water heater could interfere with the *draft hood* and block airflow.

Have a look at your water heater now and then. If there's an overhead leak onto the top of the heater, the blanket can funnel the water under the cover and the whole jacket can turn into a lace of rust.

Insulate the Pipes

A great water heater won't save you much water or energy if hot water frequently gets cold in the pipes. If you use hot water throughout the day, and often wait a long time for hot water, insulating your pipes might be a good idea. It will be easiest to do this when you're changing the plumbing, since pipes inside walls and ceilings are harder to wrap with insulation.

Pipe insulation sheaths are made of foam or fiberglass. They usually come with a lengthwise slit, so you just snap them onto the pipe. Use 3/4"-thick foam or 1"-thick fiberglass (1/2" in a tight space) as a minimum, and seal all joints carefully with acrylic tape.

Insulate all the hot-water pipes in the house and the first 5 feet of the cold-water inlet at the water heater. Hot water tends to float up into the cold-water inlet, cool off, and drop back into the tank; adding insulation or installing a heat trap reduces this effect.

Use Less Water

Using less hot water is the cheapest and easiest way to save water and energy. You can save hot water by remodeling an inefficient hot-water system and by using hot water more efficiently. An inefficient system can be made more efficient by reducing the length of the piping and by sizing it for the available water pressure, but this can be expensive. However, it costs little or nothing to change your habits:

- Take shorter showers.
- Use cold water for washing your hands and doing laundry.
- Don't leave water running while brushing teeth or doing dishes.

Save Water in the Landscape

If you haven't been water aware, it will probably be easy for you to cut a lot of water waste in your yard. Growing regionally *native plants*, which are accustomed to the rainfall in your area, costs far less than keeping up a lawn. You can reduce evaporative water losses by

- replacing sprinklers with drip irrigation;
- watering early in the morning or late at night; and
- adding several inches of *mulch*, such as wood chips or straw, to the bare ground around plants.

A LITTLE MAINTENANCE MAKES A BIG DIFFERENCE

Larry Weingarten serviced water heaters for over 20 years, making around 4,000 service calls. "I got heaters to last over 50 years," says Larry, "and the failure rate remained under one-half of 1%. From a longevity perspective, you can do MUCH better with maintenance—which also solves most performance problems."

Recycle Your Water

Graywater is any wastewater that has been used in the home except water from toilets. Dish, shower, sink, and laundry water make up 50–80% of residential wastewater. This water may be reused for other purposes, especially landscape irrigation. It's a waste to irrigate with great quantities of drinking water when plants thrive on used water containing small bits of compost. (Note: Codes in most states do not allow water from dishwashers and kitchen sinks to be reused.)

Here are some of the benefits of using graywater:

- It reduces the use of fresh water.
- It reduces strain on the septic tank or treatment plant.
- It reduces energy use and the use of chemicals.
- It recharges underground water supplies.
- It promotes plant growth.
- It reclaims otherwise wasted nutrients.
- It increases our awareness of, and sensitivity to, natural cycles.

Use *biocompatible* soap in water intended for reuse, and don't recycle diaper-washing water. Look for a plumber experienced in installing systems that divert shower or laundry water into your garden. Some techniques, such as bucketing water from your kitchen or shower, won't require a plumber. A *laundry-to-landscape system* can be installed by a do-it-yourselfer.

STEP TWO: INSTALL WATER-SAVING DEVICES

Many devices can help you save water in the home. These include low-flow faucets and toilets, as well as toilet tank adapters. Many water companies offer free water-saving tools and rebates on water-efficient toilets.

Recirculation Systems

In order to get hot water at the faucet faster, some people with large homes put in recirculation systems that keep hot water constantly circulating in the pipes. This saves both time and water, but also wastes a lot of energy, since the hot water continually loses heat—even with insulated pipes, as explained above. It also takes energy to pump water through the system, though this energy loss is much smaller than the loss from escaping heat.

Things can be slightly improved by adding a timer to control the pump, which will cut run time by about two-thirds. Somewhat better results are achieved by adding a thermostat to keep water temperature in the lines down to 105–110°F. Best of all is demand pumping, which turns on the pump only when you want hot water, cutting run time to minutes daily instead of hours.

An improvement on demand pumping is a device installed under the sink that circulates water from the hot pipe into the cold pipe and back to the water heater. Examples include the Chilipepper and the Metlund Hot Water D'MAND System. When hot water arrives at the device, it automatically switches off and hot water is supplied at the tap. This doesn't require the extra pipe runs used by other recirculation systems, reducing heat loss.

Growing regionally native plants can require little or no irrigation, as in this Berkeley, California, hillside home garden. Courtesy of Luke Hass, Friends of Regional Parks Botanic Garden.

Drip irrigation delivers water directly to the root zone, minimizing evaporation losses.

Covering soil around plants with mulch helps retain moisture.

Drain Water Heat Recovery

When we shower, we heat cold water and then run it over ourselves and down the drain. A *drain water heat recovery (DWHR)* unit captures up to 60% of that heat and puts it back into the shower water or the hot-water tank. These units can also triple the recovery rate of a water heater, making hot water available much sooner and extending the life of the heater.

Drain water heat recovery units consist of a central core, through which warm wastewater flows, wrapped with copper heat exchanger tubing, through which the cold incoming water flows. Fresh cold water is thus preheated before it goes to the water heater—or better yet, to the cold-water side of the shower. (Preheating the cold shower water means you need less fuel-heated hot water.) It's a relatively simple system with no moving parts and no maintenance, but it does require sufficient room below the drain to allow gravity to work; it may not be usable in a single-story home without a basement. Some brands are Power Pipe, ThermoDrain, and Retherm. Utility rebates are available in several states, paying up to 40% of the cost of these units.

A well-designed faucet aerator can help lower water consumption.

STEP THREE: SELECT A WATER HEATER THAT IS COMPATIBLE WITH YOUR NEEDS

Now that you've reduced waste, you may still need to buy a new water heater, but you probably won't have to get a big, expensive one. The first step in deciding what type and size of heater to buy is to determine how much hot water you really need. If you are considering sizing your water heater to accommodate more people than live in the home at present, don't get a bigger tank. Instead, get the same-size tank with a bigger burner.

To select the right size of water heater, first figure out how much water your family needs during the busiest hour in your house (for instance, when everyone is getting ready to leave in the morning). This is called the *peak-hour demand*; see "What's Your Peak-Hour Demand?" to calculate yours.

Then look for a water heater with a *first-hour rating* (see the *EnergyGuide label*) that matches your peak-hour demand. This tells you how many gallons of hot water a given model can deliver in an hour, starting with a full tank of hot water. To check the first-hour rating of your old water heater, look at the EnergyGuide label or the nameplate, or call the manufacturer (providing the model number).

What Type of Water Heater Should You Buy?

The best water heater for your circumstances depends on many factors. We'll introduce the four categories of water heater suitable for renovation projects, describing their advantages and disadvantages.

Once you know what type of system you want, it's wise to get the most efficient unit you can afford. Compare the estimated yearly operating cost (on the EnergyGuide label) for two different water heaters to get an estimate of how much money one will save you each year over the other. Then

When the hot-water faucet is turned on, this under-sink device recirculates the cold water that's first delivered—just until hot water starts to flow, saving both energy and water. Courtesy of ACT, Inc. D'Mand Systems.

look at the difference in purchase price between the two units and divide that difference by the yearly energy savings to compute how many years it would take to recoup the cost of the more-efficient unit.

And pay attention to these other efficiency features:

- How many inches of insulation does it have? Look for R-16 for a gas unit, R-22 for an electric-resistance unit.
- How long is the warranty on the heater? If it's a short warranty and you have to replace the heater, it wasn't very energy efficient.
- Is there an accessible anode rod? Better yet, are there two?

Tank-Type Water Heaters

Most tank-type water heaters have steel tanks, lined inside with a glass-like coating and insulated outside with fiberglass or rigid foam, covered with a sheet-metal jacket. Heat is usually supplied by a gas flame or an electric heating element; both types are ther-mostatically controlled.

An especially energy-efficient option is the gas *condensing water heater*. It captures heat from combustion gases and uses it to further heat the water. An ENERGY STAR-rated condensing water heater can save over $100 a year compared with a standard model.

Tank-type water heaters are common, but they may not be the best choice for a vacation cottage that gets intermittent use. Because this type of water heater has a finite capacity, they're also not great for meeting big demands, as for a spa, or for filling bathtubs. The best tank-type water heater for your home will depend on what fuel you use, how much water you use, and whether you plan to include a solar water-heating system.

WHAT'S YOUR PEAK-HOUR DEMAND?

Step 1: Identify the one hour in the day when your family uses the most hot water.

Step 2: Mark on the worksheet how many times each water-using activity takes place during that hour.

Step 3: Calculate the total gallons used for each activity by multiplying gallons per use by number of uses.

Step 4: Add up the gallons used for all activities. The total is your peak-hour demand.

Activity	Gallons of Hot Water per Use	(multi-plied by)	Times Used in Peak Hour		Gallons Used in Peak Hour
Showering (w/ low-flow showerhead)		x		=	
Bathing		x		=	
Shaving		x		=	
Washing hands and face		x		=	
Shampooing hair		x		=	
Hand dishwashing		x		=	
Automatic dishwashing		x		=	
Preparing food		x		=	
Washing clothes (w/automatic washer)		x		=	
TOTAL PEAK-HOUR DEMAND					

Example: If 7 am is your busiest time, your hot-water use might look like this:

3 showers	15 gal x 3 = 45 gal/hr
1 shave	2 gal x 1 = 2 gal/hr
1 shampoo	4 gal x 1 = 4 gal/hr
Hand dishwashing	4 gal x 1 = 4 gal/hr
Peak-hour demand	55 gal/hr

Result: This family would want to look for a water heater with a first-hour rating of 53–57 gallons per hour.

Source: AHRI: Air-Conditioning, Heating, and Refrigeration Institute (ahrinet.org/water+heaters.aspx).

A tankless water heater heats water just before delivering it, avoiding the energy losses that come from storing hot water in a tank until it's needed.

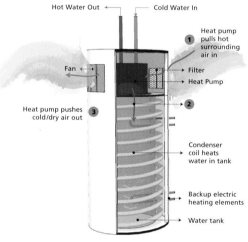

A heat pump water heater pulls heat from the surrounding air to warm water, and is about twice as efficient as a conventional electric water heater. Courtesy of Steven Winter Associates, Inc.

Tankless Water Heaters

A tankless water heater doesn't waste energy by storing hot water until it's needed, or by losing heat from a storage tank. When a faucet draws hot water, the gas burner or electric heating element turns on, heating water as needed.

However, tankless water heaters are not appropriate for every situation. Electric units are limited in their flow rates, which average 1 gpm. (Units with higher flows exist, but their application is limited by their high electrical demand.) Gas units have flow rates of 1.3–3 gpm, but they require venting for combustion gases, which limits placement.

A tankless water heater may be your best choice if

- you don't have many people in the house, and you need a steady flow of hot water during "rush hour";
- you're remodeling a guest cottage or summer home; or
- you're adding new faucets far from the current water heater and want to add a tankless heater near the distant end use.

Heat Pump Water Heaters

Heat pump water heaters work like a refrigerator in reverse: They pull heat from the surrounding air to put into the water. They are roughly twice as efficient as conventional electric water heaters, with a comparable first-hour rating. A backup electric-resistance heating element responds to high-demand situations that exceed the capacity of the heat pump.

By taking heat out of the air, a heat pump water heater also dehumidifies the space and cools the air. So locating this type of water heater inside a home's conditioned space is advantageous in hot-humid climates. The positive summertime effect outweighs the negative wintertime effect.

A heat pump water heater is somewhat noisier than a conventional water heater, so locate it in a garage or an unoccupied basement if possible. The filter on these units should be cleaned periodically.

Solar Thermal

You may be able to use the sun to heat much of your water. The simplest and most cost-effective use of solar is to heat a pool. Solar collectors with no glazing are normally used for this purpose, and they are relatively inexpensive. They may be metal (usually copper) or plastic; plastic holds up better to treated water, and copper holds up better to the sun's exposure.

Spa heating is similar, but requires higher water temperatures. Glazed plastic collectors can deliver these temperatures, but they are more expensive than unglazed collectors. It's best to place the collectors higher than the pool or spa water, so they can drain down when the pump shuts off. This gives freeze protection in winter and prevents summer overheating.

For pool or spa, have a pro size your collector. Be sure to get a well-insulated spa—and use an insulating cover to keep the heat in the water.

There are two basic types of solar water-heating system. *Active-solar* systems use a pump and controls to circulate a fluid that collects solar heat. *Passive-solar* systems use natural convection and may have no mechanical parts. Passive systems aren't as thermally efficient as active systems, but they're generally more durable, since there are fewer parts that can fail.

Of the active systems, the *drainback* and the *closed-loop* are the two most durable. Drainback systems let water drain back into a tank when the pump to the collectors shuts off, while closed-loop systems remain full of an antifreeze fluid, such as glycol, oil, or alcohol.

Of the passive systems, the two main types are *thermosyphon* and *batch heaters*. A thermosyphon system is more efficient, as the heated water is stored in an insulated tank, usually on the roof. A batch heater collects heat when the sun shines on it, but loses much of that heat overnight, unless it has an insulated lid. The thermosyphon system can suffer from freeze damage, so it comes with antifreeze fluid in the collector; for milder climates, a freeze valve lets cold water out and warm water in to prevent damage.

A solar water-heating system will probably not meet all your needs, so you will need a backup water heater. The solar system usually needs its own storage tank, from which preheated water flows to the fuel-fired water heater. Building codes, and the amount of solar hot water generated daily, may require a storage tank of up to 120 gallons, for which you'll need room.

Another possible use of the sun is called *simple solar*—for example, an uninsulated water storage tank in a warm attic. Cold water run into this tank could be heated by the warmth of the attic to 120° or more in summer. A tank in a greenhouse space, or a coil of large-diameter tubing in the attic, could do the same job. Drain simple systems in winter to avoid freezing.

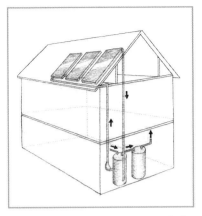

An active-solar thermal system includes one or more collectors, a pump and controls to circulate a solar-heated fluid, and a storage tank linked to the backup water heater tank.

WATER PROJECTS YOU CAN DO TODAY:

- Insulate your water heater tank and pipes.
- Save hot and cold water with a few simple changes in your behavior.
- Reuse graywater in your garden.
- Set up a maintenance schedule for your existing water heater.
- Install a demand control on your existing recirculation system.

WATER PROJECTS THAT WILL TAKE MORE TIME:

- Purchase a new water heater based on your new needs.
- Install native landscaping.
- Recover wastewater heat with a drain water heat recovery system.
- Replumb your hot-water distribution system to make it more efficient.
- Install a solar-thermal system for preheating domestic hot water.

DEPENDABLE HOT WATER

For a teenager, taking 30-minute showers is second nature. For a parent who cares about resource efficiency, those showers cost a lot in water and energy. Danny Orlando of Kennesaw, Georgia, knows this all too well. He and his family recently switched from a 40-gallon gas water heater to a more efficient tankless water heater.

Although their behavior hasn't changed, the family have seen an almost 11% reduction in gas usage, and they're very happy with the new system. "I don't know if the unit will last as long as claimed," says Danny. "But I do know that tomorrow morning, my hot shower will last as long as I want, even if the dishwasher is running."

Danny is only slightly re-thinking his decision, thanks to those teenage-length showers. "Maybe endless hot water wasn't such a great idea," he laughs.

RESOURCES

Print

Solar Hot Water Systems: Lessons Learned 1977 to Today. Tom Lane, Florida Solar Energy Center, 2003

The Water Heater Workbook: A Hands-On Guide to Water Heaters. Suzanne Weingarten and Larry Weingarten, self-published, 2011 (available at waterheaterrescue.com)

Online

"An Affordable Heat-Pump Water-Heater Retrofit." Alex Wilson, *Environmental Building News* 17, no. 7 (2008): buildinggreen.com/auth/article.cfm/2008/6/27/An-Affordable-Heat-Pump-Water-Heater-Retrofit

California Energy Commission's Guide to Selecting Water Heaters: consumerenergycenter.org/home/appliances/waterheaters.html

Directory of Certified Product Performance (Air-Conditioning, Heating and Refrigeration Institute): ahridirectory.org/ahridirectory/pages/home.aspx

ENERGY STAR-Rated Heat Pump Water Heaters: energystar.gov/index.cfm?fuseaction=find_a_product.showProductGroup& pgw_code=WHH

"Estimating and Comparing Water Heating Costs" (DOE): energysavers.gov/your_home/water_heating/index.cfm/mytopic=12780

Graywater Laws: greywateraction.org

Green Plumbers USA: greenplumbersusa.com

Oasis Design: oasisdesign.net

Information on graywater, water, and sustainability.

"Optimizing for High-Performance Solar Water Heating Systems." Gary Klein, *Solar Today,* September/October 2010, p. 60: solartoday-digital.org/solartoday/20100809#pg60

Under-Sink Recirculating Demand Pumps:

- chilipepperapp.com
- gothotwater.com

U.S. Department of Energy/Energy Efficiency and Renewable Energy:

- Water Heating Overview: eere.energy.gov/basics/buildings/water_heating.html

Water Heater Rescue: waterheaterrescue.com

Guidance on buying, maintaining, and troubleshooting water heaters.

Water Heating (American Council for an Energy-Efficient Economy):

- aceee.org/topics/water-heating
- aceee.org/consumer/water-heating

WaterSense (an EPA Partnership program that promotes water efficiency):

- Showerheads: epa.gov/WaterSense/products/showerheads.html
- WaterSense-labeled toilets: epa.gov/WaterSense/pubs/toilets.html

Chapter 16
CODES, PERMITS, AND CONSTRUCTION

How can understanding permitting and construction make your life easier? It can

- help you find and work well with a good contractor;
- promote a productive relationship with your building department;
- keep the cost of your remodeling project under control; and
- help you and your family stay sane during construction.

It's time to assemble your construction team and turn your house dreams into reality. Communicating with construction professionals and your building department can make or break a project. Here are some guidelines for getting through your project with mind, spirit, and finances intact.

WORKING WITH CONSTRUCTION PROS

Some remodels are great DIY projects, some require one or two specialists, and others require a whole team of pros. Knowing whom to call on is the first step to getting it right.

Select your construction team carefully. Check out a contractor's background and references; visit their projects; and determine whether their communication style will make for a successful project.

No Competitive Bidding

Competitive bidding is generally a waste of time. When contractors bid against each other to win a job, they sometimes guess at the price you want to hear and set impossibly low *allowances* for anything not specified in the bid. Contractors have been known to underbid a job, expecting to make up the difference on *change orders* (documents that record changes made after the contract is signed). An accurate bid for a kitchen remodel takes over ten hours to prepare, and most contractors won't spend that much time without either being paid or having some assurance of getting the job.

Set your budget before you begin to design, and tell your designer to work within it. During the design phase, it's a good idea to pay a contractor to do a preliminary cost estimate. This will help determine whether you're close to your budget and encourage open discussion of costs and options.

Get It in Writing

Always have a written contract. Construction contracts come in three flavors, and the best one for you depends on your circumstances.

With a **fixed-sum contract**, the price of the job is locked in, barring unforeseen conditions or homeowner-driven change orders. Pros: The project will

NURTURE YOUR CONTRACTOR RELATIONSHIP

It isn't like you're getting married . . . or is it? From the vows (the contract) to the morning greetings (hammers and machinery at 6 am), from the good times (framing) to the bad times (demolition, drywall, and everything after painting), you are in a serious relationship. And this relationship involves that number one relationship killer: money.

Here are some tips for keeping your relationship with your contractor going strong:

- Set the tone. You are not friends. You can be friendly, but this is business.
- Respect the profession. Think about your own job. How do you like to be treated? Extend that same courtesy to your contractor.
- Respect the contractor's boundaries. Weekends and evenings are for family. If you expect a contractor to meet with you after 5 pm, don't expect that contractor to show up before 10 am the next day.
- Have a conflict resolution plan in place, such as a binding arbitration clause in your contract.
- Keep expectations real. Your house is not perfectly square, and your walls are not plumb. There will be surprises. Unless you're paying $800 per square foot, don't expect old-world craftsmanship. Imperfections are beautiful.
- Don't micromanage the subcontractors or question the contractor's ability to do the job—especially in front of a subcontractor. (If you hire a GC, communicate through the GC. Never communicate directly with a subcontractor, unless the GC asks you to.)
- Say thank you. Leave a plate of cookies, buy the crew lunch, send a card, throw a party when the work is done. Small gestures go a long way.

cost exactly what the contract states. Cons: The price is presented as a lump sum without itemization. The contractor might try to make a higher profit by taking shortcuts.

With a **cost plus contract**, you pay the actual cost of the work plus an agreed-upon markup (usually around 20%). Pros: The project is closely estimated, there's a high level of transparency, and the profit is controlled. Cons: The cost of the project may go higher than expected, and you'll be billed for any items overlooked in the estimate.

With a **time and materials contract**, you pay an agreed-upon rate for labor and the cost of the materials, without markup. Pros: It's a fully transparent process. Profit for the contractor is limited to costs contained in wages. Cons: The price is a loose estimate with considerable opportunity for changes and cost overruns, and there is no incentive for the contractor to control costs.

WORKING WITH YOUR BUILDING DEPARTMENT

Building codes exist to keep you safe. They may seem bothersome, but they are important. Most states have adopted a set of codes known as the International Residential Code (IRC), often with additional regionally appropriate provisions. Ask your local building department which codes your project needs to meet.

Building codes represent the minimum standards for avoiding disaster. Whether you DIY or hire a contractor, it's often desirable to exceed code requirements.

Permits: Don't Get Caught without One

Everyone bemoans the building permit, but failing to pull a permit is breaking the law. If you're caught doing unpermitted work, a fine will probably be added to the cost of your permit. If you are caught after the project is complete, you may be required to tear out work to allow inspection.

Permits, like building codes, are there for your protection. Permits can be obtained only by licensed pros and homeowners. If a builder suggests that you obtain your own permit, that's a red flag. If you get the permit, you assume full liability and the warranty laws of your state fall on your shoulders, not the contractor's.

Green Building and the Codes

While building codes address things like fire safety, ventilation, structural strength, and insulation, they historically have not addressed green-building criteria. This is beginning to change, as green criteria are finding their way into codes and standards.

Green building promotes energy efficiency, resource efficiency, and indoor health. It rarely conflicts with building codes, except in the case of innovative green products or systems such as a graywater system, rainwater harvesting, or composting toilets.

Serious about Going Green? Certify Your Project!

More and more local governments are requiring that building projects meet minimum green-certification levels. Others encourage but don't mandate certification. Even if it's not required, you may want green certification for your own peace of mind and to increase your home's value (Chapter 4).

Find out which green-building programs are available in your area. For remodeling projects, the options are limited. If your area doesn't have a program, look for one in a state with a similar climate and use it as a guide. Let your code officials know that you are doing a green remodeling, and you may find that they offer special services, such as expedited plan review, extra assistance from inspectors, and reduced fees.

When interviewing contractors, say that you want green certification. Some contractors will resist; this is another red flag, since the only requirement on the part of contractors is documentation, testing, and third-party verification that they did the work properly. These procedures generally add little to the cost of your project, while significantly increasing its value. During construction, you may need to remind the contractor and crew of your green-certification requirements.

Building inspectors know a lot about codes and construction, and can be a real asset to your project. Photograph by Lou Dematteis.

STAYING SANE DURING CONSTRUCTION

Remodeling is an emotional process. While the pros are comfortable banging away at your precious home and living in clouds of dust and debris, most homeowners are not. Despite their best efforts, dust will get into your home and things will go wrong. Prepare yourself emotionally for the worst and smile at the minor mistakes.

The demolition stage is exciting. The project is under way. You have never felt your house shake like that before, but no worries—you took the pictures off the walls and packed up everything fragile.

The framing stage goes fast as the space takes shape. The architect verifies that work is going according to plan and makes minor modifications.

Things slow down a bit as the plumber, electrician, and HVAC contractors cut holes in the framing and run pipes, wires, and ducts. Daily progress isn't always apparent, and inspections can add downtime.

Drywall goes up, and wow! Big changes!

They mud and tape the drywall and everything looks better—but the dust gets everywhere. "The end is almost in sight," you think—but it's not true. The finicky work is just starting: trim, tile, cabinets, countertops, painting, hardware, plumbing, and installing the electrical fixtures. Days go by when

YOUR FRIEND THE BUILDING INSPECTOR

Building inspectors are misunderstood and often vilified. In truth, inspectors are your friends. Their job is to check that your remodel is constructed according to building codes and the approved plans. On DIY projects, inspectors can provide a wealth of knowledge. Share the details of your project and solicit their input rather than trying to hide things.

INTRODUCING UNFAMILIAR PRACTICES

The remodeling industry largely comprises independent types who love working with their hands and for themselves. They may meet new materials, systems, and inspections with distrust: "This is the way I've always done it!" But with our current understanding of building science and materials, the old way isn't always best.

Start by acknowledging your builder's experience, and find something the two of you have in common. Build rapport by talking about the changes in your own industry and how you had to relearn techniques.

If you need outside help, a building science professional, engineer, or green-building consultant can bridge the gap between homeowner and building professional (Chapter 4). Mistrust often stems from misunderstanding, and an explanation from an expert can clear things up.

There are also times when a homeowner doesn't fully understand a material or methodology, and the builder is right to reject it. This book, outside consultants, and a healthy dialogue can get you past this hurdle. Be receptive and willing to give up on misguided or inappropriate solutions.

Check to confirm that things were done the way you requested and not the "old way."

nothing seems to happen. Everyone gets frustrated, but knowing that is half the battle. Take a deep breath.

The secret to sanity lies in having a clear schedule that indicates when each step of the process will take place; your GC should provide this.

Stick to Your Plan

Making changes during construction is a surefire way to extend the length of your project and increase its cost. Trust the design and avoid last-minute changes. The exception, of course, is the unexpected condition that shows up during demolition (carpenter ants, termites, dry rot, mold, missing footings, and so forth). In such cases, a change order is a necessary tool for making legitimate modifications.

Quality Assurance

The inspections your building department provides are important, but they often miss crucial details and they generally don't go far enough.

Unless you are taking your remodel through a green-certification process, you will probably have little review or evidence of what took place. Retaining your architect to perform construction oversight is well worth the minor cost.

In addition, include three simple items in your contract:

- Require third-party review and documentation, measuring the home's airtightness, combustion safety, and proper appliance and duct installation.
- Require photo and written documentation at each step of the process. Be specific about which materials and stages should be documented.
- Include warranty language in compliance with your state's laws. Require that subcontractors in each trade sign off, stating that their work was performed as specified.

If your project involves framing, this can be an exciting stage of the process—but don't fool yourself that you're almost done.

Progress may not be obvious while the plumber, electrician, and HVAC contractor do their work, but have faith that the project is moving forward.

CONSTRUCTION-RELATED PROJECTS YOU CAN DO TODAY:

- Decide whether to go for green certification.
- Research and interview contractors.
- Make a construction sanity plan with your family.

CONSTRUCTION-RELATED PROJECTS THAT WILL TAKE MORE TIME:

- Select a contractor, agree on a price, and sign a contract.
- Have your contractor pull a building permit.
- Set up a quality assurance program with your contractor.
- Do your part to keep up good relations with your construction team.

As part of your project, have a home performance assessor test for airtightness, combustion safety, and proper appliance and duct installation—both before and after construction.

RESOURCES

Print

Be Your Own House Contractor: Save 25% Without Lifting a Hammer. Carl Heldmann, Storey Publishing, 2006

Green Building Products: The GreenSpec Guide to Residential Building Materials. Alex Wilson and Mark Peipkorn, eds., New Society Publishers, 2008

What Your Contractor Can't Tell You: The Essential Guide to Building and Remodeling. Amy Johnston, Shube Publishing, 2008

Online

Angie's List: angieslist.com

   User reviews of remodeling (and other) professionals in your area.

The Home Improvement Help Center: remodelhelp.org

   Advice and how-to's on a wide range of home improvement projects.

International Residential Code: shop.iccsafe.org/2012-ircr-code-and-commentary-combo-vol-1.html

National Association of the Remodeling Industry (NARI): nari.org/homeowners

   Provides remodeling tips for homeowners and helps you find a certified remodeling professional in your area.

TRUST, BUT INSPECT

Otogawa-Anschel Design-Build has been using sprayed-foam insulation for a decade, with over 200 installations. "A visual inspection can't detect possible voids inside the foam," notes owner Michael Anschel, "so we have an auditor inspect using a blower door and infrared camera—after insulating, but before drywall. Ninety percent of the time we find an area that was not installed properly, and can fix it without disrupting the project time line."

ABOVE: Closed-cell foam was sprayed in between wooden sleepers, which were applied over the old composition shingle roofing. Here, OSB is being nailed to the sleepers before new roofing is added. ABOVE RIGHT: The family added 700 square feet of conditioned space (without significantly changing the house's appearance from the street) by going out 6 feet and moving the back roofline up.

WILSON CASE STUDY

OWNERS: *Jeff Wilson and Sherri James*
LOCATION: *Athens, Ohio*
CLIMATE ZONE: *Cold*

Jeff and Sherri's original plan was to buy a house in town, do a quick aesthetic remodel, sell the house, and build a brand-new green home for themselves in the country. In 2001, they bought a 1,000 ft^2 Cape Cod-style house, built in 1942, and set to work on it. Jeff brought a lifetime of building experience to the project, as well as his background as host of numerous home-building shows on HGTV and the DIY Network.

ABOVE: The back of the house before the retrofit was complete. RIGHT: The new outdoor kitchen keeps cooking heat out of the house in summer, and the screened porch allows bug-free outdoor relaxation. The decking is sustainably harvested cedar.

Phase I (2001–2005)

- installed blown-in cellulose insulation in the walls and attic;
- caulked and weather-stripped;
- replaced the failed HVAC with a high-efficiency model;
- replaced 80% of the incandescent lightbulbs with CFLs;
- replaced old appliances, as they failed, with ENERGY STAR models;
- updated the kitchen and single bath, and added a half bath downstairs;
- restored the old wood windows;
- added an outdoor kitchen, dining area, and screened porch; and
- painted inside and out.

Phase I Results

The family saved about 15% on their energy bills, but they were still cold in the winter and hot in the summer. Humidity levels were uncomfortably low in winter and high enough in summer to grow mold on the basement walls. There was radon in the basement; the attached garage was falling down; and the roof, windows, doors, and siding were old.

Meanwhile, Jeff and Sherri bought country property and realized that people out there "weren't so green and carefree as we had thought." Those people were spending a lot of time driving back and forth to school, work, and shopping. But Jeff and Sherri and their two daughters could walk to almost everything they needed and felt engaged in their community. "We couldn't see leaving that to be alone in the country," says Jeff. So they got serious about making their in-town home comfortable and energy efficient.

ABOVE LEFT: The kitchen before remodeling. LEFT: The kitchen after remodeling: improved daylighting, energy-efficient appliances, garden access, more practical layout, and durable concrete counters.

ABOVE: The 4kW PV array brought the family's electrical consumption from the utility company to zero. ABOVE RIGHT: The Wilson-James house after its deep energy retrofit.

Closed-cell foam was also sprayed between sleepers applied directly to the original siding.

Phase II (2007–2012)

Deep energy retrofit:

- encapsulated the entire house in closed-cell sprayed-foam insulation;
- replaced the rotting single-pane windows with triple-pane, krypton-gas-filled, high-end vinyl windows;
- replaced the cracked wooden doors with insulated fiberglass models;
- added a 4kW PV array on the rear dormer roof;
- added 700 square feet of super-insulated living space by extending the house 6 feet in one direction and up two stories; and
- retrofitted the basement into comfortable living space, with foam insulation on the walls and floors; and

- installed
  - an R-19 garage door;
  - an UltimateAir ERV;
  - EcoStar faux slate roofing made of recycled rubber;
  - Cree LED can lights and track lighting;
  - Kohler low-flow fixtures;
  - a 16 SEER A/C and a 97 AFUE gas furnace;
  - a Bosch tankless water heater;
    - ENERGY STAR appliances and electronics; and
    - LED lighting and some CFLs.

Triple-pane, krypton-gas-filled windows not only look better than the old rotting single-pane windows but also make the house noticeably more comfortable.

Phase II Results

Energy use is down an average of 85%, even though the conditioned area was increased. The family has no electricity bill and a small gas bill. Jeff says, "Between the foam on the walls and floor in the basement blocking radon, and the ERV constantly bringing in fresh air and exhausting stale air, we believe we've licked the radon issue in the basement. The house now performs like a new home, but with all the community, neighborhood, and convenience of an old house."

You can follow the story of this remodeling project and find information about deep energy retrofits at Jeff's web site (thegreenedhouseeffect.com) and in his book, *The Greened House Effect* (Chelsea Green, 2013).

TOP: Jeff and daughter Sylvie demolish the old, damp basement. BOTTOM: Basement after: warm, dry, and cozy.

Chapter 17

MANAGE YOUR HOME AND YOUR ENERGY USE

What can good home management do for you? It can

- save you more energy and money;
- give you greater control over your energy use;
- lower the likelihood of power blackouts;
- help you avoid costly repairs by doing regular maintenance; and
- help you stay organized and plan for future improvements.

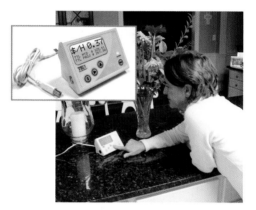

The Energy Detective monitor provides a good idea of how much energy you're using, though it doesn't indicate where that energy is being used.

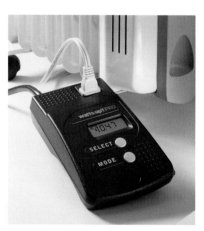

The Watts up? PRO measures voltage and current, allowing you to see the power surge when an appliance is turned on, evaluate changes in energy use over time, and download data to a computer.

After you've completed your remodeling projects, there are lots of other ways to save energy and money. In this chapter, you'll learn about new technologies to help you monitor and control your energy use. We'll also show you how to create and use a Homeowner's Manual to help you manage household maintenance and retrieve important information.

BE YOUR OWN HOME ENERGY MANAGER

There are many new household meters, monitors, and sensors, or *smart energy devices,* that can help you manage your energy use. Some of them can also help you manage your hot water, heating, and air conditioning.

Managing your energy use has far-reaching effects. Did you know that the cost of electricity to your utility company changes constantly throughout the day, depending on supply and demand? Prices go up when electricity demand is high and down when it is low. You may not see these price changes if your utility charges you a fixed rate for electricity. This is good, because it spares you from paying exorbitant bills when prices spike. But it's bad, too, and here's why.

Several times each year, your utility reaches what we call *peak power* (also called *peak demand* or *peak load*). These are the times when we place the most demand on the *electrical grid*—the system of wires and poles and power plants that deliver electricity to you—and it usually occurs during the hottest part of summer when we run our A/Cs or during the coldest part of winter when we use our heating systems the most. To prevent blackouts at these times, extra power plants must be available. But for most of the rest of the year, we don't need them. Those very expensive power plants sit idle—and we're paying for them. If we didn't need them, the cost of electricity would go down—and we'd have less air pollution, too.

Smart Meters

Inventors have come up with an array of new technologies to help us reduce electricity use during periods of peak demand. That's where the *smart meter* comes in. A smart meter is a high-tech replacement for the old-fashioned meter that your utility company put on your house to measure your electricity use. With this digital device, you can track your electricity use in real time, often via the web. It also allows your utility company to charge you something close to the actual price of electricity. During off-peak times, that price will be lower than the price you now pay; during peak times, you'll pay more than you now pay per kilowatt hour (kWh).

The smart meter makes it easier to change your habits to save money. If you see that electricity costs the most at 2 pm, you can choose to do your laundry at night. You save yourself and your community money by *shaving the peak*, which reduces the need for more power plants and allows your utility to purchase less of the more expensive fuels used during peak times.

Because a smart meter measures energy use in shorter intervals, it can help you ferret out the big energy users in your house far better than an ordinary meter can. For example, if your meter shows a sudden spike in electricity use every time you watch your plasma screen TV, try keeping your television off one night. Then compare how much electricity you use with and without the TV on. You'll be able to pinpoint just how much watching TV costs you.

A smart meter lets you track your energy use and choose off-peak times for using optional appliances, saving you money on your utility bills.

Are Smart Meters Safe?

Some consumers are concerned that smart meters may be unsafe because they emit low-level microwave radio frequency radiation. As a result, several state utility commissions have opened investigations into the health effects of smart meters, and in some cases now let consumers refuse to have one installed. However, industry research to date has not identified health problems related to smart meters. In fact, smart meters create far less exposure to wireless signals than do cell phones.

Beyond Smart Meters

Other smart energy management devices help us make the most of our smart meters, or even to manage our energy use without them:

- **In-home display monitors.** Typically small boxes that you can set on a countertop or hold in your hand. The screen shows your home's energy use and what it costs. Some monitors are easy to add to your meter or circuit box; others must be installed by an electrician. Monitors are a popular choice, because you can put them inside your home for quick access (unlike your smart meter, which is outside), and they are typically easy to read and understand. Some eliminate numbers altogether and just glow different colors to show how much energy you are using.
- **Online analytics.** Programs for your computer, tablet computer, or cell phone that analyze smart-meter data. Many of these programs recommend ways to save more energy.
- **Cell phone and computer apps.** Programs that monitor your smart-meter data remotely via your cell phone or computer, or control your thermostat or appliances from afar.

HOW MUCH MONEY CAN A SMART METER SAVE YOU?

The amount of money you'll save by using a smart meter (and other smart energy devices) depends on how you use the technology, where you live, and what your utility charges for electricity. Some pilot programs show savings as high as 20–25% and payback of the original investment (about $100) in four to six months.

Not everyone who uses a smart meter saves energy. Some people feel encouraged to use *more* energy if a feedback device shows them that a particular appliance uses very little energy. But if your goal is to use less energy, and you study your energy use patterns and make smart changes, you will save energy and money.

An in-home display monitor lets you easily view your energy use from indoors.

Data loggers record the output from instruments that measure energy use, temperature, and humidity, which can then be downloaded to a computer for analysis.

BUT I'M ALREADY SO BUSY!

If your time is tight, or energy management doesn't interest you, see if your utility offers *demand response programs* for homeowners. With these programs, your utility does most of the work by remotely curtailing an appliance's energy use when electricity prices are high. Often this involves having the utility company put a special electronic device on your water heater or A/C. Many utilities compensate customers for participating.

- **Smart appliances.** Washers, dryers, refrigerators, ovens, and A/Cs that communicate directly with your utility. No need for you to watch the meter; these appliances will find the cheapest time to operate. You can override the program, though, whenever you like. Smart appliances are still under development; field tests have been conducted, but these appliances are not yet generally available.
- **Data loggers.** Devices that keep a record of the output from an instrument. In a home, data loggers might be used to record output from instruments that measure humidity, energy use, and temperature. A favorite among engineers and techie homeowners.

Before you choose an energy management device, ask yourself the following questions:

- Is your household motivated to reduce energy use or to meet a carbon emissions goal?
- What does your utility offer free of charge?
- Are the monitoring and display devices you want compatible with your meter? (Ask the vendor or your utility company.)
- How much time do you have to manage your energy use?
- Are you tech savvy, or not?

CREATE—AND USE—AN OWNER'S MANUAL FOR YOUR HOME

Now that you know how energy is used in your home, you can create a one-stop reference for maintaining comfort and efficiency. A Homeowner's Manual is an important wrap-up to your remodeling project—a tool to make sure that the benefits of your work are sustained into the future.

Your Homeowner's Manual will organize numerous useful documents and reminders to keep your home operating smoothly, maximize your comfort and pleasure, and minimize worry and waste. It will also hold your vision for future upgrades and remodeling plans; help you keep on top of periodic maintenance to prevent problems and keep your home's systems working longer; and remind you to take health and safety precautions, such as changing the smoke detector and CO alarm.

Keep your Manual in a handy location. You may not need it often, but when you do, it's going to be invaluable.

What's in the Manual?

Putting together your Homeowner's Manual should be as fun as it is useful. Get as creative as you want, but make sure you include these items:

- Appliance manuals and warranties
- Photographs and construction drawings
- Maintenance schedule
- Your own "Best Contractors" contact list
- Summary of historical energy use and cost information

- Home performance assessment and recommendations
- Home energy manager guidelines
- Your 5/10/20-year plan

Appliance Manuals and Warranties

Appliance and equipment owner manuals aren't needed often, but when they are, it's great to know exactly where to go (especially with electronic devices like thermostats that occasionally need to be reset or reprogrammed). As for warranties, you may have a special location in your personal filing system for these, but copies can also find a home in your Manual.

Photographs and Construction Drawings

You may have put together a picture album as a coffee table chronicle of your remodeling project, but make sure some of those photos make it into your Manual; it could help you avoid trouble in the future. The most useful photos will be the details of electrical, plumbing, and insulation work before they are covered by the finished wall. If you have construction drawings that can be placed in the sheet protectors, include those as well.

Maintenance Schedule

Regular maintenance for your home, like exercise for your body, keeps things running and prevents early deterioration. This applies to the entire house, from the landscape to the bathroom faucets. The list below focuses on maintenance that relates to energy savings, comfort, safety, and durability. Set up a calendar that includes reminders for these things:

- Appliances and other major equipment, such as water heaters, should be maintained on the schedule recommended by the manufacturer. So be sure to import that schedule into your schedule.
- Each spring, conduct a visual inspection. Check your house inside and out for signs of moisture damage; look for cracks in the caulk around windows; check the slope of the surrounding ground and inspect the interior if you suspect that water is getting in. If you have gas or oil heat, check the flue for signs of backdrafting. This can show up as discoloration around the base of the flue or on top of the unit.
- Replace the filter on your furnace and A/C as needed. If your house is full of dust or pet hair, you will need to do this more often. When you change your filters, test your smoke and CO detectors and vacuum the sensors. Replace the batteries once a year.
- If you have a wood-burning fireplace or a woodstove, have the chimney cleaned and inspected after every heating season.
- If your home has a boiler, set back the temperature in summer.
- Clean your gutters and downspouts at least once each rainy season. Make sure that water drains away from the foundation.
- Clean your mechanical ventilation fans (including bath fans and range hood) to be sure they are venting at their maximum airflow.

ORGANIZING YOUR HOMEOWNER'S MANUAL

Your Manual is a living document, one that you will add to and modify over time. If you're print oriented, invest in a couple of three-ring binders—the 3-inch size—and the heavy-duty three-hole plastic sheet protectors. The sheet protectors will hold your equipment manuals, warranties, and other resources. Tab dividers will come in handy for quick reference.

If you're more digitally inclined, you'll probably want to keep your Manual on your computer. (Make sure you back it up!) You can create documents in a word-processing program, and drop in photos and links to useful web sites (products, equipment, utility company). Many appliances have owner manuals and repair manuals online. You can also input your maintenance schedule to an online calendar with automatic reminders.

HOW ONE FAMILY SMARTENED THEIR HOME AND SAVED MONEY

When Will and Carolyn Brownsberger moved into an old house in Belmont, Massachusetts, they knew it needed major upgrades. The Brownsbergers did a deep energy retrofit (Chapter 4) and installed several smart energy devices. They now control heating and cooling from a computer or cell phone using an ecobee wireless thermostat, which also provides custom energy analysis and advice via the Internet. A separate Powerhouse emonitor lets them see circuit by circuit how much energy each appliance uses. To evaluate comfort and air quality, the family use Onset HOBO data loggers, which gauge temperature and humidity in individual rooms. CO_2 monitors log ventilation levels.

The Brownsbergers spent $258,000 on the energy-related remodeling, and expect to save all of that and more over the life of the upgrades. They received incentives totaling $90,000 from their utility, National Grid, and federal and state tax credits.

Will and Carolyn used to raise the thermostat from 58°F to 65°F each winter morning, but ecobee's web report told them that this was unnecessary. The house would automatically warm to that temperature from sunlight, computer use, and other home activities. "We're managing this building to achieve high energy savings, and ecobee was a valuable tool," Will says.

Your Own "Best Contractors" List

Keep an updated list of contractors and maintenance technicians with whom you've developed a good relationship or who come with good recommendations. Having confidence in their advice and in the quality of their work adds to your peace of mind. Remember: You get what you pay for.

Summary of Historical Energy Use and Cost Information

Include a record of your home's preupgrade energy use. Use this as a baseline to monitor your energy-saving progress. Your record could take any of the following forms:

- past utility bills (at least one year's worth);
- an annual summary provided online by your utility company;
- your own annual summary of utility bills in spreadsheet format.

Make sure these records indicate both the amount of energy used (in therms or kWh) and the cost per unit of energy. Monthly and annual total costs are helpful, but don't stop there. With price fluctuations, the best way to see how much less energy you are using will be by comparing units of energy, not price. Once you get a smart meter, you can include more-detailed information.

Home Performance Assessment and Recommendations

Your home performance assessment and recommendations (Chapter 4) will lay out the game plan for making your home as efficient as possible. Whether you get a comprehensive home energy assessment, get a free or inexpensive assessment from your local utility, or take on the task yourself using Internet resources, doing an assessment has three benefits:

- It gives you a record of where you started and the improvements you have made. This can be helpful if you sell your home.
- It identifies energy improvements you might make in the future.
- It provides guidelines for panic purchases, so that when you need to buy something like a new water heater quickly, you'll have the research in hand to help you choose the most efficient model.

Home Energy Manager Guidelines

When you decide what combination of strategies and techie tools you want to use to manage your home energy use, record them in your Manual.

Your 5/10/20-Year Plan: Insert Dreams Here

If you have a long-term vision for your home, or if you phased your improvements, store those future plans in your Manual to keep you on track.

WHAT YOU'VE ACCOMPLISHED

As you enjoy the fruits of your labor, let's consider the larger implications of your home remodeling project. You've done something not only for yourself but also for the rest of us. By becoming more energy independent, you are making an important contribution to our country's economy. Our dependence on foreign oil creates economic turmoil. In fact, 10 out of the 11 *U.S. recessions* since World War II occurred after oil *price spikes*. We can free ourselves from this cycle if more households take the kind of action you did.

Managing household energy use can lower peak demand, lessening the need for extra power plants.

You've probably also increased the resale value of your home. Your Homeowner's Manual will demonstrate to future buyers that you've upgraded the home in ways that will save them money. Your energy-monitoring tools and utility bills will prove it.

But you've done even more. You've taken your first step into the future. The Internet gives each of us tremendous access to, and control over, information—a power that, as we've seen, can revolutionize governments. Now, new technologies offer us the same kind of control over our use of energy—the lifeblood of the modern economy. With solar panels, fuel cells, advanced efficiency, conservation, smart energy devices, and more, you can produce, and control your use of, energy in ways once only accessible to large corporations and governments. Call it the democratization of energy, and give yourself a pat on the back for being among the first to join the movement.

RESOURCES

"Deep Energy Retrofit in Belmont" (Will Brownsberger): willbrownsberger.com/index.php/archives/4155

A Discussion of Smart Meters and RF Exposure Issues. An EEI-AEIC-UTC White Paper, March 2011: eei.org/ourissues/electricitydistribution/Documents/Smart_Meters_RF_exposure.pdf

Healthy Homes Maintenance Checklist (HUD): hud.gov

Search for the checklist by title.

"Take Your Average Utility Bill and Learn Where to Save Energy" (Home Energy Pros): homeenergypros.lbl.gov/profiles/blogs/take-your-average-utility-bill-and-learn-where-to-save-energy

Congratulations! Your efforts to make your home more comfortable, healthful, and energy efficient are good for you and your family—and for the rest of the world.

GLOSSARY

Accent lighting: emphasizes a specific object or draws attention to a particular area, usually using lights with narrow beam control.

Active-solar heating system: the use of fans, pumps, and controls to distribute solar heat by moving air, water, or another fluid.

Air barrier: a continuous layer of materials that blocks the movement of air.

Air Conditioning Contractors of America (ACCA): certifies HVAC contractors, provides educational resources, and lists local air-conditioning contractors.

Air handler: the part of a forced-air heating or cooling system that moves the air through the conditioning and distribution components.

Air leakage: the uncontrolled movement of air in or out through the house structure. Air leakage carries heat with it by convection. Also called air infiltration, infiltration, and air exfiltration.

Airtight-drywall approach: an air-retarding technique that uses gaskets and caulk to seal drywall at its perimeter and penetrations.

Allowance: an amount of money set aside in a construction contract for items that are not specified explicitly in the original contract and therefore can't be accurately bid.

Ambient lighting: lighting designed to provide uniform illumination.

American Society of Heating, Refrigerating, and Air Conditioning Engineers (ASHRAE): a building technology organization that focuses on building systems, energy efficiency, IAQ, and sustainability.

Annual fuel utilization efficiency (AFUE): a laboratory-derived number for rating heating appliances; it accounts for chimney losses, jacket losses, and cycling losses, but does not include distribution losses or energy used to operate fans or pumps.

As-builts: architectural drawings that document the conditions of a home before renovations.

Assembly: a group of building materials that function as a system.

Assumable loan: a mortgage loan that allows a buyer to undertake the preexisting loan.

Backdraft damper: a damper installed in a duct that allows air to flow in only one direction.

Backdrafting: the pressure-induced spillage of exhaust gases from combustion appliances into the living space.

Backer rod: vinyl tube or foam rope placed in large cracks, so less caulk is needed.

Balanced pressure: see Neutral pressure.

Ballast: a device used with fluorescent or high-intensity discharge lights to provide the necessary circuit conditions for starting and operating the light. See Electronic ballast, Magnetic ballast.

Base load: the steady amount of energy or water consumed by a household year-round, not including peak use.

Batch water heater: a passive-solar water heater made of an insulated box with a glazed top exposed to sunlight.

Biocompatible: harmless to living tissue.

Blocking: horizontal framing (2 x 4 or 2 x 6) placed between wall studs to facilitate fastening items to the wall.

Blower door: a variable-speed fan mounted in an adjustable frame that fits snugly in a doorway; used to pressurize or depressurize a house to measure air leakage.

Blown-in blanket (BIB): loose-fill insulation installed in an exposed wall cavity and contained by a covering.

Blown insulation: any loose-fill insulation propelled into building cavities by air pressure.

Boiler: a device that heats water for use in heating the whole house; not usually intended to heat domestic hot water for consumption.

Borrowed light: a daylighting technique that transmits sunlight from brighter to darker rooms via an interior glazed opening.

Brass ball valve: a durable valve, operated with a lever, that opens or closes fully with a 90° turn.

British thermal unit (Btu): the amount of energy required to raise 1 lb of water 1°F at a specified temperature.

Building envelope: the boundary between conditioned and unconditioned spaces, consisting of the walls, roof, and floor, including air barrier and insulation material.

Building Performance Institute (BPI): certifies home energy professionals, specializing in assessments and energy retrofits of existing homes.

Building science: a body of knowledge about the physical phenomena that affect buildings. Includes analyses of building materials, building envelope systems, and mechanical systems for heating, cooling, and ventilating.

Can light: a cylindrical light fixture installed through a hole in the ceiling and providing downward-focusing lighting, either as a broad floodlight or as a narrow spotlight.

Carbon calculator: a tool for estimating the carbon footprint of a given activity.

Carbon footprint: the quantity of CO_2 (and other greenhouse gases) emitted by a given activity, such as operating a home.

Carbon monoxide (CO): a colorless, odorless toxic flammable gas formed by incomplete combustion of carbon.

Cash-out refinance: a refinance of the first mortgage on a property that allows the borrower to take out additional cash.

Cathedral ceiling: a sloped or vaulted ceiling, usually with the rafters serving as the ceiling joists.

Caulk: sealer applied from a tube; dries to an airtight, flexible seal in cracks and holes.

CFM_{50}: cubic feet per minute of airflow with a 50 Pa pressure difference between indoors and out.

Change order: a client's written order to the contractor, issued after execution of the construction contract, authorizing a change in contract terms.

Chase: an enclosed passageway, often used to carry ducts, plumbing, and telephone and electrical lines.

Clerestory window: a vertical window higher than eye level that can be used for lighting, ventilation, and collecting solar heat.

Closed-loop solar system: a solar hot-water system that uses an antifreeze heat transfer fluid (glycol, oil, alcohol) to heat the domestic hot water.

Cocoon: one or two rooms with increased insulation, where one spends most of one's time during extremely cold or hot weather, shutting down heating or cooling to other rooms.

Coefficient of performance (COP): a measure of a heat pump's efficiency; the amount of energy transferred to or from the space divided by the amount of energy used to make that transfer occur.

Coil: a heat exchanger in a heat pump or A/C that absorbs or rejects heat to transfer heat from indoors to outdoors (air conditioning) or from outdoors to indoors (heat pump in heating mode). The coil typically consists of copper tubing with aluminum fins; the tubing carries a refrigerant.

Color rendering index (CRI): indicates the effect of a light source on the color appearance of objects.

Color temperature: a measure of the color appearance of light as warm (reddish) or cool (blue-white). Color temperature is measured on the Kelvin scale; a lower temperature indicates a warmer color.

Combustion air: air that chemically combines with a fuel during combustion to produce heat and flue gases, mainly CO_2 and water vapor.

Combustion chamber: the box where the fuel burns in fossil-fueled water heaters or furnaces.

Commissioning: verifying that all the building systems (e.g., HVAC, plumbing, electrical) function as designed.

Compact fluorescent light (CFL): a type of fluorescent light designed to replace an incandescent light.

Competitive bidding: soliciting bids from several contractors in order to get the lowest price for a project.

Composting toilet: uses no water and does not flush to a septic system or sanitary sewer system. It is self-contained and breaks down the waste using natural biological processes.

Compressor: a motorized pump in an A/C or heat pump that compresses the gaseous refrigerant and sends it to the condenser, where heat is released.

Condensation: the conversion of a fluid from a vapor to a liquid state, usually initiated by cooling.

Condenser: the outdoor coil in an A/C or heat pump where the refrigerant condenses and releases heat, which is carried away by air moving through the coil.

Condensing clothes dryer: uses a heat exchanger to cool the moisture-laden exhaust air from the dryer, condensing the water vapor into a drain and capturing the waste heat for reuse.

Condensing water heater: captures heat from flue gases to further heat the water; can exceed 80% fuel efficiency.

Conditioned space: the part of a house that is heated or cooled.

Conduction: heat transfer through a substance from one molecule to another.

Construction documents, Contract documents: drawings and specifications assembled by an architect that provide details of construction.

Contractor: a professional who contracts to perform labor and/or supply materials for construction work (see General contractor).

Controlled ventilation: mechanical ventilation for general IAQ improvement, controlled by a time, temperature, or humidity monitor.

Convection: circulatory motion in a fluid (gas or liquid) due to uneven distribution of heat in that fluid.

Convection oven: an oven that accelerates cooking time using convection currents.

Cool roof: a roof with a higher solar reflectance than a standard roof.

Cove lighting: indirect lighting built into ledges, recesses, or valances in a ceiling or high on the walls of a room; directs light up toward the ceiling and down adjacent walls.

Crawl space: space between the bottom floor and the ground, usually with very low vertical clearance.

Cross-ventilation: the passage of outdoor air from openings on one or more sides of a building through openings on the opposite sides.

Cubic feet per minute (CFM): unit of measurement for airflow.

Damper: a device in a duct or vent to limit or stop airflow.

Damp-spray insulation: see Wet-spray insulation.

Daylighting: illumination of indoor spaces by sunlight.

Deciduous: denotes plants that lose their leaves in cold seasons.

Deep energy retrofit: a home retrofit that aims to reduce energy use by 50–90%, which is more than is usually achieved by conventional energy retrofits.

Demand response programs: allow the utility or grid operator to remotely curtail an appliance's energy use during periods of high demand.

Dense pack: a method of installing loose-fill insulation at a high density to improve its ability to slow air leakage.

Details: architectural drawings, usually large scale, that show construction of particular building elements.

Diffuser: supply grille that directs and speeds the flow of incoming air, mixing it with air already in the room.

Dimmer: a device used to vary the intensity of electric light.

Dip tube: the cold-water inlet that runs inside the hot-water tank, from the top to the base.

Directional lighting: the distribution of all or most of the light from a fixture in one direction.

Direct-vent: denotes a combustion appliance ducted to the exterior, with exterior air intake.

Distribution system: a system of pipes or ducts used to distribute energy or a fluid to and from a heating or cooling device, such as a furnace, boiler, or central A/C.

DIY: do-it-yourself.

Domestic hot water: the hot water that comes out of taps or appliances, as distinguished from the hot water circulated through the radiators and pipes of a hydronic heating system.

Downlight: see Can light.

Draft hood: a device built into an appliance, or made a part of the vent connector, that provides for the ready escape of the flue gases from the appliance and prevents backdrafting.

Drainback system: a solar water-heating system that allows fluid to drain out of the collector and into a tank when the pump to the collector shuts off.

Drain pan: a small basin under a water heater for catching minor spillage.

Drain valve: valve at the bottom of a water heater or other appliance, used to drain the appliance.

Drain water heat recovery (DWHR): a device that recovers heat from warm drain water (e.g., a shower or clothes washer) and uses it to preheat fresh water.

Drywall: a prefabricated panel with a gypsum plaster core sandwiched between layers of heavy paper, generally used to create finished surfaces on interior walls and ceilings. Also called wallboard, gypsum board, plasterboard, or Sheetrock.

Dual-flush: denotes a toilet with two flush volumes, one for liquid waste and one for solids.

Duct: a tube, often of sheet metal, that delivers air from the air-handling unit(s) throughout the home, and from the home back to the air-handling unit(s).

Ductless range hood: see Recirculating fan.

Electrical grid: an interconnected system of power plants, transmission and distribution lines, and other equipment through which electricity is produced and transmitted.

Electric-resistance heater: a device that heats water or air using electric-resistance elements (like those in electric stoves).

Electronically commutated motor (ECM): a highly energy-efficient, reliable electric motor used to power furnace and A/C blowers; the blower speed can be electronically varied; often called a variable-speed blower motor.

Electronic ballast: the electronic circuitry that provides the voltage and current needed to start and operate a fluorescent light.

Elevations: architectural drawings that show the vertical face of an interior or exterior wall.

Energy efficiency: a measure of how much useful work output results from a given energy input.

Energy efficiency ratio (EER): term used to rate efficiency of room A/Cs; equals capacity in Btu/h removed from indoor air divided by electrical input in watts.

Energy-efficient mortgage (EEM): an extension of a 30-year FHA first mortgage that provides an additional amount (up to 5% of appraised value as of this writing) to pay for specific energy-saving improvements. Requires a HERS audit.

EnergyGuide label: a large yellow sticker that appears, by law, on new appliances, making it possible to determine which model uses the least energy.

Energy modeling: process for calculating how much energy a building uses for heating, cooling, lights, appliances, water heating, and/or miscellaneous loads.

Energy recovery ventilator (ERV): a ventilation device that exchanges equal amounts of indoor air with outdoor air, transmitting heat and humidity from one airstream to the other for improved energy efficiency.

Energy vampire: see Phantom load.

Evaporative cooler: mechanical cooling equipment that forces dry outdoor air through moist pads, lowering its temperature and raising its humidity, and then delivers that air to the conditioned space.

Exfiltration: leakage of air from inside the conditioned space to outside.

Exterior insulation and finish system (EIFS): a system of rigid foam insulation and synthetic stucco finish that can be applied to the exterior of a building.

Federal Housing Administration (FHA): agency within the U.S. Department of Housing and Urban Development that administers loan programs, loan guarantee programs, and loan insurance programs designed to make more housing available.

FICO (Fair Isaac Corporation) credit score: a number by which lenders determine borrowers' credit risk.

First-hour rating: the number of gallons of hot water a given tank-type water heater can deliver in an hour, starting with a full tank of hot water.

Flashing: thin, continuous sheet metal (or other impervious material) used to deflect water from an angle or joint on the outside of a building.

Flexible duct: air duct comprising a plastic inner core supported by a helical metal wire, surrounded by a layer of fiberglass insulation and an outer jacket that acts as a vapor barrier.

Flue: a channel or pipe through which combustion gases exit to the outdoors.

Fluorescent: an efficient electric light, usually in the form of a tube, in which illumination is produced by the action of ultraviolet rays on the inside fluorescent coating. See Compact fluorescent light (CFL).

Foam-in-place insulation: insulating material that is applied as a spray with a blowing agent under pressure; when cured, results in an airtight rigid foam insulation conforming to the shape of the assembly.

Foot-candle: a unit of measure of the intensity of light falling on a surface, equal to 1 lumen per square foot.

Fossil fuel: a natural fuel such as petroleum, coal, or natural gas, formed in the geological past from the remains of living organisms.

French drain: a trench or underground passage, filled with gravel or rock and sometimes incorporating perforated pipe, that redirects both surface water and groundwater away from a designated area, such as the exterior of a house.

Full-spectrum light: an electric light source (typically fluorescent) designed to simulate the appearance of noon sunlight.

Furring strip: a small slat or strip of wood used for spacing or nailing.

Gas fill: a gas (usually argon or krypton) sealed between the panes of an insulating glass unit to improve its insulating value.

Gasket: a rubber, plastic, or foam seal between two objects.

General contractor (GC): the contractor with primary responsibility for a construction project, who hires all of the subcontractors and suppliers.

General lighting: see Ambient lighting.

Glazing: the component of windows that allows for the direct transmission of radiant energy, often made of glass or plastic.

Gravity damper: a damper used to control the inflow of outside air down a chimney or exhaust flue. It naturally falls shut when the fan is off; when the fan is on, the air pressure blows the damper open.

Graywater: any wash water that has been used in the home, not including water from toilets.

Green building: the practice of creating buildings using environmentally responsible processes and products.

Grille: a louvered plate attached to either the entry point or the termination of an air duct to cover the hole, look attractive, and (sometimes) direct the airflow.

Gut rehab: a renovation in which finishes (such as drywall) are removed to expose the structural materials.

Halogen light: an incandescent light with a quartz bulb and a gas filling that includes halogen; provides a brilliant light from a compact unit.

Heat exchanger: a device that transfers heat from one medium to another, physically separate medium at a different temperature.

Heat pump: a mechanical device that removes heat from one medium, concentrates it, and distributes it in another medium to heat or cool indoor space.

Heat pump water heater: a heat pump that pulls heat from the air to heat water; about twice as efficient as a standard electric water heater.

Heating load: the amount of heat that must be provided in a given amount of time to maintain building temperature at a given level during the coldest weather.

Heating seasonal performance factor (HSPF): a rating for heat pumps that indicates the number of Btu transferred per kWh of electricity consumed during the heating season.

Heat recovery ventilator (HRV): a ventilation device that exchanges equal amounts of indoor air with outdoor air and exchanges the heat from one airstream to the other for improved energy efficiency.

High-performance window: a window that outperforms conventional windows by lowering energy consumption and increasing occupant comfort.

Home energy professional: a home energy auditor, rater, or contractor who takes a whole-house approach to providing diagnostic and performance testing, energy modeling, air sealing, insulation, and HVAC design.

Home Energy Rating System (HERS): a standard for evaluating a home's energy efficiency and expected energy costs. HERS professionals are trained and certified by RESNET.

Home performance assessment: a professional evaluation of how your home uses energy.

Humidistat: a sensor used to control a device (such as an exhaust fan) based on the interior humidity level; it keeps the device running until the humidity level drops to an acceptable level.

HVAC: acronym for "heating, ventilation, and air conditioning."

Hydronic: denotes a heating or cooling system that uses a fluid to transfer heat.

Hydropower: the use of flowing water to generate electrical power.

Ice dam: accumulation of ice at the eaves of a sloped roof, formed as snow is melted by heat leaking from the attic and refreezes at the overhang; allows water to penetrate under shingles.

Incandescent lightbulb: a glass bulb in which a metal filament is heated until it glows to produce electric light; generally less energy efficient than fluorescent or LED lighting.

Indirect lighting: lighting in which the light source is reflected diffusely off the ceiling or walls.

Indoor air quality (IAQ): the quality of air inside a space, especially as it relates to health and comfort.

Induction cooktop: an electric cooktop with an element that produces an oscillating magnetic field, which transfers energy to a cooking vessel without heating up the cooktop itself.

Infiltration: air leakage from outside to inside a conditioned space.

Infrared (IR): the portion of the invisible electromagnetic spectrum that has wavelengths slightly longer than the light human beings see as red.

Insulating concrete forms (ICFs): assemblies of rigid insulation that serve as forms for poured concrete, and remain as permanent insulation.

Insulating glass unit (IGU): a window configuration consisting of two or more glazings separated by a space. Insulation is achieved by thin coatings of metal oxides on the glazing, and by dead air space or inert gases between glazings.

Insulation: material that slows heat conduction.

Integrated control motor (ICM): see Electronically commutated motor (ECM).

Interest: money charged for the use of money.

Interest rate: the percentage of a borrowed amount of money that is charged for the use of that money for a specified time.

Joists: the horizontal structural framing for floors and ceilings.

Jumper duct: a duct connecting grilles in two rooms, allowing air to move between the rooms to prevent pressure imbalances within the conditioned space.

Kelvin (K): temperature scale used to describe the correlated color temperature of a light source.

Kill-a-Watt® meter: a portable meter used to measure electrical energy use of appliances.

Kilowatt: 1,000 watts.

Knee wall: a short wall, generally erected to separate a living space from an attic or to join two rooms with different ceiling heights.

Laundry-to-landscape system: a simple graywater system that reuses laundry water for irrigation.

Lien: a charge against property making it security for the payment of a debt.

Light-emitting diode (LED): an energy-efficient semiconductor device that emits visible light when an electric current passes through it.

Light tube: see Tubular skylight.

Load: the amount of heat that must be provided or removed by an HVAC system to maintain a desired temperature within a building.

Loan: a sum of money lent to one who promises to repay the sum plus interest.

Loan-to-value ratio (LTV): the ratio between the amount of money borrowed and the appraised value of the property.

Loose-fill insulation: fibrous or granular insulation that can be poured or blown into place.

Low-e: low-emissivity; for example, a coating fixed to one of the surfaces of a multipane window that allows short-wavelength visible and near-infrared solar radiation through the window, but reflects back inside longer wavelengths of infrared heat.

Lumen: the unit for measuring light output.

Magnetic ballast: a ballast that uses a magnetic core and coil to provide the voltage and current needed to start and operate fluorescent and high-intensity discharge lights.

Makeup air: air supplied to replace air removed by an exhaust appliance, such as a kitchen range hood.

Manifold: a central branching unit that splits one stream of air or liquid into several channels.

Manual D: industry manual that describes the code-required ACCA method of designing duct systems.

Manual J: industry manual that describes the code-required ACCA method of calculating cooling and heating loads.

Manual S: industry manual that describes the code-required ACCA method of selecting air-conditioning equipment to meet design loads.

Mastic: a thick, creamy, latex-based sealer for ducts and cracks; dries to form a permanent, flexible seal.

Mechanical damper: a damper in a duct, chimney, or flue used to control airflow, operated by a motor that opens or closes the damper on command.

Microclimate: a small, local area with climate characteristics that differ somewhat from those of the average surrounding climate.

Micro-hydropower: hydropower from a generator small enough to be used in a creek.

Mil: a unit of length equal to 0.001 inch.

Mini-split: a heat pump with refrigerant loops connecting an air handler in each room or zone to an outdoor compressor/evaporator; pipes carrying refrigerant thus replace ducts carrying air.

Moist-spray insulation: see Wet-spray insulation.

Moisture barrier: waterproof material, such as polyethylene or house wrap, used to prevent the passage of moisture.

Motion detector: a device that is sensitive to movement; can be used to conserve electricity.

Mudsill: the horizontal framing member that sits on the foundation in a wood-framed house.

Mulch: a protective cover placed over soil to retain moisture, reduce erosion, provide nutrients, and suppress weed growth.

Native plants: plants indigenous or naturalized to a given area.

Negative pressure: a condition in which air is exhausted from a space faster than it is replaced; the resulting drop in pressure can pull in pollutants and cause backdrafting.

Net zero energy (NZE): denotes a home that produces as much energy on-site as it uses over the course of a year.

Neutral pressure: a condition in which the airflow into and out of an area is balanced in volume, and the air pressure differential is zero.

Optimum-value engineering (OVE): a method of framing houses that minimizes the use of wood while improving the builder's ability to insulate effectively.

Oriented strand board (OSB): engineered wood made of chips or flakes of wood fiber pressed and glued together.

Outgas, off-gas: the process whereby a solid material releases volatile gases as it ages, decomposes, or cures.

Pascal: a metric measure of pressure used by home energy pros to measure air leakage, duct leakage, and other air-related diagnostics.

Passive House standard: a voluntary standard that promotes extreme levels of energy efficiency through a superinsulated, supertight, well-ventilated building envelope, so that the heating-and-cooling system can be radically downsized.

Passive-solar heating: the direct use of solar energy to heat a building.

Peak demand, Peak load, Peak power: a period when power use on the electric grid spikes above normal levels.

Peak-hour demand: the demand on a water heater during the one hour of the day when the most hot water is used.

Perimeter drain: a French drain that collects and drains water away from a building's foundation.

Permanent-magnet motor: an electrical motor that uses permanent magnets instead of field windings to create torque; far more energy efficient and longer-lasting than older, capacitor-driven motors.

Phantom load: a plug load that uses energy even when nominally turned off or in standby mode. Also called standby load or vampire load.

Photosensor: a device that converts light to electrical current.

Photovoltaic (PV): denotes solar cells that convert the sun's energy into electricity.

Plug load: the energy used by a product that is powered via an ordinary electrical plug.

Positive pressure: a condition in which air pressure in one area is higher than air pressure in another area, causing the air to migrate from the first area to the second one.

Power strip: a block of electrical sockets that attaches to the end of a flexible cable.

Pressure drop: the decrease in pressure from one point in a pipe or tube to another point downstream.

Programmable timer: a device that allows the user to program when and for how long a given function will occur.

Radiant barrier: a layer of metallic foil, reflective paint, or other material that reflects or reduces the emission of radiant energy.

Radiation: heat transfer in the form of electromagnetic waves from one surface to an unconnected colder surface.

Radon: a colorless, odorless, radioactive, naturally occurring gas that is present in soils and groundwater in varying amounts.

Rebate: a predetermined sum of money returned to the homeowner after purchase of an appliance or building component.

Recessed light: see Can light.

Recirculating fan: a fan, usually over a cooking surface, that does not exhaust the contaminants to the outside, but rather concentrates them and blows them back into the room.

Recirculation system: a distribution system that keeps hot water in the pipes to provide immediate hot water at the taps; generally saves water, but consumes energy to do so.

Register: a grille covering a duct outlet, usually containing a damper to control airflow.

Renewable energy: energy from sources that will last indefinitely, such as the sun, wind, tides, and the earth's heat.

Residential Energy Services Network (RESNET): a recognized national standards-making body for building energy efficiency rating and certification systems.

Return ducts: the ducts in a forced-air heating or cooling system that bring house air to the furnace or A/C to be heated or cooled.

Rim joist: the outermost joist around the perimeter of the floor framing.

R-value: the resistance of a material to heat transfer by conduction; a higher R-value indicates better insulation.

Sacrificial anode: a replaceable magnesium or aluminum rod that corrodes before steel can rust, preventing damage to the water heater tank.

Sconce: a wall-mounted electric light fixture that washes the wall with light in an upward and/or downward direction.

Sealed-combustion: denotes a fossil-fuel heater that provides outside air directly to the burner, rather than using household air.

Seasonal energy efficiency ratio (SEER): a rating for central A/Cs and heat pumps representing the cooling output for a season in Btu divided by the electrical input in kWh required to achieve that cooling.

Section: an architectural drawing of a vertical slice through the building, depicting spatial, structural, and finish features.

Secured loan: a loan backed by property in case of default.

Sensible heat ratio (SHR): an A/C rating that indicates the fraction of the evaporating coil's capacity used for reducing temperature, as opposed to condensing moisture from the air. The higher the SHR, the smaller the fraction of capacity used to remove moisture from the air.

Setback thermostat: combines a clock and a thermostat so that heating and cooling can be reduced during periods when less is needed—for example, at night.

Shaded-pole motor: an old-fashioned, inefficient blower motor.

Shaving the peak: reducing peak demand by reducing energy use.

Simple solar water heating: an uninsulated water storage tank placed in a warm environment to preheat the water simply and inexpensively.

Smart energy devices: digital gadgets and tools, often Internet enabled and wireless, that measure, manage, or control consumer energy use.

Smart meter: a digital meter that records household energy consumption in or near real time, and transfers the data to the utility through a communications network; also called advanced metering.

Smart power strip: one that can shut down power to devices when they go into standby mode.

Smoke pencil: a tool that releases a smoke-like substance used to detect air leaks.

Smooth metal duct: air duct constructed of either rigid round or rectangular sheet metal; the smooth surface allows air to move through with little frictional resistance.

Solar heat gain coefficient (SHGC): the fraction of solar radiation falling on a window, glazed door, or skylight that is admitted into the house as heat; the lower a window's SHGC, the less solar heat it admits into the house.

Solar radiation: radiant energy from the sun, including ultraviolet, visible, and infrared wavelengths.

Solar-thermal: denotes a system that converts sunlight into heat, typically by using the sun to heat water or air.

Solar tube: see Tubular skylight.

Solar water heating: uses energy from the sun to heat water directly.

Sone: a sound rating; fans rated at 1.5 sones and below are considered very quiet.

Split-capacitor motor: an older type of blower motor; not very energy efficient.

Spot ventilation: ventilation provided in a limited area to remove contaminants produced in that area, such as smoke in the kitchen or steam in the bathroom.

Sprayed foam: see Foam-in-place insulation.

Stack effect: the upward movement of air in a building or chimney due to the tendency of warm air to rise.

Standby load: see Phantom load.

Steam oven: a midsize oven that cooks via steam, reducing cooking time in comparison to that of a standard oven.

Stem wall: the vertical portion of a foundation wall or retaining wall, designed to carry a structural load above it without lateral support at the top or bottom.

Structural insulated panel (SIP): a composite building material consisting of rigid insulation sandwiched between two layers of structural board.

Subcontractor: a trade professional who specializes in a particular aspect of a construction project, such as electrical, plumbing, or painting.

Subfloor: a rough floor (typically plywood) over which finished flooring is laid.

Sun pipe: see Tubular skylight.

Sun space: a glazed room designed to collect solar heat, which is used to heat the rest of the house.

Supply ducts: the ducts in a forced-air system that supply heated or cooled air from the furnace or A/C to the house.

Swamp cooler: see Evaporative cooler.

Tankless water heater: a water heater with no storage tank that heats water as needed, using large electric elements or gas burners.

Task lighting: light directed to a specific work area or surface.

Tax credit: an amount that is subtracted from the tax due.

Temperature and pressure relief valve: a safety device on storage water heaters that reduces dangerously high temperatures or pressures if they build up inside the tank.

Tempered glass: glass that has undergone a heat treatment that strengthens it and decreases likelihood of breakage.

Termite barrier: a continuous material between the foundation and the structure of a building through which termites cannot tunnel.

Thermal boundary: the border between conditioned and unconditioned space where insulation is placed.

Thermal break: a relatively less conductive material used as part of an assembly to reduce thermal transmittance through more conductive materials.

Thermal bridge: a break in the continuity of insulation in a wall, ceiling, or floor that allows heat to flow more readily between inside and outside.

Thermal mass: materials inside the building envelope (e.g., masonry, stone, tile, concrete, or water) that absorb heat during the day and release the heat as the space cools at night.

Thermal resistance: the ability to retard heat flow, expressed as R-value.

Thermal traps: the curved pipes or check valves that prevent hot water from rising into the cold-water inlet pipe (also known as heat traps).

Thermosyphon: a system in which a heat-storing liquid is circulated by convection, not requiring a mechanical pump.

Tint: a mineral coloring incorporated into the glass pane of a window to reduce solar heat gain.

Title insurance: a policy that protects the property owner from loss sustained by defects in the title to the property.

Tons of cooling: a measure of A/C capacity; one ton of air conditioning is 12,000 Btu/h.

Torchiere: a floor lamp that provides indirect light by sending most of its light upward.

Track lighting: a lighting system with an electrically fed linear track that accepts one or more track heads.

Trade contractor: see Subcontractor.

Transfer grille: see Jumper duct.

Transformer: a small electronic pack that plugs into an electrical outlet to transform house electrical current to the form required by a computer, phone, or rechargeable device.

Tubular skylight: a cylindrical skylight with a small diameter that fits between existing roof framing members. The walls of the cylinder are highly reflective, bouncing a strong beam of sunlight into the living space.

U-factor: a measure of how much heat is conducted through a window. U-factor is the inverse of R-value; the lower the U-factor, the better the window insulates.

Ultraviolet (UV): describes radiation beyond the violet end of the visible spectrum, with wavelengths shorter than those of visible light and longer than those of X-rays.

Unconditioned space: any space that is enclosed by the walls, roof, and foundation of a house and that is not heated or cooled. Examples include an unfinished basement, attic, garage, or crawl space.

Underwriting: the part of the loan approval process that entails guaranteeing or assuming liability for the loan amount.

Unsecured loan: a loan backed only by the consumer in case of default, with no real property asset as security.

Unvented crawl space: one that does not provide vents to the outside.

Vampire load: see Phantom load.

Vapor barrier: a material that is impermeable to water vapor.

Vapor retarder: a continuous layer of materials that resists the passage of water vapor by diffusion (e.g., polyethylene, aluminum foil, low-permeability paints, vinyl wall covers, impermeable rigid insulations, sheet metal, plywood, or waferboard).

Variable speed: an electromechanical feature that allows pump or fan speeds to be changed, either continuously or in increments, thereby increasing efficiency, comfort, or both. See Electronically commutated motor (ECM), Integrated control motor (ICM).

Vented crawl space: an unconditioned crawl space that allows outside air to bring in heat and/or moisture.

Ventilation: the controlled movement of air into and out of a house.

Visible transmittance (VT): the fraction of visible light falling on a window, glazed door, or skylight that is transmitted through it.

Wall cavity: the space between the studs of a wall.

Wall sheathing: a structural component, such as plywood or OSB, installed as part of the wall assembly. Sometimes rigid insulation board is also called nonstructural wall sheathing.

Waterless urinal: a urinal that uses no water to flush; minimizes odors using a sealant cartridge or deodorant block.

Watt (W): a unit of power.

Watt-hour: the work done by 1 watt in one hour.

Weather shell: the outer layer of a home that keeps rain, wind, and snow from getting into building assemblies or conditioned space.

Weather strip: foam, bronze, or vinyl strips or gaskets attached around the moving parts of doors and windows to reduce air leaks.

Wet-spray insulation: loose-fill fiber insulation mixed with water and sometimes adhesives that can be blown into open cavities or on irregularly shaped areas. Damp-spray and moist-spray insulation are mixed with less water and dry faster.

Whole-house fan: a large fan, commonly installed high in a wall or in the opening to an unconditioned and ventilated attic. It flushes the house by pulling outdoor air in through open windows as it exhausts hot air to the outside.

Wind power: the conversion of wind into electricity via a generator called a wind turbine.

Work triangle: an arrangement of stove, refrigerator, and kitchen sink that provides adequate work space, with no more than two of the three appliances along the same wall.

Zero peak: denotes a home designed to draw no electricity from the power grid during peak hours.

Zoning (zoned): designing the HVAC system so that different areas of the house can be set to different temperature levels.

GENERAL RESOURCES

This is a listing of resources with broad application to no-regrets remodeling. For chapter-specific resources, see the end of each chapter.

Print

The Consumer's Guide to Effective Environmental Choices: Practical Advice from the Union of Concerned Scientists. Michael Brower and Warren Leon, Three Rivers Press, 1999

Discussion Guide on Global Warming: Changing CO$_2$urse. Meg O'Brien, ed., Northwest Earth Institute, 2007

The Greened House Effect. Jeff Wilson, Chelsea Green, 2013

Green Remodeling: Changing the World One Room at a Time. David Johnston and Kim Master, New Society Publishers, 2004

Green Restorations: Sustainable Building and Historic Homes. Aaron Lubeck, New Society Publishers, 2010

Insulate & Weatherize for Energy Efficiency at Home. Bruce Harley, Taunton, 2012

Natural Remodeling for the Not-So-Green House: Bringing Your Home into Harmony with Nature. Carol Venolia and Kelly Lerner, Lark Books, 2006

Online

Alliance to Save Energy: Creating an Energy-Efficient World: ase.org

Building Envelopes Program (BEP): Handbooks & Fact Sheets: ornl.gov/sci/roofs+walls/facts/index.htm

Information on retrofit best practices, insulation, radiant barriers, foundations, moisture control, attics, and radiation.

Consortium for Energy Efficiency (CEE): Residential Sector: cee1.org/content/cee-program-resources

Click on Residential for initiatives that address energy-saving opportunities for appliances, lighting, HVAC systems, and gas heating.

The Energy & Environmental Building Alliance (EEBA): eeba.org

Houses That Work program, SmartTools Bookstore (including Builder's Guides on building science for specific climate zones).

ENERGY STAR for Home Improvement: energystar.gov/index.cfm?c=home_improvement.hm_improvement_index

Environmental Building News: buildinggreen.com/news/index.cfm

GreenBuildingAdvisor: greenbuildingadvisor.com

Green-building information, including product and technique reviews.

Home Energy Efficient Design (HEED): energy-design-tools.aud.ucla.edu/heed

A free, easy-to-use program that shows you how much energy and money you can save by making various design or remodeling changes to your home.

Home Energy magazine: homeenergy.org

Serving professionals and laypersons in residential energy management for nearly 30 years.

International Code Council: iccsafe.org/Pages/default.aspx

National Association of Home Builders (NAHB): nahb.com

National Center for Healthy Housing: nchh.org

Educational programs, tools, and resources to help the public create and maintain a healthy home.

Pharos: pharosproject.net

A database of products and research to promote the construction of healthier, more environmentally sound buildings.

Rocky Mountain Institute Residential Building Library: rmi.org/search-category/Built+Environment/Buildings—Residential/sharepoint

Scroll down to "Home Energy Briefs."

U.S. Department of Energy/Energy Efficiency and Renewable Energy:

- eere.energy.gov
- Building America: buildingamerica.gov
- Publications: www1.eere.energy.gov/library/default.aspx?page=2
  - *Vol. 14: Energy Renovations: HVAC: A Guide for Contractors to Share with Homeowners* (2011)
  - *BSC Information Sheet 001: Residential Best Practices Criteria for All Climates*
- Building Technologies Program: www1.eere.energy.gov/buildings/information_resources.html

  Publications, webinars, software, links; look for Technology Fact Sheets and Building America Best Practices Series.
- Energy Efficiency: Homes: eere.energy.gov/topics/homes.html

  Information about how to save energy and money at home; DOE programs and initiatives to improve energy use in homes; efficient- and renewable-energy technologies; and financial incentives.
- Energy Saver: energy.gov/energysaver/energy-saver
- *Energy Savers: Tips on Saving Energy & Money at Home:* energy.gov/energysaver/downloads/energy-savers-guide

WXTV: A Weekly Show on Energy Efficiency: wxtvonline.org

ACKNOWLEDGMENTS

This second edition of *No-Regrets Remodeling* was created by experts from all over North America. We are especially grateful to our authors:

Michael Anschel is the founder, owner, and principal designer for Otogawa-Anschel Design-Build, LLC, in Minneapolis, Minnesota; CEO of Verified Green, Inc.; and a green blogger for *Remodeling Magazine*.

Architect George Beeler's passion is exploring the frontier edge of green living and how that applies to our built environment, including new and rehabilitated homes, offices, schools, universities, and wineries. aimgreen.com

Ann Edminster, author of *Energy Free: Homes for a Small Planet* and principal developer of LEED for Homes, consults to design firms, builders, investors, start-ups, utilities, public agencies, and nonprofits.

Doug Garrett has extensive background in IAQ and green building; he owns Building Performance & Comfort, Incorporated, and is a Certified Energy Manager and an ACCA Certified Instructor. bldgperformance.com

David Hales is a building scientist, researcher, trainer, and contractor. His research at Washington State University's Extension Energy program includes central forced-air system efficiency, crawl space performance, and high-performance homes.

Leslie Jackson, former assistant editor at *Home Energy* magazine, coauthored *Rocket Mass Heaters* with Ianto Evans. This manual for building fuel-efficient wood-burning stoves is now in its third edition and is published in four languages. rocketstoves.com

Larry Kinney is the president of Synergistic Building Technologies, a Boulder, Colorado, firm that develops window and daylighting systems and associated controls. Kinney has written over 200 energy-related articles and reports.

John Reynolds has taught architecture at the University of Oregon since 1967. He is coauthor of *Mechanical and Electrical Equipment for Buildings* (6th–11th eds.) and *Courtyards: Aesthetic, Social, and Thermal Delight*.

Barbara R. Saunders, an award-winning writer, specializes in educational and marketing materials about science and technology, including energy, health and fitness, and software. barbararuthsaunders.com

Doug Seiter coined the term "green builder" in the early '90s, developed and managed the country's first green builder program, in Austin, Texas, and then took Denver's program statewide as Built Green Colorado.

Carl Seville is a recovering remodeler who teaches, speaks, writes about, consults on, and certifies green buildings. He is coauthor of *Green Building, Principles & Practices in Residential Construction*. greencurmudgeon.com, sevilleconsulting.com

Larry Weingarten has done hot-water- and energy-related work since 1978, has developed tools and methods for maintaining water heaters, and coauthored *The Water Heater Workbook*.

Rick Williams is a mortgage loan officer. He leads the Realtor Outreach campaign and teaches energy efficiency financing for Santa Clara County, California.

Elisa Wood has written for many years on energy-related topics in the industry's top publications. RealEnergyWriters.com

Edward Wyatt has degrees from UC Berkeley in both economics and mechanical engineering. He has worked in energy conservation and analysis, efficiency, and manufacturing for 25 years.

We also leaned heavily on a top-notch team of technical reviewers:

John Broniek, building science engineer, Broniek Consulting; Peter Byrne, Setanta Energy and Water; Jim Cavallo, principal, Midwest Energy Performance Analytics, Inc.; Jeff Christian, Christian Crafted Conservation; Robert Clear, former staff, Lighting Research Group, Lawrence Berkeley National Laboratory; Abram Conant, assistant chief engineer, Proctor Engineering Group; Gord Cooke, P.E., president, Building Knowledge Canada, Incorporated; D. Charlie Curcija, deputy group leader of the Windows and Envelope Materials Group at Lawrence Berkeley National Laboratory; David Eisenberg, cofounder and director of the Development Center for Appropriate Technology; Don Fugler, building scientist and researcher, Ottawa, Ontario; Howdy Goudey, researcher in the Windows and Envelope Materials Group at Lawrence Berkeley National Laboratory; Robert Hart, researcher in the Windows and Envelope Materials Group at Lawrence Berkeley National Laboratory; Marye Hefty, Michael Baechler, and Theresa Gilbride of Pacific Northwest National Laboratories; Mary James, publisher at Low Carbon Productions and former editor and publisher of *Home Energy* magazine; Tina M. Kaarsberg, team leader, Building Technologies program, DOE; Ann Kelly, energy efficiency programs manager for San Francisco's Department of the Environment and former publisher of *Home Energy* magazine; David Legg, energy performance consultant; Brennan Less, graduate student researcher in the Residential Building Systems Group at Lawrence Berkeley National Laboratory; Jim Lutz, researcher at Lawrence Berkeley National Laboratory; Steve Mann, energy consultant, Home Energy Services; Kelley McKanna, project manager, Renewable Funding, LLC; Evan Mills, staff scientist, Lawrence Berkeley National Laboratory; Courtney Moriarta, senior project manager, SRA International; John Proctor, P.E., CEO Proctor Engineering Group, Ltd.; Mike Rogers, president, OmStout Consulting; William Rose, senior research architect, Illinois Sustainable Technology Center; A. Tamasin Sterner, president and chief coach of Pure Energy Coach, LLC; Chris Stratton, research associate at Lawrence Berkeley National Laboratory; Leah Thayer, founder and publisher of daily5REMODEL.com; and Linda Wigington, principal, Lind M. Wigington Associates.

We couldn't have created this book without support from the staff of *Home Energy* magazine: Alan Meier, senior executive editor; Iain Walker, executive editor; Jim Gunshinan, editor; Macie Melendez, assistant editor; Tom White, publisher; Kate Henke, design and production manager; Carol Markell, advertising and marketing manager; Mark Barroll, marketing intern; Maggie Forti, office manager; Alana Shindler, fulfillment manager; and Toni White, office assistant.

Carol Venolia served as project manager, coordinating the efforts of all the players and bringing her background as an eco-architect, coauthor of *Natural Remodeling for the Not-So-Green House*, and author of the ebook *Get Back to Nature Without Leaving Home*. Marie Narlock assisted with conceptual planning; Devin Kinney created the chapter icons and many illustrations.

The book was brought to life by the highly capable team of Phyllis M. Faber, book publisher; Beth Hansen-Winter, book designer; Irene Elmer, copyeditor; Karen Stough, proofreader; and Theresa Duran, indexer.

Last but not least, we would like to acknowledge the support of the staff of Oak Ridge National Laboratory who helped fund and guide this second edition: Pat Love, Tracie Curtright, LaTonya Jordan, Roderick Jackson, Kaushik Biswas, and William Craddick.

INDEX